The Tropical
Freshwater
Aquarium
Problem Solver

Practical and Expert Advice on Keeping Fish and Plants

Gina Sandford

Tetra Press
No 16063

Contents

AN ANDROMEDA BOOK

Copyright © 1998 Andromeda
Oxford Limited

Planned and produced by
Andromeda Oxford Limited,
11–13 The Vineyard, Abingdon,
Oxfordshire,
England, OX14 3PX

Published in North America by
Tetra Press,
3001 Commerce Street.
Blacksburg, VA 24060

ISBN 1–56465–197–5

Advisory Editors LEE FINLEY (US), BRIAN WALSH (UK)

Project Manager and Designer	Frankie Wood
Editor	Peter Lewis
Picture Research Manager	Claire Turner
Indexer	Ann Barrett
Production Director	Clive Sparling
Publishing Director	Graham Bateman

Film origination by Pixel Tech, Singapore
Printed by Acumen Ltd, Singapore

AQUATIC PLANTS • 186

Introduction

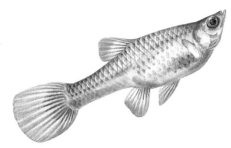

*A*n aquarist colleague of mine is fond of remarking that she keeps her fish in jail! Although this image may appear startlingly negative, it is, in truth, a very accurate description of the business of fishkeeping.

To pursue the analogy: a prisoner's food is provided, and he is obliged to eat what is supplied; his environment is regulated; his recreation is monitored; and the area he inhabits is restricted. The same conditions apply to your fish. They don't have the option of moving downstream because there is no suitable food available; they are entirely dependent on what you offer them. Likewise, if the temperature of the water doesn't suit them or if the water quality deteriorates, they must put up with it. Even if they are migratory fish that are accustomed to swimming long distances, their exercise is confined to within the four glass walls of the aquarium. The inescapable fact highlighted by this stark image is that we humans are solely responsible for the well-being of the fish in our charge.

This book is a contribution to raising the awareness of those involved in the tropical fishkeeping hobby. Its aim is to help you solve the problems that you will encounter in every aspect and at every stage of this challenging and fascinating endeavour. For the novice, it outlines the basic principles of tank set-up and fish husbandry, while for the experienced aquarist, it contains a wealth of detailed information on a broad range of topics. One of the book's distinctive features is its use of the "question and answer" format to troubleshoot specific concerns. These are based on *real* questions that are frequently asked by hobbyists, and are drawn from my own 30-year experience as an aquarist, and from my columns dispensing advice to others in a number of fishkeeping magazines.

Throughout this volume, you will come across my refrain that the key to successful fishkeeping is forward planning. By this, I mean that you *must* research thoroughly what is required to create your chosen set-up and make sure that conditions in the tank are right before you introduce any livestock. This is not a new insight, but I make no apologies for repeating it here.

◄ *A selection of Guppies,
one of the most popular
fish in the hobby.*

The author of one of the very first books
on the hobby (H. Noel Humphreys:
*Ocean and River Gardens – A History of the
Marine and Freshwater Aquaria*) was at pains to alert fishkeepers to their
responsibilities in maintaining good water quality and not overstocking their
tanks. When this early book was written – in 1857 – the technological aids
available to aquarists were few and rudimentary. Now that we have a vast
array of filters, pumps, heaters, thermostats and sterilizers at our disposal,
and can diagnose problems accurately with a sophisticated armoury of test
kits, how much less of an excuse there is for bad practice on our part!

As the popularity of the aquarium hobby has grown, so has the level of
awareness of the wider role we play in conservation. Irrespective of whether
your fish are wild-caught or tank-bred, being a conscientious aquarist
means reproducing as safe and natural an environment as possible for the
species you are keeping in your aquarium. This book provides you with the
knowledge you need to do this.

Finally, a note on measurements; tank sizes have been given in the most
accessible form of LxWxH (in both inches and centimetres) rather than
their capacity in gallons. Where liquid measurements are used, for example
in dosage information, they are expressed in imperial, metric, and US units.

This book will serve as an indispensable tool to help you become a
successful aquarist. Enjoy your fishkeeping!

GINA SANDFORD

Aquarium Care

The most basic prerequisite for keeping tropical fish
is to set up a suitable tank and ensure that the many systems
essential to supporting aquatic life are all bedded in and running
smoothly. It cannot be overemphasized that this groundwork *must*
be laid well in advance of buying and introducing any livestock.
Carelessness and impatience will result in disillusionment for the
prospective hobbyist and – *far more importantly* – the demise
of living creatures. By contrast, careful forward planning
and preparation will pay dividends in the form of a well-
appointed aquarium containing happy, healthy fish.

The first part of this section leads you through
the stages of setting up your aquarium. Primary concerns of
where to site it, and how best to supply it with heat, light and air
are followed by a description of the principles and techniques of
water management. Once in place, some tank systems are difficult
or even impossible to alter, so the advice offered here will help
you get the fundamentals right first time.

After a safe and appropriate environment has been
established, it is time to introduce your fish. The second part
of the section covers all aspects of tropical freshwater husbandry:
choosing suitable tankmates, teaming the right fish with the right
surroundings, feeding the correct foods and – most vital of
all – coping with health crises. Because fishkeeping is almost
synonymous with fish breeding, special emphasis has been
given to this most rewarding (though sometimes
most frustrating!) part of being an aquarist.

▶ *Black Neon Tetras* (Hyphessobrycon
herbertaxelrodi) *see page 133.*

Aquarium Design

A WELL-PRESENTED AQUARIUM MAKES A TRULY impressive sight, and can become the focal point of a room. The ever-changing vista within the tank has a calming effect on the viewer – little wonder that aquaria are often to be found in doctors' and dentists' waiting rooms! Moreover, for those people who live in apartments, where having a dog or cat might be impractical, it is the only viable way of keeping pets. Unsurprisingly, then, fishkeeping ranks among the world's most popular hobbies.

Tanks used to be made from glass panels set in angle-iron frames with special lime-free putty. To resist corrosion, the frames were painted or coated. This method of construction limited the range of shapes and sizes in which tanks were generally available. There was also continuing concern over the effectiveness of the watertight seal between the putty, frame and glass.

Modern Aquaria

The invention of silicone rubber in the US radically altered aquarium construction and design, and rendered framed tanks obsolete. Stored in a mastic form that hardens in air, silicone rubber fuses with the panes of aquarium glass by forming a molecular bond with the silica sand of which the glass is composed. This bond gives years of trouble-free service. What is more, the elastic consistency of the hardened rubber even allows the glass to move slightly, so reducing the possibility of stress points that might cause it to fracture. A small bead of silicone rubber around the inner corner of the tank also helps ensure an effective seal. There are now a number of different tank shapes on the market that have only been made possible by the advent of this versatile material.

▶ *This interestingly shaped modern aquarium displays an alluring collection of plants and fish. However, many aquarists still prefer the traditional rectangular shape of tank for ease of maintenance and viewing.*

Weight Considerations

Time spent planning a new aquarium, particularly a display tank, will always pay dividends. Weight is a major consideration; glass thickness increases the deeper and longer your tank is, to ensure it will hold the greater weight of water. Before filling your tank, install it in its final location. Water, gravel and rockwork will make it impossible to move thereafter without dismantling it. A finished aquarium is extremely heavy; one (imperial) gallon of water weighs 10lbs, so even a modest 36-gallon (165-litre/44-US gallon) tank will contain 360lbs (165kg) of water alone. Add the weight of the tank – around 55lbs (25kg) – plus any heavy rocks, and the aquarium will soon exceed 440lbs (200kg). Clearly a solid

Q&A... ● *Can I make my own aquarium using silicone rubber?*

Yes, but first you should try making small "practice" tanks. Do not use silicone rubber intended for sealing baths and wash-basins, which contains fungicides that are toxic to fish. Use the correct thickness of glass for the dimensions of the tank you are constructing. In the first instance, you would be well-advised to buy a ready-made tank, or, for less conventional designs, to have one built to your individual specifications. Detailed advice on tank-building can be found in specialized publications.

● *I have just purchased a new all-glass tank, but am concerned by the slightly acrid smell it gives off. Is it safe to use?*

New tanks often smell of vinegar. This arises from the curing of the silicone rubber, which takes around 24–48 hours to harden, but continues to exude a pungent odour for much longer. By the time you buy the tank, the smell will usually have worn off in storage. But if it does still linger, it will disappear once immersed in water. Fish and plants seem unaffected by it.

● *Which is preferable, a glass or an acrylic tank?*

There is little to choose between these two materials. Acrylic has the advantage that it can be moulded into a variety of attractive shapes that require no joins. Jointed glass tanks bonded with silicone rubber are now extremely reliable, however, so you need have no worries about leakage. Glass is also generally more scratch-resistant than acrylic.

● *Why choose a rectangular box tank, when there are now so many more interesting designs?*

There is no denying that the more irregularly shaped modern aquaria are aesthetically pleasing objects in their own right and can enhance the overall decor of a room. But bear in mind that the prime reason for having a tank in the first place is to keep, breed, and view fish. And the shape that affords the maximum clear viewing area is the rectangular box! Angled or curved designs also run the risk of creating viewing distortion, which can be very frustrating when you are trying to observe or photograph your fish. Another factor in favour of conventional designs is that they can accommodate tank life-support systems more easily.

base will be required. Purpose-built cabinets and stands guarantee that the load is evenly distributed, but if you are adapting existing furniture, make sure it will take the load and remain stable. Also consider the strength of your floor. If the tank stand has slender legs and the floor is made of wooden boards, then the legs should be placed above the joists. Of course, no such problems arise with a concrete floor. If you live in an apartment, be on good terms with your downstairs neighbours in case of leaks!

Safety

If you opt for a frameless or all-glass tank, it is important that you place some cushioning material between the underside of the aquarium and the surface on which it is to sit. This will prevent any slight imperfections or pieces of grit on the top of the cabinet creating localized stress-risers on the flat glass base of the tank, which can cause it to crack. The most usual form of cushioning is a sheet of expanded polystyrene, approximately 0.2–0.25in (5–6mm) in thickness. Often the shop from which you purchase the tank will offer you this, but if not, it is readily available from hardware stores.

Siting Your Aquarium

Do not place your tank in front of a window, or in direct sunlight, where excessive light will cause algal problems that can only be overcome by relocation. Nor should you site a tank in a draught, or where the fish will be disturbed by constant human activity. Also consider how the tank blends with the rest of your room; it is best to try the empty tank and its stand in the desired position to help you envisage the finished result.

The planning stage should also be used to decide on the method of tank filtration (see Filtration, pages 24–25). If an external unit is to be used, then where is it to be located? Gravity-fed rapid sand filters can be concealed in the cabinet below the main tank. Power filters must be installed near the tank and on roughly the same level, whereas air pumps should be placed above the water level, unless they are fitted with in-line one-way check valves, and should not be positioned where they will vibrate against the side of the aquarium.

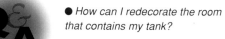

● *How can I redecorate the room that contains my tank?*

... It is best to do this before installing the aquarium as, once full, it will be impossible to move without completely dismantling it. Subsequent decorating will mean leaving the wall behind the tank unpainted or unpapered, unless you have allowed for this by leaving a small gap. Fumes from paint and other decorating materials can have an adverse effect on fish. So, ensure the tank is well-covered, and provide an air supply from an adjacent room via an aquarium air pump.

● *What should I put on the back of the tank?*

Seeing wallpaper through the rear of the tank does look rather unnatural. It is best to address this issue before installation. Rolls of photo-realistic tank backgrounds are available that can be stuck to the outside rear face of the aquarium. Alternatively, three-dimensional vacuum-formed panels resembling rockwork can be attached inside the back of the tank. Resist the urge to paint the back of the tank light-blue, which looks most unrealistic. Black paint is better, giving an impression of greater depth. Needless to say, the paint should be applied on the outside, and for durability should not be water-based.

● *What advice can you give me on installing a free-standing tank?*

In homes with open-plan rooms, aquaria are sometimes used as room dividers. This sounds quite straightforward, but it takes considerably more planning than the conventional method of siting a tank against a wall. If the divider is going to consist solely of an aquarium and stand, then consider the proximity of the power source. Decide on the type of filtration for your tank, and whether to use a hood to house the lighting or suspended spotlights. You must also plan how to conceal the electrical cables and the pipework. On the other hand, if the aquarium is to be incorporated into a shelving unit or cabinet, then the prime concern will be whether the furniture will take the weight of the tank. The same considerations as above then still pertain; in addition, ask yourself how easy it will be to carry out regular maintenance tasks. As free-standing aquaria are viewed from both sides, careful attention must be given to the internal layout. A wider than normal tank facilitates the planting and placement of decor, since it allows you to create a central "spine" of tall plants and/or rockwork and wood. This will effectively form the background when the tank is seen from either side.

Aquarium Decoration

ONCE YOU HAVE SITED AND INSTALLED YOUR tank, your thoughts will turn to the question of interior decor. This will, to some extent, be dictated by the fish you are planning to keep. Some require lots of rockwork with caves, while others need open areas for swimming. Their demands on the water chemistry will also influence your choice. Further details are given in the entries relating to individual species.

The best place to start is the substrate. There is a wide selection, so choose with care; once set up, it cannot be changed. Most popular is gravel, approximately 0.125in (3mm) in size. Unless you intend keeping hardwater fish, it should be lime-free; so be sure to buy from a reliable source such as your local aquarium supplier. It comes in a variety of colours, some natural, others not. Avoid very light colours, particularly white and yellow, as these can lead to the fish becoming poorly coloured as it attempts to blend with its surroundings. Honey or black substrates are preferable, though ultimately it is a matter of personal choice. The gravel should not be sharp, particularly if you are keeping bottom-dwelling fish or species that dig, as it can damage their barbels or mouths.

Another possibility is sand, but again be sure of its origin and intended purpose. Builders' sand is inappropriate as it is usually sharp, compacts too easily, and may well contain toxic additives. Use filtration sand instead, which is available in varying grit sizes, and is chemically inert, smooth and non compacting. Its main drawback is that it tends, over time, to find its own level – more so than gravels – so terracing it effectively can prove a little tricky. On the other hand, its non-compacting nature makes plant growth and propagation simpler, as the roots can easily penetrate it.

▼ *Carefully selected materials can greatly enhance the appearance of your tank. Whatever your particular set-up, you should always aim to create a natural effect with your tank decor.*

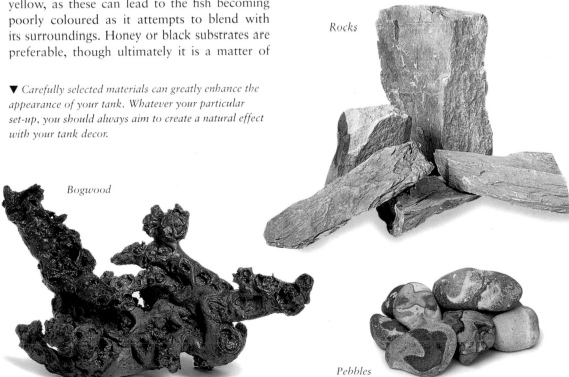

Rocks

Bogwood

Pebbles

Pebbles are rocks approximately 2in (50mm) in diameter upwards that have been rounded by erosion. They can be used as a substrate, but are better employed as a feature with gravels or sand, by placing selected pebbles in a small area of the tank. Don't use pebbles from the seashore, as they will require substantial cleaning to remove traces of salt, and may contain other pollutants. Instead, if possible, collect them from freshwater streams.

Rockwork lends an element of height to your tank's decor. Select your rocks carefully. If the tank is to look natural, then the rocks (and any pebbles) should appear to be of the same material. If there are any striations (strata) visible in the rock, they should run in a similar direction when placed in the aquarium. Not all rocks are suitable. For example, limestone will leach alkalis that have a detrimental effect on soft water tanks, and may not be controllable even in hard water systems. Ensure that any rockwork structures you build in the tank are robust enough to withstand being undermined by fish. Seat the base rocks directly on the bottom glass of the aquarium, infilling around it with the gravel or sand substrate. Rocks above the base layer can be cemented together using special silicone rubber for aquarium use.

Wood can be used as an alternative or a supplement to rocks. Here, again, you should exercise caution; some species of tree can leach harmful toxins into the water. There are two main choices of wood, so-called bogwood and vine roots. Bogwood is tree root that has remained submerged for centuries in marshy conditions. Each piece is individually sculpted by nature. Bogwood does leach tannins that can stain the water brown, so it is advisable to scrub and soak it for two weeks before use, with regular changes of water, to remove the majority of these. The tannins do not harm most fish, and particularly in soft acidic water systems, such as those for many of the popular South American species, are positively beneficial. Vine roots, which are exactly what the name implies, are often used as ornamental media by flower arrangers, and are equally suitable as decor for the home aquarium.

Aquatic plants can be as much a part of the living aquarium as the fish, and will lend a certain

colour balance to the overall effect created by the tank decor. Be aware of the differing needs of the plants; some are more suited to hard water systems than others. Similarly, some species grow larger, or have large leaves, and so are unsuitable for planting at the front of the tank. Also, when planting, take into account that different plants require different levels of lighting (see Plants, pages 186–199).

Arrange your aquatic plants in such a way that, as they grow, all their leaves will receive light from above. Generally speaking, large broad-leaved plants are best planted as individual specimens, while fine-leaved varieties should be planted individually in groups. Red-leaved plants usually demand a greater intensity of light than green plants. Plants are often sold potted in a fibrous material that should be carefully removed, to avoid damaging the roots, before planting in the tank. Some plants, such as Java Fern (*Microsorium pteropus*), prefer to anchor themselves to wood. To help their roots gain an initial foothold, drill small holes in the bogwood

▲ Simple arrangements can be used to great effect. Here, granite rocks and Hair Grass (Eleocharis acicularis) *make an imposing environment for Platies.*

or vine root and pass through short lengths of gardening wire to attach the plant to.

Artificial tank decor can be used. Plastic plants have the advantage of not being eaten by herbivorous fish, nor are they dependent on lighting quality. Yet, although some are quite realistic, they never match the full beauty of the natural plant. Imitation wood and rock can also be purchased, which is convincingly realistic and contains no trace elements. It is available in a variety of shapes and sizes, but the drawback is that you are bound to end up with the same shape and colour as someone else.

Plastic novelty ornaments, such as sunken galleons, castles, divers, and so on, can be bought for the aquarium. Whether you choose to add them is, of course, a question of personal taste, but bear in mind that they inevitably detract from the realistic appearance of the tank.

Q&A...

● *How do I know if the wood I have selected will look appropriate, or fit the aquarium?*

Ask you aquatic dealer if you can place the wood in a similar sized bare display tank in the shop – most will be happy to oblige. If, once you get it home, the piece of wood is too large, avoid using a saw, as the sawn surface will look unnatural. Instead, try breaking it, or fracturing it by tapping it lightly with a wood chisel.

● *Despite soaking and scrubbing my bogwood, the water still has a slight stain to it. Can this be removed?*

A power filter containing a small amount of activated carbon will remove much of the stain.

● *How can I gauge whether or not the gravel or sand is too sharp or will compact?*

Thrust your unclenched hand into the dry gravel or sand. If it penetrates with little resistance, then you should have no problems.

● *Are pieces of coral suitable as freshwater tank ornamentation?*

Lumps of coral should only be used in marine aquaria. Coral is particularly sharp, and could easily damage freshwater fish. Also, bear in mind that its high calcium content makes the water hard, which would harm softwater fish and plants. However, for this very reason, coral shells or coral sand (which is made from crushed coral) are ideal as substrates in a hard water set-up, such as an African Rift Valley cichlid tank.

● *The gravel I have bought as a tank substrate looks a little dusty. Should I somehow pre-treat it?*

There is nothing you can do to avoid dust accumulating in gravel; it is the inevitable result of individual grains rubbing together. Before adding it to the aquarium, all gravel and sand should first be rinsed through to remove this dust. The same applies to wood and rock, which should be thoroughly scrubbed.

● *Is there any risk in collecting rocks?*

Yes. Unless you are geologically trained, and can determine the chemical characteristics and effect of various rocks in water, and have knowledge of any pollution they may have been subjected to, the safest course of action is to leave them alone. It is a false economy if the rocks you have gathered for free kill the contents of your aquarium.

Heating

FISH ARE ECTOTHERMS, OR, TO USE THE MORE common term, cold-blooded. The temperature of the blood of such creatures is determined by their environment. This in turn affects the metabolic rate and the amount of dissolved oxygen in the water, which affects their rate of respiration. The warmer the water, the less dissolved oxygen, and the more active the fish become. In cooler water the amount of dissolved oxygen increases, and the fish grow sluggish. The implications of this for the aquarist is that fewer fish should be kept in warmer waters than in cooler conditions due to the demand on the limited oxygen supply.

In the tropics, water temperature remains reasonably constant. In large bodies of fresh water in these regions, overnight temperature changes are only slight and, unlike in northern climes, there is no cold season. To replicate these natural conditions, the water temperature in the domestic aquarium needs to remain uniformly high within a fairly narrow range – generally 22–29°C (72–84°F). The optimum temperature for particular species will be found in the separate entries relating to them.

The modern aquarium heating system has two main components – the heater, which heats the water, and the thermostat, which controls the level of heat by switching the heater on and off.

Selecting Your Heater and Thermostat

When purchasing a heater, tank capacity is your prime consideration. A heater of the wrong size will cause a small tank to heat too rapidly, or will struggle to maintain the correct temperature in a larger tank. Follow the manufacturer's advice; for general guidance, the recommended heater sizes for various capacities of aquaria are given in the table opposite. Note that two or three heaters are advisable for larger tanks. This is a wise precaution against the water cooling excessively if one heater should fail. Moreover, when placed at different points in the aquarium, multiple heaters make for better heat distribution.

▶ *A tank heater with a built-in thermostat is the most popular type of aquarium heating.*

Undertank heaters are also available; the tank rests on these external elements, which (like more conventional types) are regulated by a thermostat. The advantages of such heaters are that they warm the roots of plants and are very robust. But do consider in advance how easy it would be for you to replace them in the event of failure.

Many thermostats, whether heater-combined or separate units, have mechanical switches. A bi-metallic switch reacts to the surrounding temperature, opening or closing the contacts through which the power flows to the heater. Internal (submersible) thermostats have a small sealed dial to set the desired temperature. A similar dial is fitted to external thermostats, but is made tamper-proof to prevent young children from inadvertently altering the temperature.

Though expensive, the latest thermostats with microchip technology offer unrivalled accuracy

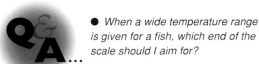

● *When a wide temperature range is given for a fish, which end of the scale should I aim for?*

Higher temperatures generally make the fish grow faster, but will shorten its lifespan. They can also adversely affect plant growth. It is therefore advisable to select a temperature at the lower end or the middle of the range. Raise it to induce spawning, and thereafter gradually revert to the original level.

● *How do I prevent fish from leaning against heaters and burning themselves?*

This is a constant problem with some sedentary fish. If using a separate gravity-fed rapid sand filter (see Filtration, pages 26–27) the heaters can be housed in the filter tank rather than with the fish. Or you can surround the heater with a suitable plastic mesh that allows water circulation but avoids direct contact with the fish. You can buy plastic tank decor incorporating an airstone in which you can secrete the heater without suffering overheating or circulation problems. On the other hand, just making the heater more obtrusive can sometimes help, as the fish feel a little more secure among the rockwork than near the exposed heater. Of course, the root cause of fish approaching the heater may be that you have the thermostat set too low; check the thermometer.

● *What should I do in the event of a power cut?*

The larger the tank, the less the heat reduction. For the duration of the power cut, cover the tank with some form of insulation, a blanket for instance (but not fibrous material, such as roof insulation). Some aquarists prefer to place polystyrene tiles or panels on the sides and back of the aquarium as a permanent feature, which can both be decorative and act as an insulator. A tight cover glass should also help. When the power returns, let the tank heat gradually under its own thermostatic control, as too rapid heating will harm your fish.

Heater Specifications

Heater size	Aquarium size
75 watt	to 15 gal (68 l; 19 US gal)
100 watt	to 20 gal (91 l; 25 US gal)
150 watt	to 30 gal (136 l; 38 US gal)
200 watt	to 50 gal (227 l; 63 US gal)
300 watt	to 80 gal (364 l; 100 US gal)
2x200 watt	to 100 gal (455 l; 125 US gal)
2x300 watt	to 150 gal (682 l; 188 US gal)

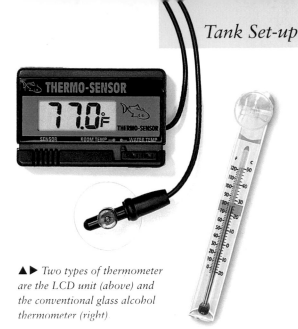

▲▶ *Two types of thermometer are the LCD unit (above) and the conventional glass alcohol thermometer (right)*

and reliability. Their sensor is a small element placed in the water and connected to the external thermostat by a thin cable. (Some units have pressure sensors that attach to the outer surface of the tank.) The sensor passes information on the water temperature to the thermostat, which switches the heater on or off. On some units the sensor also gives a reading of the temperature which is displayed on a small liquid crystal display (LCD) panel on the thermostat.

Thermometers

There is little point heating and regulating the water temperature if you cannot tell how warm the water is. The thermometer is both the most useful and the cheapest fishkeeping tool. Every aquarist should have at least one; two are even better, so that you can check one against the other. There are many different types. A conventional glass alcohol thermometer containing red or blue fluid gives a quick reading. Avoid mercury thermometers; though more accurate, they have a slow reaction time and will poison your livestock and plants if one breaks in the tank.

You can also buy thin plastic strips with sections that light up in response to specific temperatures (sometimes incorrectly called LCD strip thermometers). Permanently attached to the front of the tank, they give early warning of any heating problems. More recently, inexpensive battery-powered external (true) LCD thermometers have become available.

Lighting

ONE OF THE FIRST POINTS TO CONSIDER WHEN lighting your tank is that light does not penetrate water easily. The deeper the water, the greater the loss of illumination. So, the same intensity of light that you use in your room will, in most cases, be the minimum that is required to illuminate an aquarium. Regardless of whether you are planning to grow plants in your aquarium or not, some form of tank lighting will be necessary just to view the fish.

Ensure that you get the right kind of lighting. Tungsten lights, which are common in general domestic use, are not really suitable for the aquarium. These bulbs run at a high temperature, and quickly fail if splashed by water. They are also liable to overheat when installed under a close-fitting hood. Moreover, their light has an orange hue, imperceptible to the human eye, that is unsuitable for many aquarium plants. A far more practical solution to aquarium lighting is offered by the fluorescent tubes of varying spectral hues that are now widely available. They run more cheaply and at a lower temperature, and emit up to three times the amount of light of a tungsten bulb. A single fluorescent tube running the full length of the aquarium will generally suffice if you are not aiming to grow plants in your set-up.

However, if you want to take on the challenge of creating a beautifully planted aquarium, then your lighting requirements will be more complex. Aquarium plants not only need the proper amount of illumination, but also the right type of light as regards its colour frequency emission. As the phenomenon of a rainbow, or light shone through a prism, readily demonstrates, natural light is made up of a spectrum of different colours. Artificial light has difficulty in recreating the spectrum, and is often a compromise. Advances in lighting technology mean that certain parts of the natural spectrum can be enhanced, but absolutely faithful reproduction of daylight remains elusive.

● *Could I reduce my tank's dependency on a fluorescent tube by siting it in direct sunlight?*

This is not an ideal solution, as it invariably promotes algal growth. The light is not sufficiently intense – having been reduced by passing through a window, the tank glass, and then the water – to support higher plant life. At least with artificial light you have full control over its intensity and duration.

● *There are many types of fluorescent tube on the market, each claiming advantages over others, but which is best for a single-tube installation?*

Quite honestly, no one type offers an all-round solution. Some tubes emit a somewhat cold light; these work well for around 6 months, after which the light intensity seems to fall off quite rapidly, but nonetheless promotes good plant growth. A standard warm-white tube, available from the local hardware store, is also reasonably effective. It all depends on the type of plants you wish to grow (see Plants, pages 188–199).

● *If I am keeping fish that require subdued lighting conditions, how can I also grow plants in my tank?*

Subdued lighting is not just about the amount of light emitted, but more about the tank set-up. It is possible to provide subdued lighting for your fish without stunting the growth of your plants. Aquarium decor should be chosen with this in mind. A piece of wood or rockwork forming an arch will meet the fishes' lighting needs. Some large broad-leaved plants will also act as a "parasol" for them. In many instances, it is enough to provide the fish with a place of refuge if they should become alarmed.

● *I have heard mention of using a tungsten bulb both as a light source and water heater in small tanks. What is your opinion?*

This practice is both dangerous and ineffective. Moisture eventually forms on the electrical contacts in the lamp holder, leading to a substantial electric shock. The heat differential between the surface of the bulb in contact with the water and that above the water level is sufficient to drastically reduce its life. The likelihood of the bulb breaking and exposing the internal filament to the water is thus increased.

Aquarists in the Netherlands, who are renowned for their planted tanks, often use a series of full-length tubes spaced at around 4in (10cm) intervals from front to back of the aquarium. This system appears to work very well. Each tube covers a different part of the spectrum, emitting slightly warmer or cooler tints, and the end result is the closest possible reproduction of natural sunlight.

In addition to light intensity and colour, the duration of lighting is an important consideration. A traveller to the tropics quickly becomes aware of the very short periods of dawn and dusk; 12 hours of daylight are followed by a 12-hour night. Also, unlike more temperate zones, where daylight hours vary with the seasons, in the tropics no such change affects the length of the day. As tropical plants are accustomed to such conditions, these need to be replicated in the aquarium. If you are using just a single light, then it should stay on for 12 hours. Additional lights, of differing colour output, can be sequenced to come on for a duration of between 2–4 hours less per day. This is best achieved with time switches, and mimics the intensity of the tropical sun as midday approaches and recedes.

Alternative Forms of Lighting

Good alternatives to fluorescent tubes are high-intensity mercury vapour and metal halide lamps, which are expensive both to buy and to run, but are extremely effective. Take care when using them; so bright is the light they emit that they must be properly screened from people's direct line of vision to prevent damage to their eyesight. The eyes of your fish, however, are protected by the filtering effect of the water through which the light has to pass. These types of lighting are often used in conjunction with fluorescent tubes.

Bear in mind that the useful life of all forms of aquarium lighting, whether fluorescent tubes or specialized lamps, is strictly limited. Although they may still appear to be emitting enough light, the difference will be noticeable as soon as you fit a replacement. The working life of most tubes is around 12–18 months, after which they should be replaced. Metal halide lamps have a similar life, while mercury vapour lamps should be changed more frequently. Early tell-tale signs of the imminent failure of a fluorescent tube are burn marks at one or both ends. Shortly after these appear, it will begin flickering; once this happens, the tube is long overdue for replacement.

◀ *This striking octagonal aquarium is lit by a single high-intensity lamp. In this set-up, the lighting has been made into a feature; other aquarists prefer to conceal it under the tank hood.*

Air Pumps and Aeration

THE MAIN FUNCTION OF AN AIR PUMP IS TO cause water movement, either by powering an airstone to give a cascade of small rising bubbles, or through moving water in an upright tube by creating larger bubbles of air that push the water up the tube. This latter function is normally referred to as an airlift.

First, it is important to dispel one myth. The air stream from an airstone in the aquarium does not in itself increase the amount of dissolved oxygen. The length of time the air bubbles take to rise to the surface is insufficient to diffuse oxygen into the surrounding water. An airstone's function, rather, is to disturb the water surface, causing ripples that increase the area of water in direct contact with the air. It is only here that oxygen exchange takes place, as witness the fact that, when something has caused the level of dissolved oxygen in the water to drop, fish congregate at the surface to maximize their oxygen intake. An airstone improves water circulation around the heater and introduces fresh water to replace that at the surface; it also enhances the amount of dissolved oxygen in the tank.

Air pumps are also used to power undergravel filters (see Filtration, pages 25–26) that employ the airlift principle to pass water through the filter medium. This principle works by displacing water from the up-pipe; to replace it, more water is drawn through the filter bed and back into the airlift tube. Simple corner filters use a similar system, though here the medium is not the gravel substrate, but filter wool or an equivalent.

Air pumps for domestic aquaria are invariably of the diaphragm design. Inside the pump casing is an arm, fixed at one end, which is made to vibrate rapidly (50–60 times per second) by an electronic coil. The free end of the arm is attached to a rubber diaphragm stretched over a cavity. As the diaphragm vibrates it sucks in air through one port and expels it through another. These ports are fitted with small flap-type check valves to ensure that the air travels in the right direction. Usually there is some form of filter pad through which the air is ingested into the pump. Air from the pump then passes along a plastic pipe to the airstone or airlift.

The vibrating action of these pumps makes them rather noisy, though more modern designs have gone a long way to minimizing their obtrusiveness. Inevitably, wear and tear occurs on the moving parts, principally the diaphragm, but also the flap valves. These are not usually difficult or expensive to replace, so when purchasing an air pump it is a wise investment to buy a spare diaphragm in case of emergency. If your filter is

● There are two outlets on my air pump. Does this limit the number of devices I can connect to?

Not at all; there are low-cost T-pieces and adjustable flow valves that you can buy to increase your pump's versatility, but bear in mind that there is a limit to how many devices can be powered off the one pump.

● Can I suppress the noise of my air pump by putting it in the cabinet below the aquarium?

Yes, provided there is enough airflow both into the pump and around it to prevent overheating. Also ensure an in-line check valve is fitted between the pump and the airstones to stop water back-flowing.

● Why has the air flow of my pump dropped off since I first installed it?

The diaphragm may need replacing, though that is usually signalled by an increase in noise level as the actuating arm inside the pump flails around untethered. Check that the flap valves in the pump are seated on a clean surface. Also check the condition of any flow valves or T-pieces fitted to the system; these can become blocked after a while. Alternatively, the airstone may have got blocked, or the air line kinked. Filter pads can also become clogged and need to be replaced regularly. In addition, standard airstones deteriorate and clog over time (some in 6–12 months) and need to be replaced.

dependent on an air pump, then all the while it is out of action the vital microbacteria in the filter medium will be decaying.

One key point when using an air pump is not to locate it below the water level without using an in-line check (one-way) valve between the pump and the airstone or airlift. This small, inexpensive item stops the water back-siphoning, which can flood the pump and ruin its electronic components. When you fit the valve, make sure

that it is the right way round, allowing free passage from the pump, not to the pump. Also, never locate the pump on top of the aquarium, lest the vibrations cause the pump to "walk" and fall off, or even worse, drop into the tank.

▼ *Here, air from an air pump passes through a plastic pipe into the airlift tube via an airstone. The deeper the water in your tank, the more powerful the air pump needs to be to run the airstone, filter, etc.*

Aquarium Maintenance

As an aquarist, your prime concern is for the health and longevity of the living creatures in your care. To provide the best conditions for your fish and plants, a regime of regular aquarium maintenance is essential. In the broadest terms, the key to running a successful tank is knowledge and efficient application of water management; the precise details of what needs to be done and how often are matters that you must decide for yourself, as every aquarium is different. Most tank maintenance takes less than an hour a week for an average-sized domestic tank, and can spare you the distress (not to mention the financial outlay) involved in having to replace livestock.

Aquarium maintenance is greatly facilitated if you keep an accurate log. Enter what you have done and when you did it, be it adding a new fish, feeding a new food, or whatever. Then if something goes wrong, you will be able to check back and identify the probable cause. A log is invaluable should you need to dose the aquarium, as exact details of the amounts of chemicals used can be noted. This should prevent you overdosing in future or, at worst, mixing a lethal cocktail of medications.

Effective water management need not entail buying an array of expensive equipment. Apart from regularly consulting the thermometer that you will already have installed in your aquarium

Q&A...

● *I keep a spare heater/thermostat, but is there anything else I should have on hand?*

Yes, filter media for whatever system you are using, O-seals and bearings for power filters, diaphragms and filter pads for air pumps, starters for lights, fuses (of the correct size) for plugs and in-date test kits for nitrites, pH and hardness. These replacement parts and diagnostic aids can literally be life-savers in the event of equipment failure when your aquarium store is closed.

● *What types of abnormal fish behaviour are the most common signs of problems with the water?*

If your fish are at the surface then they probably do not have enough dissolved oxygen in the water. To aid respiration, they are coming towards the surface where the dissolved oxygen is richer. Conduct a partial water change and check the filter for blockage. If all the fish are listless and not eating, test the temperature. Your heater or thermostat may be faulty. Clamped fins can also be indicative of low temperature, but is more often related to ill health or disease.

◄ *Kissing Gouramis (Helostoma temminckii) are easy fish to keep, as they are very adaptable and tolerate most water conditions. Close scrutiny of fish behaviour for any abnormalities is a good "early warning system" for identifying imminent problems. Most difficulties can be resolved by efficient water management.*

● *I am confined to a wheelchair, and find maintaining my tank a real struggle. Can I get someone to help me with this?*

Yes; if you feel uneasy about asking aquarist friends to help you, then you could employ someone on a commercial basis. Aquarium stores often organize maintenance services – shop around for a competitive rate, and make sure that you employ a reputable operative with full insurance cover. It is also important that they detail in writing the precise tasks to be carried out under the agreement.

● *I have a skin complaint that is aggravated when I get my hands wet. Is it all right to use rubber gloves in the aquarium?*

Yes, but first check that they are not coated with anything that may harm the fish, and don't use the same pair that you use for washing up or cleaning, which will have potentially harmful chemical residues on them. Lower the water level before planting plants; there are tongs available that allow you to work in deep water, but these take some practice to work with.

● *Are commercial siphons worth using?*

Yes – a commercial siphon system is a good investment if you are concerned about the possibility of inadvertently ingesting tank water while siphoning. They are relatively easy to use and especially convenient if you are changing water in quarantine or hospital tanks, where pathogens and/or medications may be present.

✓ AQUARIUM MAINTENANCE CHECKLIST

DAILY
1 Check the temperature
2 Check the fish
3 Check equipment to ensure it is working and mend or replace as necessary

WEEKLY
1 Carry out a 20–25% water change
2 Siphon the substrate, stirring the upper half-inch if necessary, to remove faeces and any other debris
3 Remove any dead vegetation
4 Check nitrite levels
5 Clean condensation trays and cover glasses to remove any build-up of algae and salts, otherwise light to plants will be reduced

6 Clean front glass with a scraper
7 Trim plants as required

MONTHLY
1 Clean filter(s) including the pipes, which can become furred up with algae. Use a pin to clear holes in spray bars
2 Check airstones are still effective

BIANNUALLY
1 Service power filter motors
2 Service air pumps and replace filters
3 Replace half the fluorescent tubes on planted aquaria (six months later replace the remainder)
4 Replace UV sterilizer tube

(see Heating, pages 14–15), the simple practice of touching the tank will help you, over time, gain an instinctive awareness of whether the water is at the correct temperature. Cleaning or replacing the filters is also quite straightforward (see Filtration, pages 26–27); remember that doing this disturbs the bacteria beds, so you should refrain from adding any new fish to the tank for a few days.

Maintenance, then, is not simply about the physical upkeep of your tank. It also means developing a "feel" for the aquarium and for the well-being of its occupants. For example, fish behaviour is a very good indicator of actual or potential problems. You will find that as your experience grows, so you will quickly notice even the most subtle changes in your fish. Spots and cuts will be immediately apparent, but other less obvious abnormalities – clamped fins, loss of appetite, change of colour, shimmying, gasping at the surface, rapid respiration and scratching – can also be signs that something is wrong. An environmental crisis (for instance, a sudden deterioration in water quality) or a medical emergency (such as an outbreak of disease) may be imminent. There is no "sixth sense" involved in anticipating such problems, rather it is a question of keen observation and accurate analysis. Prompt action on your part can avert a disaster; in some cases, all that may be required is a simple water change.

Water Changing

No matter how effective your filtration system, regular water changes are vital. The precise frequency will depend on the fish being kept; consult the Tank Conditions and Care features on each individual species for guidance.

Never replace all the water in the aquarium at one time. Unless the new water were suitably aged and consistent with the existing tank water, this would seriously damage the health of your fish, and most likely kill them. Normal changes

◄ *Calcium deposits have been allowed to build up on this heater, making it unsightly and drastically reducing its efficiency. Poor tank maintenance can result in the deterioration of your equipment, which may ultimately put the lives of your fish at risk.*

► *Removing detritus such as excreta and uneaten food from the substrate is an essential maintenance task. Here, a power cleaner is being used, but the siphon hose can also be passed over the substrate when you do a water change.*

● *How can I avoid sucking up fish with the pipe during siphoning?*

... This can be a real problem if you have several small, inquisitive fish in your tank. The best solution is to purchase a commercial siphoning gravel cleaner equipped with a safety screen.

● *Every week I find I am getting a high nitrite reading. After a water change it drops again. What might be the cause of this?*

The most common causes are overfeeding or an interruption in filtration, possibly as the result of a power cut. It may also be the case that your tank is overstocked. In the short term, you can reduce the nitrite level to zero with daily 25% water changes, but the root cause will ultimately need to be addressed. If the level increases again, institute larger (30%) or more frequent water changes, coupled with a reduction in feeding and a lowering of stocking levels.

● *Should I carry out any water tests before or after I have done a water change?*

Always test before doing a water change; if you leave testing until after, the new water introduced at the water change will influence the readings. If you wish, you can test again afterwards to see what has changed.

● *Is it safe to do water changes twice a week?*

Yes, provided you replace no more than 10% of the water each time; it is also essential that you use aged water on each occasion.

◄ *When using an algae scraper, take care not to scratch the glass with gravel, as algae growing in these scratches is almost impossible to remove.*

(10–12mm) bore, long enough to reach from the bottom of the aquarium to a bucket placed on the floor. A length of about 6ft 6ins (2m) should suffice for the majority of set-ups A piece of normal garden hose can be used, but a transparent hose is better, both for detecting any blockage and for creating the siphon. To siphon the water, place one end of the pipe in the water, and with most of the remainder of the hose outside the tank and below the water surface, initiate the flow of water by sucking briefly on the free end. Once the water passes along the pipe and below the water level, take the hose from your mouth and direct the water into the bucket. Now you'll realize why a pipe that shows the water movement is preferable to a garden hose!

are limited to around 20–25% volume of water every 7–14 days. The replenished water should be approximately the same temperature as that already in the tank; yet another reason to invest in a good thermometer!

Ideally, the replacement water should also be aged, though in most instances tap water will do, provided the chlorine levels are not too high. To age water, leave it to stand at least overnight (or preferably for 48 hours) to release additives such as chlorine that are added to tap water. Alternatively, spray it into a bucket to dispel the chlorine, or add a commercial liquid dechlorinator. Some aquarists like to keep a large water container ready as a reservoir for water changes, equipped with an airstone and a heater/thermostat.

The best way of removing water from the aquarium is to use a siphon pipe. This is simply a flexible plastic pipe of around 0.3–0.5in

Another method for starting the siphon is to immerse the entire hose in the tank to remove all the air from it, then with one end blocked by a finger, remove it from the tank and point it at the bucket. Although this will stop you getting a mouthful of water, submerging the full length of the pipe in the tank may frighten your fish. You also run the risk of dislodging your tank decor.

As you siphon out the water, pass the end of the pipe over the substrate to pick up any debris that has not been removed by the tank filter. When you add the new water to the tank, do it gradually, and never just "dump" it straight in. This not only saves disturbance of the gravel and tank decor, but also allows the existing and new water to mix slowly, thereby avoiding any shock to the metabolism of your fish.

Filtration

THE FUNCTION OF TANK FILTRATION CAN BEST be explained in an analogy. The atmosphere in a small room containing several people, with the windows and door firmly closed and no air-conditioning, would soon become intolerable. The same is true of water, the medium inhabited by fish; like the room, an aquarium is a minia-ture, enclosed ecosystem, totally reliant on the effectiveness of its filtration system. Filters per-form a similar function to air conditioners in maintaining the quality of the water and creating healthy conditions for both fish and plants.

The question of filtration must be addressed right at the outset of planning any aquarium. The choice and price range is large and varied; keep uppermost in your mind that your live-stock's interests are paramount, and cost consid-erations only secondary. The theme or purpose of the tank will to some extent determine your choice of filtration. Thus, a different solution is

▼ *A newly set-up tank with cloudy water. This is not injurious to the fish, but is unsightly, and can be cleared in a few days by an efficient filtration system.*

required for a densely planted Amazonian tank than for a rocky Rift Valley aquarium. In addition, special filtration may be needed for the purposes of breeding and rearing. Tank size is also a determining factor.

Many tank filters utilize the nitrogen cycle (see Maturation, pages 40–41) to a greater or lesser degree in their operation. This is a process that converts waste pollutants back into less harmful, even useful, forms. It occurs in the natural environment, and helps keep the water in a state that supports life. If it fails, then the water becomes stagnant, and is unable to sustain fish and plants. The same principle applies to aquarium filtration. Prolonged lack of filtration through power failure or defective operation can soon turn a healthy aquarium into a disaster zone. Once the aquarium is dependent on a filter system, it should only ever be turned off briefly for maintenance or cleaning.

In many instances, filters provide the catalyst for the conversion part of the nitrogen cycle to work, while the return water from the filter is harmless to the fish and contains useful nutrients for the plants.

A seemingly bewildering array of filter types is available. Many can be used in combination to increase the filtration efficiency and purity of the water. In some ways, their efficiency in filtration far exceeds the conditions the fish would find in their natural environment, where water clarity is much lower than that desired in the aquarium. Do not, however, confuse water clarity with water quality, which is the true function of filtration.

Biological Filters

Biological filters depend principally on the nitrogen cycle to perform their task. The system works by passing the water through a gravel or sand bed. Provided the water is well-oxygenated, which it will be if fish are living and thriving in

the aquarium, the oxygen will feed the bacteria in the filter media, which in turn will assist the breakdown of organic waste through the nitrogen cycle. If maintained properly, these filters are highly efficient, but only reach this state after a maturation period of around one month.

Undergravel filters are the simplest form of biological filter. They are relatively cheap, and comprise a single plate or series of connecting plates placed, as the name suggests, under the tank substrate. The gravel or sand is the medium through which the water is drawn and in which the waste is converted into a harmless form. Water movement is generated either by airlift tubes or submersible pumps (powerheads) fitted to the lift tubes, which draw water from under the plates.

The performance of these simple filters depends on the free passage of water through the largest possible surface area of substrate. They are not suitable for use in tanks where the fish are likely to dig, for instance many of the Central American cichlids, as the depressions in the gravel provide a short-cut for the water flow, which seriously impairs the filter's efficiency.

While the undergravel filter might appear to be a "fit-and-forget" system, it does require periodic maintenance. After a while the gravel can become fairly heavily laden with waste material

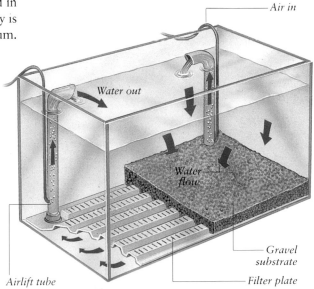

▶ *A tank fitted with a conventional-flow undergravel filter. In this system, water is drawn down through the filter bed (substrate) and returned via the airlift tube to the top of the aquarium.*

Air in

Water out

Water flow

Airlift tube

Gravel substrate

Filter plate

that has not completed conversion. So, when conducting a water change, gently disturb the upper layers of the gravel to free some of the dirt, and remove the suspended debris during siphoning. Another word of caution – if the flow of water is too fast, it has been known to draw freshly hatched fry into the gravel.

Gravity-fed rapid sand filters are a superior type of biological filter. This is essentially an undergravel filter installed outside the tank. Instead of being fitted in the main aquarium, the filter is housed in a separate tank concealed beneath it. The filtration tank, which need not be as deep as the main aquarium, is divided into compartments (see diagram) through which the water flows through differing density filtration gravel and sand, after which it is pumped back up to the main aquarium.

The "gravity-fed" part of its title refers to the method by which water flows from the top tank into the rapid sand filter. Instead of using a siphon arrangement, as in canister or power filters, the feed pipe acts as an overflow pipe. As water is pumped from the filter, the main tank level reaches the height of the overflow tube, allowing the water to flow by gravity back to the filter. Gravity-fed rapid sand systems are the very best biological filters for domestic freshwater

▼ *A gravity-fed rapid sand filter. This unit comprises a series of compartments containing trays, through which the tank water is passed. The filter media include coarse, medium and fine filter sands.*

aquaria. But they are expensive; in effect you are buying a second, more complex tank. They must also be designed into the tank set-up from the outset, with an overflow system inbuilt in the main aquarium. On the other hand, they do double the surface area of the set-up, allowing better infusion of oxygen into the overall water mass. General tank equipment such as heaters and thermostats can be concealed in the lower filter tank, rather than looking somewhat obtrusive in the main aquarium. They also offer the possibility of using special media at the output stage of the filter to alter the water characteristic to suit specific fish needs, such as crushed coral shells to harden the water for a Lake Tanganyikan tank set-up, or peat moss for the soft, acidic tank conditions preferred by many South American characins.

Mechanical Filters

Mechanical filters operate by removing sediment and debris. This is achieved by passing water through a canister containing a filter material, usually filter wool, which collects the debris, after which the water is returned to the main body of tank water. These filters also perform a degree of biological filtration, but the effectiveness of the nitrification process is somewhat limited due to the restricted filtration area.

Internal box filters are an extremely basic form of mechanical filter. An airlift pipe powers a simple clear or semi-transparent plastic container, filled with filter wool and weighted down with

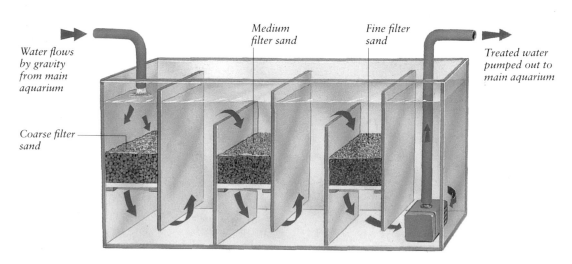

Water flows by gravity from main aquarium

Medium filter sand

Fine filter sand

Treated water pumped out to main aquarium

Coarse filter sand

Q&A...

● *Can I do without a filter in my tank?*

Theoretically, yes; water quality can be maintained by the natural nitrogen cycle. However, normal aquarium stocking levels, with their commensurately high levels of waste, preclude this option. It would be unwise to try to set up most aquaria without some form of filtration.

● *Would a simple airstone suffice?*

No; an airstone, powered from an air pump, primarily causes water movement. Little or no air is diffused as the bubbles rise in the water column. The main function of an airstone, except when used as an airlift in some filter systems for moving water, is to disturb the water surface and, through the ripples thus created, increase the area of water interface with the atmosphere.

● *I wish to set up a well-planted community tank. Would an under-gravel filter improve plant growth?*

Unfortunately not. Far from helping the plants grow, the moderately rapid downflow of water over their roots often impedes their growth. Anyway, plants do not obtain nutrients from water being drawn past the roots, but absorb it through their leaves from water that is pumped back into the aquarium after filtration.

● *How can I change my undergravel filter for a different method of filtration?*

Biological filters cannot simply be switched off – the nitrogen cycle would quickly break down, and the water turn toxic. Your only options are either to continue to use the undergravel filter but supplement it with another form of filtration, or to completely dismantle the aquarium, remove the unwanted filter plates, and thoroughly wash the gravel if you are re-using it. This again underlines the importance of choosing your filtration carefully when you first set your tank up .

● *Despite cleaning my power filter, its flow rate is far lower than when first installed. Why is this?*

Check the pump impeller bearings; if they are worn and inefficient, they usually rattle. A more likely cause is seal failure. Most external power filters use O-ring seals between the canister and the lid. When these fail, air is sucked into the canister and the pump cavitates. Only once the pump is turned off does the water leak out. Always have an emergency supply of spare filter bearings and seals.

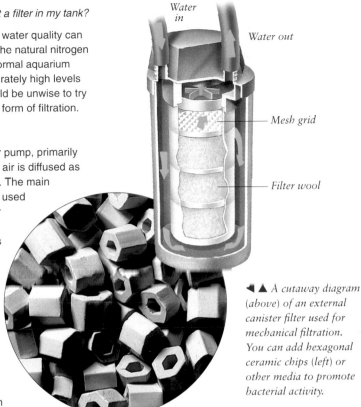

Water in

Water out

Mesh grid

Filter wool

◀▲ *A cutaway diagram (above) of an external canister filter used for mechanical filtration. You can add hexagonal ceramic chips (left) or other media to promote bacterial activity.*

small pebbles or marbles. The airlift pipe works by pumping air through an airstone near the base of the vertical pipe. As the bubbles rise and expand, the water is driven up the pipe, drawing more water through the filter media. These are often referred to as box or corner filters. Another even simpler arrangement, the sponge/airlift filter, dispenses with the box. Instead it has an inverted, walking stick-shaped pipe complete with airlift, with the short end of the pipe (not the airlift section) fitted with an open-celled foam rubber filter block through which the water passes. Both of these simple filter arrangements are often used in small breeding and fry tanks, to which their gradual flow rates are ideally suited. They are less effective in tanks larger than 1ft (30cm).

Power or canister filters provide efficient mechanical filtration for larger tanks. These use electrical pumps to convey the water at much higher flow rates than that achieved with simple airlifts. Some versions employ a totally sealed electric pump for submerging in the aquarium, while others are designed for placement outside the tank. Both types work on similar principles, but the larger filters designed for large aquaria are, by necessity, of the external variety. Like the internal box filter, the canister of the power filter contains media in which to trap particles. This may be filter wool, open-cell foam rubber, or even a block of nylon strands similar to a pan scourer. In many cases there is sufficient space within the canister to insert other media, either to improve the biological filtration effect or modify the water chemistry to suit the tank inhabitants. The internal variety is self-priming, whereas the external power filter relies on water being siphoned through to prime the pump. As the flow rate of these filters is fairly high, always fit the basket provided over the intake tube to prevent small fish being sucked up, or larger debris blocking the pipe.

Mechanical filters require more regular maintenance than biological filters. The medium, being condensed into a small area, can quickly become clogged with collected debris, slowing the water flow. The medium will require changing every three to six weeks, depending on the demands of the filter. When changing the filter wool it is advisable to retain a little of the existing wool from the cleaner side, as this will contain bacteria that help the nitrogen cycle take place, and that will quickly colonize the new replacement wool.

Certain products can be bought to improve the biological efficiency of mechanical filters, such as porous ceramic chips. With their high surface area, these provide a good foundation on which the nitrifying bacteria can propagate. The chips are generally sandwiched between two layers of filter wool, the first to strain off the bulky debris, the second to "polish" the water.

Trickle Filters and Other Types

Wet/dry filters combine biological and mechanical methods of filtration, though with a bias towards the former. They are normally applied after a power filter, acting on the water as it returns to the aquarium. Trickle filters comprise a series of stacked shallow trays containing filter wool or sand (or a combination). The trays have

Spray bar — *Filter wool or sand*

Filtered water returns to main aquarium

Plastic trays with drainage holes

▲ *A basic trickle filter system. Units such as this are sited above the main tank. They are supplied by water pumped through a spray bar from a power filter. Trickle filters help oxygenate the water flowing through them and so increase bacterial activity.*

drainage holes in their base, so that the water from the power filter's outlet flows onto and through the filter medium in the top tray, down through the successive trays and back into the tank. As the medium is never fully immersed, it is in permanent contact with the atmosphere, from where it extracts oxygen to feed the bacteria in the filter beds, hence the alternative name of wet/dry filter.

Sometimes only a single tray is employed, though they are more often used in multiples. Despite their simplicity, trickle filters are very efficient, and impart extra transparency to the aquarium water. As the flow through them is diffused, they are sometimes used to good effect on their own in small fry tank set-ups.

Diatomaceous earth filters are essentially a form of power filter, but contain a totally different filter medium – the microscopic skeletons of zooplankton. This is a very fine compound,

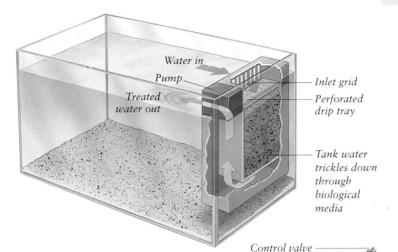

Water in

Pump

Treated
water out

◀ *Internal trickle filters are a
good idea where space around
the aquarium is extremely
limited. These units can be
adapted to contain a carbon
filter or denitrification unit.
Their main disadvantage is
that they take up valuable
space within the aquarium
and can look unsightly.*

Inlet grid
Perforated
drip tray

Tank water
trickles down
through
biological
media

Control valve
Water in

Media

▶ *Small single-tray trickle filters sited
above the tank can be used effectively on
breeding and rearing tanks, or where it is
impractical to fit a larger multi-tray unit.*

Canister filter
*(positioned below the
tank) filled with
filter wool*

Water out

which can only be used in conjunction with a
purpose-designed power filter. Its fineness also
means that it easily gets blocked. As a result,
these filters are not normally used for the main
tank filtration, but to give extra transparency to
the water, or to remove microscopic water-borne
organisms such as *Ichthyophthirius* (whitespot
or "Ich") in its free-swimming stage. Both the filters and the medium they use are expensive.

Another expensive form of filtration is the
pressure-fed filter. This is similar to the biological gravity-fed rapid sand filter, except that the
sand is contained within a pressurized container,
and the water is forced through the sand to effect
filtration. These are more commonly used on
large marine installations, though they are just
as effective on freshwater systems.

Recently, filters that combine biological and
mechanical filtration with trickle filters in a single unit have become available. Though expensive, they can easily handle the total filtration
demands of the tank. They are available both as
internal and external modules.

Q&A

● *How do I prevent small fry being
sucked into a filter?*

... The water flow on power filters is
quite significant, so if raising fry in a
small separate tank an air-operated box or sponge
filter would be more appropriate. Many box filters have
an adjustable inlet grille that can be regulated to
prevent small fry being sucked in.

● *What maintenance should be undertaken with
trickle filters?*

Trickle filters periodically require medium replenish-
ment, though generally not as frequently as power
filters. If a multiple-layer trickle filter is used, then only
replace the medium in the top tray, and relocate it to
the bottom of the stack, moving the other trays above.
In this way you will still retain the bulk of the bacterial
beds undisturbed.

Ultra-violet Sterilizers

ULTRA-VIOLET (UV) STERILIZERS DIFFER FROM filters in that they do not change the characteristics of the water, but instead kill microscopic free-swimming organisms such as bacteria and protozoa, as well as free-swimming algae and fungal spores. In the spectrum, ultra-violet light is located between visible light (blue end of the spectrum) and X-rays. Radiation from UV lamps reacts with the DNA structure of cells of pathogens. The efficiency of this radiation is governed both by exposure time and especially by the depth and transparency of the water.

Modern UV sterilizers utilize low-heat tube lamps (similar to neon tubes). Surrounding the lamp along its full length is a second clear tube made of quartz. Yet another tube, in this case opaque, provides the outer case. The water passes between this outer tube and the quartz tube in the process of ultra-violet radiation. The quartz tube is present firstly to shield the tube from direct contact with the water, a simple electrical precaution, and secondly to transmit the UV through to the water more efficiently than glass. The outer case is opaque to prevent harmful rays escaping and damaging viewers' sight, and also to prevent the build-up of algae and slime on the quartz tube, which would lower the proficiency of the sterilizer.

▼ *Diagrams showing the position of a UV sterilizer in relation to a tank filter, and the construction of the unit. Because the light they emit is extremely harmful, sterilizers are housed away from the tank, so that there is no direct line of sight to them; direct exposure would also damage the cells of your fish. Always handle UV sterilizers with care, as the quartz sleeve is easily broken.*

ULTRA-VIOLET STERILIZATION

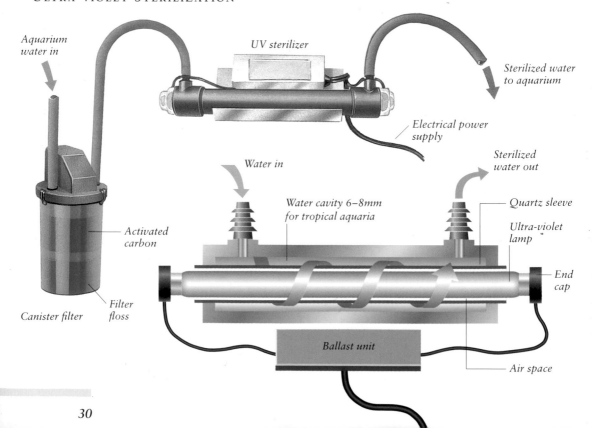

Aquarium water in

UV sterilizer

Sterilized water to aquarium

Electrical power supply

Water in

Sterilized water out

Water cavity 6–8mm for tropical aquaria

Quartz sleeve

Ultra-violet lamp

Activated carbon

End cap

Canister filter

Filter floss

Ballast unit

Air space

● *How do I know when the UV radiation of my unit is exhausted?*

... While there are specialized meters that measure the amount of UV light emitted, these are laboratory-grade instruments, and not generally available to the home aquarist. The best course of action is to note the date of installation on the side of the unit (some manufacturers provide a label) and renew the tube as appropriate.

● *In a permanent installation, should a sterilizer be turned off like the tank lighting for parts of the day?*

UV units may be turned off for a period of time, but while off they are performing no function. In freshwater systems, they are better suited for specific tasks, such as warding off fungal attack on hatching eggs.

● *I understand there are a number of different specification UV tubes. Is a specific unit required, or can I try one of these alternatives?*

Yes, there are many degrees of UV lights available. Many are not suitable for sterilization purposes, but are used for disco lighting! The most efficient tubes emit light in the 250–255 nm wavelength. Always replace the tube with a type recommended by the manufacturer.

USING A UV STERILIZER

✔ Always change the tube before it becomes ineffective. Though it may still appear sound, UV radiation will be much reduced.

✔ Ensure the quartz tube surrounding the UV tube is clear of slime and algae, otherwise its effectiveness will be reduced. If it is cracked, replace immediately. Quartz tube replacements can be obtained easily and cheaply.

✔ Always disconnect from the mains and isolate the water supply before undertaking any maintenance.

✗ Never look directly at the tube when it is on. It will damage your retina.

✗ Do not operate the UV unit for protracted periods with no water flowing through it, otherwise it may overheat and fail prematurely.

✗ Do not fit in a damp position, particularly under the tank hood – electricity and water do not mix.

As the efficiency of the sterilizer partially depends on water transparency, this unit is normally fitted in the return line from an external filter, more usually a power filter, allowing the filter to refine the water before exposing it to the UV light. As depth is also a determining factor, the annular ring of water flowing between the quartz tube and the outer casing in the system described above is rarely greater than 10–12mm, more often 6–8mm. Whereas marine systems require a maximum of around 6mm to perform, fresh water, with fewer inorganic ions, can work effectively with water depths approaching 20mm or greater. Flow rates too affect the sterilizer's efficiency. Manufacturers usually list such data as part of the specification. When buying these units, specify your tank size, state whether it is for use in tropical freshwater or brackish water (which, like marine water, requires shallower water penetration and slower flow rates).

Ultra-violet lights have an alarmingly short useful life, and while the tube may appear to be emitting light, its UV content may be much reduced. The working life of a tube is generally around 800 hours, though manufacturers usually recommend replacing it after 500–600 hours, or six months' normal use.

Ultra-violet sterilizers can either be part of permanent installation, or used periodically for a specific purpose. UV light effectively kills or weakens such pathogens as *Ichthyophthirius* (whitespot or 'Ich'), but only in its free-swimming stage. It also helps control algal blooms (a problem in new set-ups), but again, only the water-borne algae passing through the sterilizer is treated. Some aquarists use sterilizers to prevent fungal spores attacking eggs and newly hatched fry, especially when hatched in quarantined conditions separate from the parents. If quarantining new fish before moving them to the main tank, a sterilizer helps eliminate harmful bacteria and other micro-parasites. They are also used to good effect in central filter systems operated by many commercial fish stockists. This is where a number of tanks are serviced by one large filter, with the water circulating through all the stock tanks. By using a UV sterilizer in the filter system, the risk of transferring harmful parasites and protozoa is greatly reduced.

Water Chemistry and Testing

MANY FISH IN THE FRESHWATER AQUARIUM are fairly tolerant of variations in water chemistry, only requiring precisely regulated conditions for acclimatization or to induce spawning. Others, however, are more particular. African Rift Valley cichlids, for example, thrive in hard, alkaline water, whereas the South American discus cichlids require soft, acidic waters if they are to prosper and breed.

The chemical make-up of natural waters is largely determined by that of the terrain over which they flow. Rivers that are formed by rain drainage through limestone fissures and caves are hard and alkaline, while those that are fed mainly from forest drainage tend to be slightly acidic. Likewise, our domestic water supply contains minerals and salts that have either leached in at source, or been added by the supplier to ensure that the water is of drinkable quality.

All aquarists should equip themselves with a range of test kits. Most test kits work by adding chemicals to water samples to determine the pH level or hardness, or the presence of particular

▲ *Tiger Barbs* (Barbus tetrazona) *headstanding in an early stage of nitrate poisoning. Nitrates are less harmful than ammonia or nitrites, but must still be kept in check in your tank.*

◄ *A test kit used to measure the level of highly toxic nitrites* (NO_2)*. As with all test kits, the capsules of chemicals are added to a water sample, never directly to the tank.*

toxins. For measuring pH, test kits and dipsticks (thin pieces of plastic that change colour according to the water's acidity or alkalinity) are available, in addition to electronic meters that do not rely on chemical reactions and are more accurate. A number of different toxin test kits enable the aquarist to ascertain the levels of ammonia, nitrites, nitrates or copper in the tank. Testing for the presence of ammonia and nitrites is an indispensable part of setting up and maturing a new aquarium (see Maturation, pages 40–41). A test kit for nitrates will allow you accurately to assess the quality of your tap water, and a copper test kit is a useful measuring tool after you have had to dose your tank with a copper-based medication (e.g. malachite green) as a cure for whitespot. Finally, since many aspects of water chemistry can be affected by temperature, don't neglect to use the simplest test kit of all – the thermometer!

At the first sign of change in behaviour of the fish, use the appropriate test aids to find out what action is needed. Incorrect water chemistry can raise the stress level of fish, which in turn can adversely effect their immune system, and thus leave the door open to disease.

Water changes (see Aquarium Maintenance, pages 22–23) will often alter the chemistry of the water, albeit briefly. As long as the tank is mature and stable, it should self-regulate.

Water Hardness

Water hardness is a measure of the amount of dissolved salts – particularly calcium, but also magnesium – in the water. Although a variety of scales exist, the most common scale is °dH, a measure of general hardness, and not just the carbonate hardness. Soft water starts at a value of 0°dH, and becomes harder as the value rises to 25°dH and above (see table). Rainwater is generally around 0 to 2°dH, with any hardness coming from particles in the atmosphere. Tap water varies according to its source. For example, London tap water, which is drawn

from underground clay-lined natural aquifers after it has already leached through chalk strata, is generally hard, around 18 to 22°dH. Supplies from peaty moorland regions will generally be softer, 5–10°dH. (Some of these values fluctuate as the water authorities add chlorine, fluoride and other chemicals in the interests of hygiene and potability.)

As a rule, fish that require alkaline conditions also prefer harder water. There are exceptions, but this is a fairly good rule of thumb. As with pH, the hardness can be adjusted by a variety of means. Crushed coral shells in the filter or as substrate in the aquarium will harden the water, as will the addition of limestone, either as a decorative rock in the aquarium, or in crushed form in the filter. To soften the water, there are proprietary units containing ion exchange resins through which the water is pumped. Another method is to collect rainwater in a water barrel. If doing this, ensure that it is not contaminated by substances on the roof or surface on which it falls. Do not use rainwater exclusively as it does not contain certain trace elements essential to the fishes' wellbeing; instead mix with tap water to achieve the right balance of hardness.

pH

Pondus hydrogenii, or pH for short, is a measure of the acidity or alkalinity of water. It is measured on a scale of 0 to 14. Water at pH 7.0 is neutral, neither acidic nor alkaline; above 7.0 the water is alkaline in varying degrees, while below 7.0 it is more or less acidic. If the prime conditions required for a fish and plants are unknown, then a broadly neutral pH (6.8–7.2) is the recommended starting point.

▶ *Table showing the calcium carbonate (CaCO₃) content of water, the equivalent °dH number and the standard descriptions for each level.*

Water Hardness

Mg/litre CaCO₃	°dH	Description
0–50	0–3	Soft
50–100	3–6	Moderately soft
100–200	6–12	Slightly hard
200–300	12–18	Moderately hard
300–450	18–25	Hard
Over 450	over 25	Very hard

● *How often should I test the water in my tank?*

A ... Once your tank is well-established and chemically stable, monitoring once a fortnight is generally all that is needed, unless you suspect some change has occurred and corrective action is required.

● *Are the chemicals used in test kits safe to use in the aquarium?*

Absolutely not; liquid-based test kits must never be brought into contact with water in the tank, as they are toxic. The only test material that is safe to immerse in the aquarium is the non-liquid dipstick for measuring pH. Use the vial or test-tube provided to extract a water sample before using the chemicals, ensuring the vial is not contaminated with residues from previous tests, or from the water used to clean it. Ultimately, you may prefer to invest in an electronic meter.

● *How reliable are chemically-based test kits?*

While fresh test kits are accurate enough for most purposes, they do have a limited shelf life, which can be further eroded if kept in adverse conditions. Always refer to the manufacturers' instructions and recommendations. If greater accuracy is sought, use an electronic meter; these have reference samples provided with which to effect minor adjustments.

● *Does it matter which type of nitrate test kit I buy?*

No, but what you must realize is that not all test kits are the same. Some read nitrate–nitrogen (NO_3–N), while others read total nitrate (NO_3). These readings are different, and you need to be able to convert from one to the other: to convert nitrate–nitrogen to total nitrate, multiply the NO_3–N reading by 4.4 (to convert the other way, divide the NO_3 reading by 4.4). Most aquarium books give NO_3 levels; before buying a test kit, check whether it tallies with the books you own.

● *By using activated carbon or zeolite in my filtration system, can I dispense with water changes?*

No, water changes are still an essential part of aquarium management.

▶ *A basic pH test kit for aquarists. It is scaled from 4.5 to 9.0; beyond this range in either direction, freshwater fish cannot survive for long. Such liquid test kits give a rough guide to levels of acidity or alkalinity, but the more expensive electronic meters are far more accurate.*

To adjust the pH, commercially available peat granules can be placed in a power filter. These will release acids gradually into the aquarium as the water flows through them. Alternatively, there are liquid extracts available, which are mixed with water in a bucket to dilute them before being added to the tank.

Horticultural peat may also be used to acidify the tank water, but great care must be exercised when buying this, as some types of garden peat contain toxic pesticides or herbicides that would prove fatal to your fish. The safe option for use in aquaria is Irish moss peat (also referred to as Sphagnum moss). After having ascertained that it contains no harmful additives, you should pack the peat tightly into a fine-meshed bag and tie it up securely. The foot section of an old nylon stocking or pair of tights is ideal for this purpose. Rinse the filled bag under the tap or in a bucket to remove any tiny particles, and then either place it in a box or canister filter after the filter wool, or secrete it in the aquarium behind some decor.

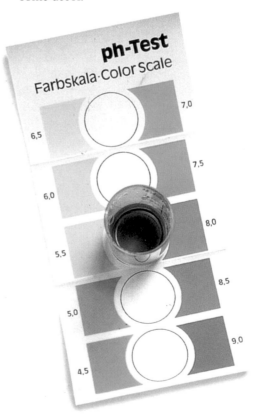

ph-Test
Farbskala·Color Scale

6,5
7,0
6,0
7,5
5,5
8,0
5,0
8,5
4,5
9,0

DO'S AND DON'TS OF WATER MANAGEMENT

✓ Wait for a while after you have conducted a water change before measuring pH or hardness, as the new water will have had an effect on the chemistry.

✓ Always measure the pH at fixed times of the day. Plants in the aquarium release CO_2 during the night and absorb it during the day, which will affect the pH value.

✓ Throw away any chemical test kits that have passed their recommended expiration date, as they will give you an inaccurate reading. Also, store all kits well away from children and animals; the toxic reagents they contain can be extremely dangerous.

✗ Never attempt rapid changes in pH or water hardness; alter them gradually over several days. Rapid pH changes, in particular, stress the fish, so weakening their immune system.

✗ Avoid extremes of pH that will adversely affect both fish and plants.

✗ Avoid mixing waters with a temperature difference greater than ± 3°C. The shock may be enough to kill the fish.

✗ Don't conduct massive water changes under normal circumstances. The water may not recover its ideal values for some time, causing stress to many fish and plants.

Pieces of wood (especially bogwood) used as decoration in the aquarium will slowly release tannins that both make the water acidic and slightly soften it. This shows as a slight tea-coloured staining of the water. It is not harmful to the majority of fish, rather beneficial.

Activated Carbon

Activated carbon is sometimes added to the filter system of freshwater tropical tanks (on the clean water side). This highly porous material, which has now supplanted charcoal, extracts dissolved organic carbon in the water through adsorption. Copper, trace elements, and heavy metals are also extracted. The water becomes more transparent, as the carbon cleanses most stains. However, it also removes many medications that are added to the water to cure disease, so its use is not advised under these circumstances. Note that excessive use of activated carbon may adversely affect plant growth.

Once they have been exhausted, the activated carbon granules should be discarded and replaced. The optimum time frame for replacing them is every two to three weeks.

▶ *Activated carbon can be used in your filtration system to reduce the discolouring that is caused by tannins leaching into the water from wood.*

Zeolites

Zeolite granules remove ammonia, both by ion exchange and adsorption. Like activated carbon, they can be added to the filter system. However, their use needs careful monitoring, as experiments have demonstrated that they can cause a harmful increase in nitrates. A small amount of zeolite granules (about a teaspoonful at most) added to fish transportation bags can be beneficial when moving fish over long distances. Granules that are a compound of zeolites and activated carbon have recently appeared on the market.

Tap Water Conditioning

Units for conditioning tap water before it reaches your aquarium are readily available. Water softeners can be plumbed into the water outlet, while filters containing resins will screen out excessive chlorine, nitrates and phosphates (increasingly added to the domestic water supply). Though initially expensive, they are a good idea if you frequently have problems with the water quality when changing the water; and they are relatively cheap and easy to recharge. A less expensive alternative is to use a liquid conditioner to neutralize chlorine and heavy metals and remove ammonia.

Hard Water Systems

IT IS ESSENTIAL, WHEN CHOOSING FRESHWATER tropical fish, to be aware both of the water chemistry of your tank, and of the particular requirements of the species you wish to keep. Some fish may suffer loss of coloration, become listless and disinclined to breed, or even die if the water conditions are not right.

For example, if you have an aquarium with water that is moderately soft (6°dH) and slightly acidic (c.6.5–6.8pH), then you will need to modify its chemical composition if you intend keeping hard water fish. This will present no problems in a new set-up, but if you are thinking of changing the water make-up in an established tank, then consider the compatibility of both the existing fish and plants. These may have to be moved to another tank.

Fresh water is regarded as slightly hard when above 6°dH, and very hard above 25°dH. Most hard water fish acclimatize more easily to soft water conditions than vice versa. Typical hard water fish are the African Rift Valley and Central American cichlids, and some Asian barbs.

Most domestic water supplies tend to be on the hard side. To measure its hardness, draw off sufficient water to conduct the test in accordance

Hard water/Alkali-loving Species

African Rift Valley Lake cichlids, such as *Julidochromis* spp., *Haplochromis* spp., Lake Malawi Mbuna, etc.

Synodontis multipunctatus catfish, also from the African Rift Valley lakes.

Some Central American cichlids, such as *Copora nicaraguensis* (Nica).

Some livebearing toothcarps, such as *Poecilia velifera* (Yucatán or Velifera Molly), and *Poecilia latipinna* (Sailfin Molly).

Astyanax fasciatus mexicanus (The Blind Cavefish).

Some of the cyprinids, such as *Epalzeorhynchos bicolor* (Red-tailed Black Shark)

Q&A

● *Can I use salt to harden the water in my tank?*

... Yes, but only use marine salts at very low concentrations. Do not add the salt directly to the tank water; instead add it gradually, dissolved in new water in the course of a water change.

● *If the water is hard, is it necessarily alkaline?*

No, but this will invariably be the case in practice. Use a test kit to monitor the level of alkalinity.

● *I live in a hard water area, so do I need to use calciferous rock as a buffer?*

No, you shouldn't need to, provided you do regular water changes.

▼ A Lake Malawi tank set-up. Its water is extremely clean and well oxygenated, and of a slight hardness and alkalinity (8–10°dH; 7.5–8.0pH). You can use Tufa rock here, as Mbuna cichlid species are mouthbrooders, which do not need smooth, flat rocks for spawning.

▼ Two types of substrate that are ideal for use in a hard water aquarium. Both contain lime, and will add both hardness and a slight degree of alkalinity to the water.

Coral sand

Coral shell

with the test kit manufacturer's instructions. Before commencing, let the sample stand for an hour or so to diffuse the chlorine and other gases added to the water in the interests of hygiene. It is worth remembering that, in the aquarium, water hardness is lowered slightly by the extraction of salts by plants. These salts can also be seen on close-fitting tank cover glasses, where they are deposited by water surface agitation, particularly near the output of a filter and above airstones. Unless special provision is made, the water will find its own hardness and pH, which may not meet the requirements of the fish.

Invariably there is a connection between the hardness (°dH) of the water and its alkalinity (pH), and those fish and plants that thrive in hard water will generally require alkaline rather than acidic conditions. To create a controlled hard water system, select a tank substrate of crushed coral shells, sand or gravel with a high calciferous content. Aquarium gravels or sands containing lime are ideally suited to this purpose, as they make the water both hard and slightly alkaline. To find out whether or not your substrate contains lime, pour a little vinegar over a small sample – if it fizzes, then it contains lime. If you are thinking of growing plants, sand is preferable, since it allows the roots to spread more easily.

The same criteria apply to the rockwork used as decoration. Ideally, this too should be calciferous (try the vinegar test). Choose your rock with care; the Tufa rock that is sometimes used to decorate hard water aquaria (particularly ones containing African Rift Valley cichlids) certainly hardens the water, but is very crumbly, and does not provide a good surface for the cichlids to spawn on. This is equally true of many types of sandstone.

Various buffer solutions can be purchased to control the hardness and alkalinity of the water. Buffers inhibit changes to the water chemistry, holding conditions stable for longer periods than would otherwise happen naturally. They are highly recommended for initial use when setting the tank up. Follow the manufacturer's advice and use your test kit to monitor the effect on the aquarium water.

Soft Water Systems

FRESHWATER BECOMES SOFT WHEN IT IS BELOW about 6°dH, and can be measured using proprietary test kits. Soft water has lower levels of calciferous salts than those found in hard water. Ideally, when setting up a soft water tank, you should use lime-free gravel or sand as a substrate. If this is not available from your local aquarium dealer, use filtration sand (available from pond suppliers); this is usually neutral and will not affect your tank's water chemistry. Also, because it has been formulated not to clog, it allows easier penetration and water circulation for plant roots when applied as a substrate. Of course, this same sand is also highly effective when used for its intended purpose, as the medium in a gravity-fed rapid sand filter!

Avoid limestone in tank decor. This calcium-rich sedimentary rock makes the water harder and more alkaline. The same is true of calciferous material in the filtration system.

Soft Water and Acidity

Soft water systems usually tend to be acidic. Wood placed in the aquarium leaches tannins that make the tank slightly acidic as well as soft. The tannin from the wood shows up as a yellowish stain in the water. This is harmless to fish, though it may reduce slightly the light for plant propagation. A small amount of activated carbon in the filter will reduce or remove this stain.

If greater acidity is required – say, for keeping killifish – then peat or peat extract (sometimes sold as "black-water tonic", as it simulates black-water conditions) should be used. Precise dosing levels of peat extract are given on the bottle. Exercise caution if you are using peat in non-liquid form; some garden peat has chemical supplements that are toxic to fish. Use Irish peat moss (Sphagnum moss) with no additives. This is often added to the power filter after the first cleaning stage. Alternatively, the peat can be placed in the aquarium. One method is to put a thin (10mm) layer of peat below the gravel

Soft water/Acid-loving Species
Many of the small South American tetras, e.g. the Diamond Tetra (*Moenkhausia pittieri*) and the Black Widow (*Gymnocorymbus ternetzi*).
Most killifish, including *Aphyosemion australe*, and *Aplocheilus lineatus*.
Loaches such as *Botia macracantha* (Clown Loach), and *Botia sidthimunki* (Pygmy Chain Loach, or Dwarf Loach).
Some South American cichlids, notably *Microgeophagus ramirezi* (Ram Cichlid), *Pterophyllum scalare* (Freshwater Angelfish) and *Symphysodon discus* (Heckel Blue Discus).
Some catfish, such as *Corydoras* spp., and many of the Loricariidae.

▶ *This tank has been set up to accommodate fish that thrive in soft, acidic water conditions. It replicates a biotope in the Amazon rainforest, and contains Ram Cichlids* (Microgeophagus ramirezi), *Black Widows* (Gymnocorymbus ternetzi) *and* Corydoras *spp. catfish.*

or sand, provided undergravel filters are not employed. The heavier gravel layer will prevent the peat from being constantly disturbed by water currents and making the water turbid. Peat also provides nutrients for plant growth. Another way of introducing peat into the aquarium is to place it in a small cloth bag through which the water can circulate, and hide it in the tank behind some decoration.

Rainwater is a good supply of soft water, so long as you ensure that it is free of pollutants either from the atmosphere or from the drainage system to the collection reservoir. Pure rainwater is virtually 0°dH, and should be mixed with harder water to achieve the right degree of hardness. Tap water can be treated by softeners fitted to your existing domestic plumbing. These work by passing the water through ion-exchange resins. Once exhausted, the resins can easily be

recharged by flushing through with a salt solution. This must not be table salt; instead, use marine or dishwasher salt.

One great advantage of an acidic tank is that fungal infections are controlled more naturally by the water chemistry. Likewise, a softwater tank will generally have fewer snails, as their shells will not be able to extract sufficient calcium from the water.

Few fish can tolerate water lower than 5.5pH, even soft water-loving species. Signs of excesssive acidity are fish gasping at the surface, or even trying to leap out. Death will quickly ensue if the problem is not remedied instantly.

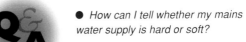

● _How can I tell whether my mains water supply is hard or soft?_

If soap lathers quickly and abundantly, then the water is soft. If not, and if there are limescale deposits in your sink and toilet, then chances are the water is hard.

● _How can I find out what water hardness is required for a particular fish?_

In this book, consult the Tank Conditions and Care features relating to the species in question. As a rough guide, lacustrine (lake-dwelling) fish tend to need harder, more alkaline water than riverine fish. But always research in depth the fish you are interested in.

Maturation

A MAJOR KEY TO SUCCESS IN FISHKEEPING IS patience, especially the realization that aquaria cannot be created overnight. This is absolutely crucial in setting up your first aquarium, when you must allow a fixed amount of time – the maturation period – to elapse before introducing your livestock. During this period, the water reaches its optimum chemistry to support life.

The Maturation Period

There is no short-cut to maturation; it is a fixed 36-day process. The only exception is where the bulk of the water is being drawn from an established tank, and the filter is "seeded" with the medium from an existing mature filter. Even in such cases, however, a 5-day delay is advised to let the tank adjust before introducing livestock

During maturation, the water and the filter undergo massive swings in toxicity. The aim is to establish an efficient mechanism for the conversion of ammonia to nitrites, and of nitrites to nitrates. High levels of both ammonia and nitrites are toxic to fish.

Initially, the level of ammonia naturally rises to alarming levels, peaking at about 9 to 10 days, after which it rapidly falls until, after about 15 days, it is negligible. As the ammonia level decreases, so the nitrites increase, until they too peak after 29 days, then swiftly decline over a further 7-day period, as they are converted into less harmful nitrates by the filtration system and other natural processes. A mature filter or tank is one in which the water has stabilized to safe levels and

▶ In the nitrogen cycle, bacteria break down waste pollutants, so keeping the water in a fit state to support life. Filtration is a vital aid to this process in aquaria, where fish densities are higher than in nature.

Q&A...

● *How can I be sure the maturation period is complete?*

The 36-day period is invariable. But if you need reassurance, see how a few fish react to the conditions over, say, a week. If they swim naturally, with no clamped fins or lifeless hanging at the surface, then the tank is ready for fish.

● *A friend has a mature aquarium. Can I use some of his water to speed up the maturation process?*

This is not advisable. The water may have a different composition to your own. In any case, the filter has to undergo its own maturation.

● *How does the maturation period affect hard- or soft-water aquaria?*

For both types, you will have used filter media and/or tank decor and substrate to modify the water chemistry to the desired level. The maturation period simply allows these processes to advance. Most first-time aquaria find their own hardness level, influenced by plants, gravel and other decor, and will generally be populated by fish with a wide water chemistry tolerance.

● *Should I change or clean the filter during this period?*

No. You must let the biological element of the filtration system develop. Even after this period is over, do not replace all the filter medium, retain a little (say 25–50%) of the old one as a starter culture for the new medium.

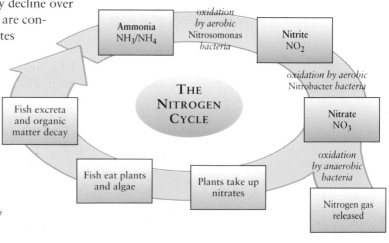

THE NITROGEN CYCLE

Ammonia NH₃/NH₄ — *oxidation by aerobic Nitrosomonas bacteria* → Nitrite NO₂ — *oxidation by aerobic Nitrobacter bacteria* → Nitrate NO₃ — *oxidation by anaerobic bacteria* → Nitrogen gas released

Fish excreta and organic matter decay → Fish eat plants and algae → Plants take up nitrates

▲ *Black Mollies* (Poecilia sphenops) *are highly tolerant of water quality. As a result, they are often the first fish placed in a new set-up by aquarists (after 20 days) to control algal growth and promote the growth of plants.*

species such as mollies, which can be introduced in small numbers after 20 days. Although the filter can take some 3–6 months to reach peak efficiency, it will be screening out most toxins by the end of the maturation period.

After the maturation period is over, algae and plants will compete for ascendancy in your tank. This struggle can take more than 6 months to resolve itself. Initially, the algae will prevail, as the plants take a while to become established and because their efficiency at extracting nutrients from the water is lower than that of the algae. Hence the "green tank syndrome" that often affects new set-ups. The way to overcome this problem is to promote plant growth so that the algae cannot compete. Some aquarists try to retard algae by reducing the lighting, but this is counter-productive, since it also stunts plant growth. A far better strategy is to remove or reduce phosphates, by passing the water through conditioning units containing ion-exchange media.

Many novice aquarists fail by trying to force the pace and, sadly, end up abandoning the hobby altogether. Success, on the other hand, engenders a feeling of well-deserved pride in your achievement, and will encourage you to take up new challenges.

The Nitrogen Cycle

A sequence of chemical reactions continues in the mature tank, in a process known as the nitrogen cycle. This works in the following way; the nitrates produced by the breakdown of ammonia and nitrites are absorbed by algae and other plants, which promotes their growth. The plants flourish, and in turn provide proteins, which fish ingest during feeding. As the fish pass the protein through their gills, and as their excreta and plant matter decompose in the tank, ammonia is produced, thus beginning the cycle anew.

the biological filter is working efficiently in breaking down metabolic waste products.

The maturation period also allows time to rid the tank of chlorine and other additives to tap water, and affords the opportunity to check that the heating system is operating correctly.

Plants should be added after 5 days, once the water temperature has stabilized and the chlorine dissipated. The plant roots will establish a good foothold without disturbance from any fish. Also, since plants are one of nature's methods of water filtration, they help produce mature, life-sustaining water. To promote plant growth, the lighting system should be in operation. No fish should be added until the 36 days are up. The sole exception are nitrite-tolerant

Fish Compatibility

THE FIRST CONSIDERATION THAT PEOPLE HAVE when keeping different fish together is their relative size; however, as fish are usually purchased as youngsters, you may not be aware of a particular species' full growth potential. The sheer size of some fish can frighten smaller species. For example, a large, very active barb or characin cruising about the tank will often intimidate the smaller species into remaining hidden among the plants around the periphery of the aquarium.

Size is often equated with predatory habits. As a very rough guide, predators have either large mouths, large eyes, long barbels or a combination of these. Clearly, if such fish are kept with smaller companions, they will eat them! But we often choose to disregard this self-evident fact.

Ignorance is frequently to blame. A novice, on seeing a small fish for sale, might mistakenly conclude that it cannot possibly pose any threat to his community fish. Only some months (and

several disappearances) later does the error become apparent. The "small fish", which has hitherto spent most of its life hiding away, is not so small any more, especially not its mouth! The lesson here is always to research specific fish before buying them.

Short-term thinking can also cause problems. Even though putting a small predator in with other fish for a brief spell may not actually result in fish being eaten, it will still seriously disrupt the social well-being of the tank.

Wherever possible, shoaling fish should be kept as a shoal. They have innate self-preservation techniques that aquarists should observe. If a predator is close by, the fish release a fright pheromone that causes the shoal to tighten and confuses the predator. Although we do not intentionally keep such predators in our community tanks, in the confines of the aquarium, fish can be frightened by external disturbances such as sudden noises, movements and so on, and should be allowed to respond naturally. Many also feed as a shoal, whereas single specimens will skulk away, uncertain whether it is safe to come out into the open to feed on their own. One of the most common beginner's mistakes is to keep Tiger Barbs in ones and twos – they can wreak havoc in a tank. Kept in tens, they behave themselves, spending more time watching one another than harassing companion species.

The most overlooked cause of trouble between aquarium fish is the need for territory. Even in the most peaceful tank, the incumbent fish each have their territory; they may not defend this aggressively, but it will still represent their small domain. Whenever you add a new fish, it will be encroaching on another's patch. For many of the community fish this will not be a problem but for others it could have dire consequences.

Cichlids are notoriously territorial but bottom-dwelling catfish and some Botias also stake out a domain. These fish need large, shallow aquaria with plenty of rocks, caves, and wood to defend.

◀ *Tiger Barbs* (Barbus tetrazona) *and Coolie Loaches* (Pangio kuhli) *have been successfully teamed in this Southeast Asian river community tank. Barbs are boisterous and loaches territorial, but each species lives in a separate water zone and will not come into conflict.*

● *Would adding a pair of dwarf cichlids to my long-established tank cause problems?*

You need to be aware that dwarf cichlids are territorial, especially when breeding. Check whether any of your other fish have similar requirements. If they do, consider whether the tank is large enough to accommodate another pair of fish with a territory. If it is, then rearrange the decor before adding the cichlids, so that all the fish have to re-establish their territories at the same time.

● *I have a 36x12x12in (91x30x30cm) aquarium in which I have a pair of breeding* Ancistrus. *I can expand the tank to 24in (61cm) deep, and would like to add a pair of a different species from the same genus. Would this be acceptable?*

No. Depth is not the critical factor here, but the tank's base area, because this is where your fish live. Although you are doubling the capacity of your tank (from 3–6 cubic feet), the dimensions of the base remain the same, allowing no room for an additional pair of *Ancistrus*.

● *What is the maximum stocking level for tropical fish?*

Population density can be calculated in terms of the oxygen requirement of the fish, based on the length of the fish (excluding tail once fully grown) relative to the tank's surface area. The recommended tropical stocking rate is 1in of fish length per 10sq in of surface (2.5cm/64sq cm). The territorial needs of certain fish may often require that the stocking level is lower than this figure.

● *I have read that killifish should be kept in species tanks. Does this apply to all species, or are there some that are suited to a community tank?*

No, segregation is not a universal requirement for killis. Several of the *Aphysemion* spp. make welcome and colourful additions to a community tank, provided there are no fin nippers. *Aplocheilus* spp. may also be kept in community aquaria; these are especially useful, in as much as they are surface-dwellers and so provide movement in a region that is often devoid of fish.

● *If I inadvertently introduce incompatible fish to my tank, what can I do to rectify the situation?*

As long as the established fish only show close interest in the newcomer(s), this is acceptable. If this interest turns into harassment, in the form of chasing, biting and fin-nipping, then swift action is called for. Remove the new fish to safe quarters in a quarantine tank, and either return it to the dealer, or pass it on to an aquarist friend who can accommodate it successfully.

Fish/Tank Compatibility

THERE EXISTS IN THE HOBBY A MYTH THAT A fish will only grow to the size of its aquarium. Thus, if we really want to own a particular species, which books assure us will grow in excess of 3ft (91cm), we persuade ourselves that if we keep it in a 4ft (122cm) tank, it will only reach about 18in (46cm) and remain at that size. Nothing could be further from the truth! One only needs look in shops or public aquaria to see how many Giant Gouramis, Pacu and Red-tail Catfish have been donated because they have outgrown their original owners' aquaria. So, if you have your eye on a big fish, do make sure that you can house an appropriately large aquarium. As a very approximate rule of thumb, the tank should be three times the length of the fish, and at least as wide and deep as the fish is long, so that it can swim and turn with ease. Note especially that catfish with long barbels that they extend in front of them need enough space to do this without the barbels hitting one end of the tank and the caudal fin the other. This can cause panic, making the fish leap out of the water or thrash about wildly.

If you are keeping predominantly bottom- or top-dwelling fish, the aquarium can be shallow, as the midwater levels will not be used. Remember that with top-dwellers (e.g. Hatchetfish) a cover glass is essential. As an alternative, you could use floating plants for cover, which would have the advantage of mimicking the natural habitat of such fish.

However, fish/tank compatibility is not simply a question of tank size and shape. You must also consider the water conditions in the aquarium before selecting your livestock. Know your pH and hardness levels, and choose fish that will thrive in your given range. For example, keeping Lake Malawi cichlids with South American angelfish would not only be inadvisable on the grounds of incompatible habits and temperaments, but would also be wrong from the point of view of water conditions.

▶ *The Red-tail Catfish* (Phractocephalus hemioliopterus) *is a truly impressive creature, which can reach a length of 39in (c.1m). Before buying one – or any other potentially large fish – you must ensure that you can accommodate it properly.*

Fish and Plants

Fish and plants can be difficult to combine – because some fish eat plants, and some dig them up. These aggravating habits can be curbed by careful choice of fish (either non-herbivores or non-diggers) and plants (well-established, deep-rooted species with coarse, hard leaves). Yet even these strategies don't always work, and you may have to resort to a sequence of potted plants, periodically removing damaged ones.

Lighting awkwardly shaped aquaria may leave some dark areas. Likewise, if the water is too deep, light is reduced and plant growth suffers. Bear in mind certain plants' light requirements, and pH and hardness needs before selecting them for your tank. Finally, your plants must be positioned with care. Fine-leaved *Cabomba*, for example, will get battered to pieces by the water flow if placed near a filter return, or damaged by fast-moving medium-sized fish chasing around the aquarium.

Points to Remember

- A long, wide tank houses far more fish than a tall, thin tank of the same water capacity
- Don't try to keep hardwater fish in a softer-water aquarium or vice versa
- If you keep herbivorous fish, grow coarse-leaved plants and feed the fish on soft-leaved lettuce – they soon get the message
- Keep top-dwelling fish (e.g. Hatchets) in covered aquaria, or they will jump out
- If your fish has long barbels, a large mouth, large eyes or a combination of these, don't keep it with smaller species, as it is quite likely to be a predator

 ● *My large catfish and barbs have dug up or eaten all the plants I have put in their tank. Is there anything they will leave alone?*

Java Fern (*Microsorium pteropus*) is safe, because this can be grown on rock or bogwood in the midwater or upper regions of the tank. It has tough leaves and most fish seem to leave it alone.

● *Aren't the lighting levels needed to grow plants successfully too high for most fish?*

Not if you plan properly, in which case the plants will actually work for you, providing shade for the fish. Moreover, certain fish have even adapted to feeding in brightly lit environments; for example, the very popular

Otocinclus and *Farlowella* species of suckermouthed catfish, along with the more specialized stingrays, have flaps that partially cover the eyes and shield the retina.

● *Is there any simple way in which I can stop my cichlids digging and moving the gravel around?*

Not really. Digging is a normal activity for cichlids, and is often a necessary part of their breeding rituals. Gravel tidies can be installed in the substrate, but once the cichlids discover them, they will excavate them and play with them.

▶ OVERLEAF *A section of a large tropical community aquarium, showing a wide variety of compatible livestock and appropriate plants.*

Fish Health

FISHKEEPING CAN SOMETIMES SEEM FRAUGHT with constant problems. Having said this, if you keep up a regime of regular, diligent maintenance, you should avoid many of the hobby's most common pitfalls. Moreover, if you train yourself to observe your fish and plants so that you can recognize normal patterns of behaviour and growth, you will be able to detect the very first signs of trouble and deal with any problem before it turns into a catastrophe.

The vast majority of fishkeeping problems are caused by something we aquarists have done – or not done! – rather than by an outside organism, or pathogen. When pathogenic diseases do occur, they are a real nuisance, because they can remain dormant in a tank for a long time until a change in the environment suddenly creates ideal conditions for them to flourish – and, quite suddenly, you are faced with an outbreak! In such cases, we tend to panic and reach for an instant remedy, when what we should really be doing is trying to ascertain what caused the outbreak, determining exactly what disease the fish has, and then treating it with the correct remedy. It is pointless medicating a fish unless you know precisely what the illness is.

Any external factor that causes stress to your fish weakens its immune system and leaves it open to viral and bacterial attack. Endeavour to keep stress factors to a minimum through regular maintenance; by doing so, you will avoid any build-up of toxic substances in the tank. Likewise, take care when choosing fish to avoid incompatible species (see Fish Compatibility, pages 42–43) and also ensure that shoaling fish are kept as shoals and not as individuals.

When you do need to use medication, read the manufacturer's instructions carefully and follow them to the letter. Remember, treatments are not instant, so allow time for them to work. Never be tempted to try a second treatment if the one you first used does not appear to have taken effect within, say, 12 hours – the resulting toxic

Q&A...

● *What should I keep in my medicine chest in case of emergencies?*

Only the bare essentials – a whitespot cure, a bacteriacide and a fungicide – and even then use these with care! Many fish are killed by patent remedies being administered one after the other in a hit-and-miss fashion by an inexperienced aquarist in a panic. First determine the illness, then treat with the correct remedy. Remember to renew medications at regular intervals; fresh treatments are far more effective than those at the end of their shelf life.

● *I treated my aquarium for whitespot and used Methylene Blue. My catfish, a Whiptail, went crazy, trying to get out of the water. Is this normal?*

Many catfish (and some other fish) react adversely to treatments containing dyes, especially if these are used at full strength. Many aquarists only use these as a last resort and then at half strength or weaker. Follow the manufacturer's instructions carefully. Sometimes, fish that are not to be treated with a particular medication are listed – check carefully before using it.

● *My fish seem to have an excess of body mucus, and their gills are haemorrhaging; what is causing this?*

These sound like the symptoms of alkalosis, a condition that occurs when the pH levels in a tank become too high. Few freshwater fish can survive for long in water above pH 9.0. The increased alkalinity may have been caused by something as simple as adding clay pipes to the tank as shelters or spawning sites. Alternatively, you may have undertaken a large water change with water that was not sufficiently well aged. Reduce the alkalinity of the tank water by adding peat granules or a liquid extract (see Water Chemistry and Testing, pages 34–35). Also, remove any objects that may be making the water too alkaline.

● *I had whitespot in one of my tanks and now there is an outbreak in another. I have not added any new fish to the other tank, so why should this happen?*

It is possible for a disease to be transferred on nets, hoses, or even on your wet hands. If you have an outbreak in one tank, sterilize all pieces of equipment before using them elsewhere – and wash your hands!

cocktail might well kill your fish. A number of treatments, such as that for whitespot, take several days to destroy the pest, as it can only be killed during its free-swimming stage. This means that you have to wait for the parasite to develop through various phases before it reaches this stage. In such an instance, it is important not just to use the correct dosage, but also to complete the full course of treatment to eradicate the pathogen.

Some treatments containing copper can be toxic to certain fish. Again, be sure to check the instructions before use to see if any of your fish are listed. Others may affect plants or the bacteria in your filters, so, depending on the pathogen involved, it may be better to isolate the affected fish in a hospital tank for treatment. As a rule of thumb, if the pathogen has a free-swimming stage, treat *in situ*, as you will need to eradicate

it from the whole tank. If it does not, it is a much better idea to use a hospital tank. This is especially important if the treatment is one that has to be applied directly to an open sore or wound, a process that involves catching the affected fish at regular intervals.

Although we always tend to ascribe the death of one of our charges to illness, we must remember that they do also die of old age! So, finding a single body of a fish you know you've had for a long time in a tank of otherwise healthy individuals is not a cause for concern.

Sadly, because of sickness or old age, it will sometimes be necessary to destroy a fish. The most humane method of doing so is to cut its spinal cord just behind the head using a sharp knife. There is no disguising the fact that this is an unpleasant task, if you can't bring yourself to do it, consult your vet.

COMMON TROPICAL FRESHWATER AQUARIUM DISEASES

Whitespot (Ich)

Symptoms: a few small, white spots initially appear on the body and fins. Highly infectious; the number of spots increases rapidly over a 48-hour period.
Comments: one of the most common diseases of tropical aquarium fish, caused by a parasite called *Ichthyophthirius multifiliis*.
Treatment: administer a proprietary treatment.

Fungus

Symptoms: fluffy, white, cotton wool-like growths on the body and/or fins.
Comments: customarily attacks areas already weakened or injured.
Treatment: treat the whole tank with an aquarium fungicide for major outbreaks; spot treatment with aquarium fungicide or gentian violet for minor outbreaks. Determine the cause (damage to the protective mucus coating, injury, environmental, etc.) and rectify.

▶ *This Corydoras sp. catfish is suffering from a severe fungal infection around the dorsal fin. Fungus may often develop on a graze or cut sustained by a fish.*

▲ *Whitespot afflicting an Uaru (Uaru amphiacanthoides). This disease causes damage to the skin and gills.*

Velvet

Symptoms: a yellow/gold, velvety covering to the body and fins. The fish may scratch and breathe rapidly.
Comments: caused by a parasite known as *Piscoödinium*.
Treatment: administer a proprietary treatment.

Finrot

Symptoms: degeneration of fin membranes and inflammation (reddening) of fin rays. In catfish it may also cause the barbels to degenerate.
Comments: bacterial infection triggered either by injury to the fins or poor water quality.
Treatment: improve water quality. Spot treat with proprietary bacteriacide (e.g. Myxazin) or gentian violet.

Skin Slime

Symptoms: very fine grey-white coating on the body. Fish may shimmy or scratch.
Comments: poor water conditions may damage the body mucus. This allows attack by various parasites, namely *Chilodonella*, *Ichthyobodo* (formerly known as *Costia*) and *Cyclochaeta*.
Treatment: correct the water conditions and administer a proprietary treatment.

Hole-in-the-head

Symptoms: light-coloured, stringy faeces. Sometimes the sensory pores on the head become enlarged and filled with pus. Mostly affects cichlids.
Comments: caused by an internal parasite called *Hexamita* that normally affects only weakened fish.
Treatment: prescription drugs; Metronidazole or Di-metronidazole at a rate of 50mg per 4.5 litres. Mix with water prior to use. Repeat the treatment after 3 days.

Constipation

Symptoms: loss of appetite; fish produces minimal, if any, faeces; may rest on bottom of tank, and may develop a slightly swollen belly.
Comments: caused either by overfeeding the

▲ *The normally flowing fins of this angelfish have been badly eroded by finrot, with secondary fungal infection.*

▲ *An advanced stage of hole-in-the-head disease is evident on this Turquoise Discus, manifesting itself as a large, open sore.*

fish or administering a poor or unsuitable diet.
Treatment: half a level teaspoon magnesium
sulphate per 4.5 litres of water. Improve diet.

Pop-eye
Exophthalmus

Symptoms: the eye sticks out from the socket,
and may appear inflamed.
Comments: most commonly a result of environmental problems. Less often caused by parasites, in which case it is incurable.
Treatment: adjust the water quality. It may take
some time for the fish to recover

▲ *Pop-eye results from a build-up of fluid in the eye
sockets of the fish. This condition is most usually
triggered by poor water quality.*

Dropsy/Malawi Bloat

Symptoms: fish develops a distended abdomen.
When viewed from above, scales may be seen
sticking out from the body.
Comments: can result from either organ failure
or a poor/unsuitable diet. Also caused by environmental factors, such as excessive levels of
sodium chloride or nitrates.
Treatment: no proprietary remedy. Improving
or correcting environmental conditions or diet
may help effect a cure.

▲ *A pencilfish exhibiting symptoms of dropsy. Note
that the body of this normally slim fish is swollen, and
that its scales are standing proud.*

Swimbladder Disease

Symptoms: loss of balance – fish may swim
upside down or on their side.
Comments: results either from poor water conditions, which allow a bacterial infection to
take hold, or the swim bladder may have been
damaged or bruised by poor handling, breeding
or fighting.
Treatment: if poor water conditions suspected,
improve them and give an antibiotic to eradicate the bacterial infection. If other external
causes suspected, isolate fish in shallow water.
If there is no improvement after 7 days,
euthanasia should be considered.

Anchor Worm
Lernaea

Symptoms: fish scratch against various surfaces.
Small worm-like creatures may be seen
attached to the fish.
Comments: caused by parasite that buries its

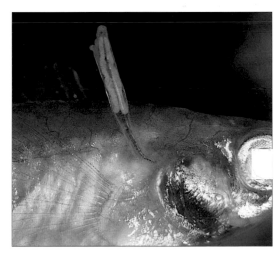

▲ *Anchor worms attach themselves to the host, in this
case a guppy (Poecilia reticulata var.), by pushing their
heads through the scales and anchoring to muscle tissue.*

▲ *An adult fish louse clinging to the skin of a swordtail. Fish lice leave their host to lay egg capsules on rocks; the eggs hatch in around four weeks.*

head into the fish. Usually found on pond fish rather than tropicals but may be inadvertently introduced to the aquarium.
Treatment: remove the worms with tweezers, taking care not to break off their heads. Treat the resultant wound with antiseptic. Serious infestations may be treated with an insecticide, Metriponate, at a concentration of 1.125– 1.8mg per 4.5 litres.

Fish Lice
Argulus

Symptoms: fish scratch themselves against rocks, wood or gravel. Small, round, almost transparent parasites may be seen attached to their skin by suckers.
Comments: usually found on pond fish rather than tropicals, but may be inadvertently introduced to the aquarium.
Treatment: remove the lice carefully with tweezers. Treat resultant wound with antiseptic. Serious infestations may be treated with an insecticide, Metriponate, at a rate of 1.125– 1.8mg per 4.5 litres.

Leeches

Symptoms: fish scratch against various surfaces. Worm-like parasites visible on skin; these attach with suckers at both ends of their body and can contract and extend their bodies.
Comments: usually found on pond fish rather

than tropicals but may be inadvertently introduced to the aquarium.
Treatment: remove the leech carefully with tweezers. Treat resultant wound with antiseptic. Serious infestations should be treated with an insecticide, Metriponate, at a rate of 1.125– 1.8mg per 4.5 litres.

Internal Parasites

Symptoms: despite eating well, the fish become emaciated. Sometimes worms can be seen protruding from the vent.
Comments: various *Capillaria* species of threadworms are the most common cause.
Treatment: a suitable anthelminthic from the vet, which is administered with food.

Gill Parasites

Symptoms: laboured breathing (also an indicator of other common problems); flicking against rocks; in heavy infestations glazed eyes, heightened colour and disorientation as the oxygen supply to the brain is reduced.
Comments: the most common gill parasites are *Dactylogyrus* (gill flukes). Infestation is fatal if not treated promptly.
Treatment: proprietary treatment, e.g. Sterazin, from your dealer.

Q&A...

● *How can I apply a treatment directly to my fish when it's flapping about in the net?*

With small fish, direct treatment is somewhat hit-and-miss. One of the easiest ways is to fold the wet net around them and apply the treatment through the net. For medium to large fish, catch them and wrap them in a wet cloth or piece of linen; a clean towel is ideal, but not for fish with large spines, as they become entangled in the material. Fish usually stop flapping about once their eyes are covered and you can then paint the affected area.

● *Why did some new additions to my well-established tank, where I change the water every 2–3 months, swiftly die (everything else in the tank is fine)?*

You are not changing your water frequently enough. Your other fish have adapted to higher levels of nitrates (or whatever), but the new ones quickly succumbed.

Quarantine

ONCE YOUR AQUARIUM IS WELL-ESTABLISHED, there will come a time when you wish to acquire more fish. Since adding new fish always carries a risk of introducing disease, it is a wise precaution to set up a quarantine tank for isolating new fish before moving them to the main tank. To do this, follow the same procedures as for your main tank. It is important that the system in the quarantine tank is mature. The tank does not have to be very large, but should be of sufficient size to accommodate the fish in question.

Some people prefer to use a bare tank, but this can traumatize fish already suffering from the stress of having been caught and transported. It is far more humane to provide some modest decor for the wellbeing of the inmate(s) – say, a fine layer of sand on the aquarium bottom, one or two potted plants and some sort of cave or other shelter. These should be arranged in such a way that you can still observe the fish with ease. Otherwise, you may only realize it has contracted a disease when its body floats to the surface!

Quarantine usually lasts two to three weeks. As well as giving you the opportunity to check for diseases and administer the appropriate remedy, it also allows you to check that your fish is feeding properly and to make any necessary adjustments to the water parameters before you transfer your new charge to the main aquarium.

Some aquarists still shun quarantine. It is true that some fish settle in more quickly when introduced directly into a fully set-up aquarium, and experienced hobbyists have separate tanks, containing only a few fish, specifically for this purpose. However, this complex procedure is not advisable for the beginner. A quarantine tank also performs another, very important function; it can serve in emergencies as a hospital tank for injured or sick fish.

▶ *A Black Ruby Barb* (Barbus nigrofasciatus) *isolated in a quarantine tank. Quarantined fish will be happier if you equip the tank with some foliage and rockwork.*

● *What sort of filtration should I use on my quarantine tank?*

... One of the air-operated sponge filters is ideal. If you use a different system that usually contains charcoal in the canister, remember to remove the charcoal when you use medications, otherwise they will be filtered out of the water.

● *Should I carry out regular maintenance on my quarantine tank?*

If possible, yes. When the tank is occupied, remember to remove all uneaten food and also carry out a small water change each week. If the tank has housed sick fish, the water needs to be changed completely before the next inmates use it. If the fish have proved free from disease, a 50% water change will suffice.

Breeding

AT SOME STAGE YOU MAY DECIDE TO TRY YOUR hand at breeding fish – more likely, your fish will preempt your decision and breed for you! Either way, hopefully, you should end up with young fish that demand your care and attention.

Before dealing with raising fry, however, let's consider your breeding stock. Although you can buy them, it is not always your best bet. Fish pass their breeding prime, and those sold to you (quite legitimately) may simply have reached this stage. In captivity, some of the *Ancistrus* species, for example, have a spawning cycle of 9–10 months, stop for several weeks and subsequently recommence. This continues for two or three years until the pair cease spawning altogether.

Most aquarists prefer to buy young stock in groups of six to ten. When they are young, egg-laying fish are usually unsexable, so a group of juveniles gives a much better chance of having a pair. It also means that you have covered all eventualities if you are unsure whether they spawn in pairs, trios or shoals. Even if you cannot differentiate the sexes in mature fish (which does sometimes happen), they should still be able to select their own partners within the group. When they do spawn, you may notice subtle differences in the sexes that will help you separate out partners for future breeding projects.

One crucial reason for starting out with young fish is that you can control their diet and tank conditions so as to produce strong, healthy fish as your breeding stock. For your breeding programme, choose fish that have no defects such as misshapen fins or bodies, or poor colour, as these traits may be passed on to their offspring.

Your breeders then need to be "conditioned". This term describes the separation of the sexes (though this is not always necessary) and the feeding regime used prior to introducing the fish to a spawning tank. Treat your fish to the very best care and attention, since even something as simple as ensuring that there are mosquito larvae in a diet can trigger a successful spawn. A steady supply of fresh foods is vital, as is the maintenance of optimal water conditions in the tank.

While conditioning the fish, you'll also need to prepare the spawning tank. The type of set-up will be governed by the spawning method of the fish, so all the various types are outlined here.

Egglayers

Substrate spawners broadly denotes fish that lay their eggs on a flat surface. Numerous fish fall into this category, for example many of the cichlids and catfish. The type of set-up varies with species; a deep tank with vertical pieces of slate or wood and tall, broad-leaved plants (real or plastic) is ideal for angels, while *Corydoras* catfish prefer slates laid flat on the substrate, round pebbles and smaller plants (e.g. *Cryptocorynes*). For cave-spawners, provide a fine gravel substrate and rocks, halved coconut shells, flower pots and so on for the fish to spawn in or under.

▶ *The leaf-spawning Angel* (Pterophyllum scalare) *is notorious for eating its eggs. Either remove the eggs or the parents, depending on where they spawned.*

● *Should I put my pair of conditioned fish into the spawning tank at the same time, or put the male in first?*

Always put the female(s) in first. This allows them time to settle down and find suitable retreats should the male(s) become too amorous. If you put them in together or – heaven forbid! – the male first, the male becomes dominant and treats the whole tank as his own, thus depriving the female(s) of any sanctuary. It is not uncommon for males to kill females in such circumstances.

● *My* Corydoras *have spawned on the aquarium glass in the community tank. How can I save the eggs?*

Use a razor blade and, holding a small tray against the glass just beneath the patch of eggs, slide the blade gently down between the glass and the eggs. The eggs will drop into the tray; remove them to hatch elsewhere.

▲ *The male Siamese Fighter* (Betta splendens) *constructs a bubble-nest and mounts guard over the eggs. Provide surface-floating plant material for such fish to spawn.*

With some of the cichlids, the parents are involved to a greater or lesser extent in caring for the fry. Never breed them in a bare tank, as their parental care involves digging pits in the substrate and moving the fry from one to another. **Bubble-nest builders,** such as the gouramis and some catfish, require plant material, a plastic lid or piece of polystyrene floating on the surface to build beneath.

Egg scatterers practice no parental care and scatter their eggs either over the substrate or among fine-leaved plants. These eggs may be adhesive or non-adhesive but the tank set-ups are the same for both. The fish need fine-leaved plants such as clumps of Java Moss through which they will spawn. Alternatively, use any of the commercially available synthetic spawning media. After the fish have spawned, you can either take away the parents (for those species that exhaust themselves on short spawning runs) or remove the plants and eggs together for hatching in another tank (for those species that spawn continuously over a longer period). Breeding tanks for egg scatterers often have a marble

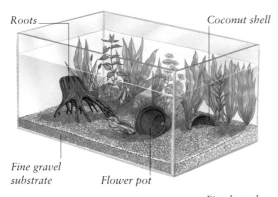

Roots — Coconut shell

Fine gravel substrate — Flower pot

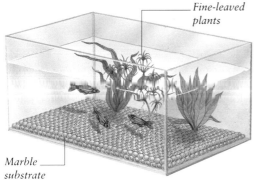

Fine-leaved plants

Marble substrate

▲ *A marble-substrate breeding tank for egg scatterers lets the eggs fall through, so the parents cannot eat them. After spawning, remove the parents, and take away the marbles to stop food decomposing between them.*

● *My Siamese Fighters spawn regularly with no trouble, but once the eggs hatch, I lose most of the fry. Why is this happening?*

Check your tank set-up carefully. With many bubble-nest builders, the most common cause of losses at this stage is the lack of a very tightly fitting cover glass. It is essential to keep the gap between the water surface and the cover glass very warm and humid so that the young fish are not chilled when they surface for air.

● *I set up a breeding tank for my Congo Tetras and placed them in it but, despite feeding them well, they have not spawned. What can I do?*

If the female is full of roe, she will appear well-rounded. In this case, try a water change and spray in cooler water, which may induce spawning. If she doesn't seem interested and is quite skinny, separate the pair and recondition them before trying again. Sometimes we aquarists are too impatient to breed our fish and get the timing wrong!

◀ *Cave-spawning fish (for example, most species of dwarf cichlids) require a number of different retreats, which can be constructed from various materials.*

substrate; another way of isolating parents from their eggs is to secure a piece of plastic mesh across the tank. A useful implement for holding pairs or trios of small fish such as Zebra Danios is a kitchen colander, in which the holes allow the eggs to fall to safety.

Egg depositors, such as some of the killifish, which lay a few eggs each day over an extended period, are best spawned using a spawning mop. This handy piece of tank equipment comprises a tangle of synthetic knitting yarn attached to a float made from a cork or piece of polystyrene. Use a light coloured yarn as the dye can bleed from dark colours unless boiled several times.

Peat divers are more specialized killifish, and their mode of reproduction demands far more effort on the part of the aquarist. They need a tank with a peat substrate. Depending on the species, the male either presses the female down onto the peat to deposit her eggs, or the pair burrows right into the substrate. Once the fish have spawned, the substrate is removed, drained until it is just damp and crumbly and stored in plastic bags in a warm, dark place for anything from one month to several months (depending on species). It is *vital* that you label the bag with the species name and the date that it was put into storage! To hatch, it is simply a matter of adding

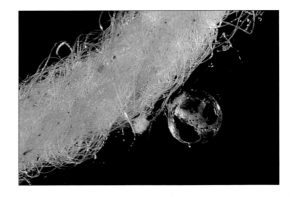

▲ *An egg attached to a spawning mop. Mops should be checked regularly, and either removed complete with eggs for hatching elsewhere, or the eggs picked off and hatched in a separate container*

water. After the first hatch, dry the peat and store again, as the eggs are designed to hatch at various times to ensure the survival of the species.

Mouthbrooders, as their name suggests, brood their eggs (and sometimes their fry) in either the male or the female's mouth. During this time, the parent concerned does not eat, so they must be at the peak of health before they breed. These fish do not need a special set-up but, if they breed within a community, you should not expect to raise all the fry. You may, however, wish to carefully remove the brooding parent and, when it spits out the fry, to rear these in another tank.

Livebearers

There are several breeding traps on the market that claim to be suitable for livebearers. These either float in the main aquarium or clip over the sides. Their principal drawback is that they are all quite small; often, a large female molly or swordtail will suffer great stress or even die in such cramped conditions. It is a far better strategy to establish a special breeding tank that will allow the female space to swim, yet let the fry escape through to the rest of the aquarium. Such a set-up is vital when breeding livebearers, which have the unfortunate habit of eating their own newborn young.

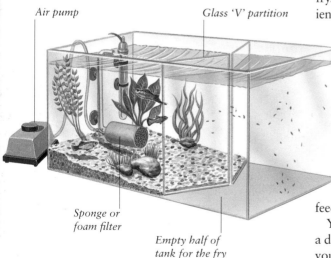

Air pump

Glass 'V' partition

Sponge or foam filter

Empty half of tank for the fry

▲ *Tank set-up for livebearers with a V-shaped insert that has a gap to let the fry swim through. You can also split the tank with a wide mesh or perforated divider.*

Triggering Spawning

Some fish will breed without more ado, whereas others need far more coaxing. There are several ways of spurring reluctant fish into action.

Chilling is used for fish that normally spawn at the beginning of the rainy season. Cooler water is sprayed into the tank to simulate rain.

Warming can be used to stimulate certain other species. Sometimes it is necessary to raise the water temperature to the high 20s°C (low 80s°F).

Food may be a crucial factor in triggering spawning. No matter how well the fish has been conditioned, it may still need a specific food (e.g. black mosquito larvae) that contains the essential amino acids for the female to produce eggs.

Another species spawning in the tank will occasionally coax difficult fish into spawning in the community aquarium; in such cases, the trigger is the release of sperm and milt by the first fish.

Confined space can sometimes induce spawning in a pair of a type of fish whose normal method in the wild is to shoal spawn. Ice-cream containers or margarine tubs are useful for this purpose.

Raising the Fry

Cleanliness is all-important in breeding or rearing tanks. The water must be filtered, but you do not want a unit so powerful that it sucks in the fry. Air-operated sponge filters are ideal; experienced aquarists usually keep one or two of these running on other tanks so that they are mature and full of beneficial bacteria. They can then be transferred to the rearing tanks as needed. They have a dual role; firstly, they break down waste products and, secondly, the sponge (being full of micro-organisms) creates the perfect feeding-ground for the young fry, though you should not rely on this alone to feed them. A small air-operated box filter is a handy alternative, but does not offer the feeding advantage of the sponge type.

You will have to feed the fry two or three times a day. It is essential to coordinate the hatching of your first foods with the hatching of the fry – 12 hours too early or too late could spell disaster. You will need thereafter to provide a continuous supply of food for a large brood; remember, it is better to raise 100 fry properly than 1,000 poor specimens. Prior to feeding, using a length of air line, siphon off the bottom of the tank to remove uneaten food. Top up the tank and feed the fry. Maintaining cleanliness in tanks where you are rearing herbivore fry is especially difficult, as vegetable matter breaks down very quickly. One answer is to use the algae on stones as their first food. Provide plenty of space for the fry to grow into, to avoid them becoming stunted. Other problems that may occur are:

Fungused eggs. Sometimes unfertilized eggs can turn white and grow fungus. Adding a few drops of Methylene Blue will help deter this. Also, remove any eggs you see turning white. Another, biological method is to put one or more *Asellus* (water louse/sow bug) in the tank, which feed on the bacteria and fungal spores on the eggs. Fungusing is less of a problem with fish that provide parental care, as the parents constantly mouth and fan the eggs, and pick out unfertilized ones.
Loss of young fry. Directly after hatching, some fry (e.g. of catfish) rest on the sides or bottom of the tank until they become free-swimming. If you feed them too soon, uneaten food can rot and breed infection. Be scrupulous about cleaning after feeding. In order to raise difficult fish that need almost sterile conditions, some aquarists use a UV filter in their rearing system.

▶ *A Red Devil* (Cichlasoma citrinellum) *guarding its fry. At this time, they can be exceptionally aggressive – it may be necessary to partition the tank or to remove other fish.*

Q&A...

● *I have lots of young Guppies in my tank; how can I set up another tank to grow them on without having to wait weeks while it matures?*

The easy way out is to use water from your main aquarium. Fill the rearing tank, over a few days if necessary, about two-thirds full with water from the parents' tank. Top up the main aquarium as you would when doing a water change and also partially top up the rearing tank in the same way. Filtration of the rearing tank will depend on what system you are using on the main tank. If you are using an undergravel filter, fill an internal air-operated box filter with some gravel from the main tank. This will be full of the bacteria needed to break down waste products and your box filter will work immediately. If using an external canister filter, fill the box filter with some of the medium in the canister and use some marbles to weigh the box filter down.

● *I am feeding my newly hatched rainbows brine shrimp nauplii but without success. What else can I try?*

The newly hatched brine shrimp is probably too big for them to eat, try as they might! Start them on infusoria. You might also try a different brand of brine shrimp, as some have smaller nauplii than others.

Foods and Feeding

A WIDE RANGE OF FISH-FEEDING POSSIBILITIES confronts the aquarist. For the carnivorous fish in your tank, live foods are the most natural nourishment; some of these can be collected from the wild, while others are easily cultivated. Fresh fish or meat are good alternatives for most carnivores. Feeding the herbivores is even more straightforward; the garden or kitchen yields a great variety of suitable fresh vegetables or fruit. In addition, aquatic outlets stock an extensive selection of commercially prepared dried and frozen foods for all types of fish.

Live Pond Foods

The most popular and well-known live pond foods are *Daphnia* (water flea), and bloodworm (midge larvae). But other pond life, such as mosquito larvae, rotifers and *Asellus* (the water louse, or sow bug) are equally good. Mosquito larvae form a vital part of the diet of some fish, especially when being conditioned for breeding.

Many aquarists are fearful of feeding live foods to their fish lest they introduce disease or parasites into the aquarium. In practice, the risk is slight as long as you choose your collecting site

● *I have lots of* Cyclops *in my outdoor water barrel. Can I use them to feed up my breeding stock?*

By all means, but under no circumstances put *Cyclops* into a tank containing fish eggs, as they will prey on them.

● *How can I cultivate infusoria for my fry?*

A culture of infusoria – a general term covering various microscopic organisms, including *Paramecium* – can be started with commercial preparations bought from your aquatic dealer. Alternatively, boil some chopped hay in water for 15–30 minutes and strain the liquid into jars. Leave them open to the air, and they will soon turn cloudy and become infected with infusoria. Be warned; the smell in preparing infusoria is pervasive and unpleasant.

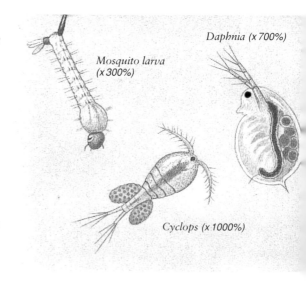

Mosquito larva (x 300%)

Daphnia (x 700%)

Cyclops (x 1000%)

carefully. Seasonal pools are ideal, as they contain no fish (the usual carriers of parasites and disease). They should be shallow, and surrounded by broadleaved woodland (the needles from conifers make the water too acidic). The leaves of deciduous trees provide food for bacteria which, in turn, nourish the pond life. Other good sources of live foods are duck ponds (without fish!) and cattle troughs. Even buckets left to stand in the garden or on the balcony of an apartment will yield mosquito larvae.

Once you have collected your live foods, be sure to sort them by size and ferocity. Certain things should never be fed to fish – the larvae of predatory pond beetles, dragonflies and damselflies will attack and eat small fish. If in doubt, don't kill it, but put it back; habitat destruction has put many frogs, newts, toads and some of the larger aquatic invertebrates under threat.

Alternatively, you can cultivate *Daphnia* in large outside water containers. Add deciduous leaves to produce the fuel for the food chain and seed with *Daphnia* (either collected or bought from a shop). This system will also produce mosquito larvae, which don't need to be seeded, as mosquitoes have a habit of finding even the smallest bodies of water to breed in.

◄ *Feeding bloodworm. These midge larvae are highly nutritious; they are sometimes found in old water barrels, but are usually bought live or frozen from aquatic stores.*

Other Live Foods

Live foods come from sources other than ponds. Worms of various kinds make good fish food. Starter kits of whiteworms and grindal worms can be bought by mail order or from shops or hobbyists. Whiteworms are easily cultured in wooden or plastic boxes of loamy soil. Put a slice of bread on top of the soil and cover the culture with a piece of glass or perspex that fits snugly inside the box. To keep the box dark, cover it with a lid, and punch holes in it for ventilation.

Tubifex are sometimes available. These small, red worms live in the sludge near sewage outfalls. Since they ingest this mud, they must be thoroughly cleaned, and not just washed, before use. Keep them in running water for at least a week to flush out their systems. Although fish like *Tubifex*, they are likely vectors of disease. Frozen and freeze-dried forms are safe to use.

Earthworms from your garden can also be fed to fish. Clean the soil off them, and offer them whole to large fish, or chopped up for smaller species. Other handy garden foods are woodlice, crickets (which can also be bought) and aphids.

Brine shrimp (*Artemia salina*) is the mainstay of fish breeders, as it is the first food of many young fry. It is imperative that brine shrimp is ready when the fry need it and that a regular supply is maintained until they are large enough to eat other things. Brine shrimp is easily hatched in large bottles (plastic soft drink bottles are ideal).

◄▼ *A selection of live foods suitable for feeding to tropical aquarium fish. You should always check the specific dietary needs of your fish – the 'Tank Conditions and Care' boxes in the Species section of this volume will help you to do so.*

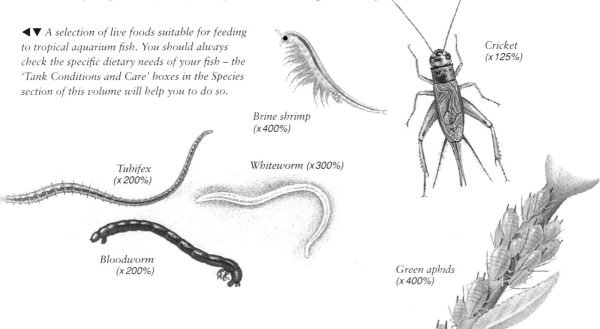

Cricket
(x 125%)

Brine shrimp
(x 400%)

Tubifex
(x 200%)

Whiteworm (x 300%)

Bloodworm
(x 200%)

Green aphids
(x 400%)

Fill them with a salt solution (25g marine salt per litre of water) and add the eggs. Keep them warm, at 18–24°C (64–75°F), and aerate them well so that they remain in suspension; if they are allowed to settle, the hatch rate is greatly reduced. They hatch in 24–48 hours, depending on the brand. To harvest the brine shrimp nauplii (tiny hatched shrimps), turn off the aeration. The egg shells will settle to the bottom, leaving the nauplii in mid-water. Siphon them off, strain them through a fine net, and rinse in fresh water before feeding to avoid adding salt to the rearing tank. Cultures last for a few days. To ensure a constant supply, start three cultures at 2-day intervals, restarting each one on its seventh day.

Live fish are sometimes needed. Use deformed or damaged fry or surplus stock (do *not* use diseased fish!); otherwise buy cheap aquarium fish. This diet, though, is strictly a last resort.

Dried Foods

Commercially prepared dried foods are a mainstay for most fishkeepers. These are processed from natural ingredients, and come in a variety of forms, ranging from a fine powder or granules for fry to large flakes, pellets and sticks for large fish. Because different species feed at different levels of the water column, the foods are designed to float or sink as appropriate. They are available in several "flavours" for carnivores, vegetarians, livebearers, and so on. One advantage of commercial dried foods is that they have been formulated to provide fish with all the essential proteins, vitamins, mineral trace elements and amino acids. Another is their obvious convenience. There is a large range available to the modern aquarist; some types of dried food even contain colour enhancers to improve the appearance of your fish.

▶ *Dried foods for fish are available in a wide variety of different forms, such as flakes, floating and sinking pellets, wafers, tablets, granules and freeze-dried.*

▶ *A group of platies gather eagerly around a pellet of dried food. Feeding time affords an excellent opportunity for you to observe your fish and check on their health.*

Frozen and Fresh Foods

Frozen foods are a more recent innovation. These small trays of food portions can be kept in your freezer or fridge icebox, and used as required. The food pieces come in various sizes from plankton, through aquatic invertebrates, cockles and up to whole lancefish. There are also blends (e.g. Discus diet) and vegetable foods (e.g. spinach). They are a good alternative to live or fresh foods, though some can be very messy and, if feeding only a small number of fry, may pollute the tank if a whole portion is fed at a time.

Fresh foods for herbivores are customarily lettuce, peas and spinach, but other suitable foods include slices of potato, cucumber or courgette (zucchini), or, for large fish (for example Pacu), chunks of banana or even whole cherry tomatoes. Carnivores can be fed shrimps, pieces of fish or lean meat cut, chopped, minced or grated to an appropriate size.

Feeding Regimes

How much and how often to feed your fish varies greatly with species. As a rule, underfeeding is preferable; a hungry fish is a healthy fish. For a standard community tank, a pinch of flake in the morning and perhaps a cube of frozen food in the evening will be ample. Always aim to provide your fish with a balanced and varied diet.

To feed correctly you first need to find out whether your fish is a carnivore, herbivore, insectivore or omnivore. Then purchase a selection of suitable foods. It also helps to know at what time of day your fish are active – there is no point feeding a crepuscular fish (active at dawn and dusk) in the middle of the day. This may mean feeding different foods at different times. A balanced

and nutritious diet is necessary if you are to breed, grow and maintain healthy fish. Many problems such as Malawi Bloat are caused by an incorrect diet or too much food (see Fish Health, page 51).

When fish won't feed, the hobbyist's ignorance is usually to blame. You may be offering it food of an unsuitable type or size. Sometimes, however, the behaviour of the fish is the root cause. This is particularly true of predatory fish that are wild-caught and imported as mature specimens. Such fish have a set feeding regime, and will only accept other fish or anything else alive that is small enough to eat. The answer is to buy young specimens. Even if they will only take live foods to start with (such as bloodworm and shrimp), most will adapt to frozen foods in time.

Live foods must be fed to certain predatory fish if they are not to starve to death. Do not buy an out-and-out predator if you are not prepared to provide it with its essential diet.

● *My arowana looks interested when I drop fresh shrimp in the tank but when they fall to the bottom it ignores them. What can I do?*

The trouble with arowana is that they are surface feeders and anything that falls more than half-way through the water column is often ignored. Try threading a piece of prawn onto a needle and cotton. Slide the prawn down almost to the end of the cotton, but don't tie a knot – you want it to slide off easily. Dangle the prawn in the water and gently jerk it against the water current. Hopefully, your arowana will think it's alive and grab it.

● *I'm having trouble getting my new Tiger Fish (Hoplias malabaricus) to feed. Can you help?*

Wild-caught fish can usually be coaxed into eating with live foods – anything that wiggles and is suitably sized to fit into their mouths will do. Once your fish is in the habit of eating, drop fresh food into the stream of water from the filter. With any luck, it will recognize this moving morsel as food and acquire a taste for it.

Holidays and Moving House

HOLIDAYS CAN BE A TRAUMATIC TIME FOR YOUR livestock, with fish dying from unintentional mistreatment by a "fish sitter" who is ignorant of their requirements. Of course, the ideal person to look after your tanks while you are away would be an informed aquarist friend. Failing this, though, your fish can still be left in the care of people with no previous experience if you make careful preparations. Spend some time beforehand running through the basics of your set-up with them (e.g. power points, timers, filters and air pumps). Alert them to signs of problems, but set their minds at ease by servicing the equipment and tank prior to your departure. Most problems arise because of poor water quality so, a week before you leave, carry out a 30% water change, then, the day before you go, do a 10% water change. Finally, leave a checklist of tasks and an emergency telephone number.

Feeding may be somewhat haphazard during your absence, but don't despair. Except for young fry, tropical fish are quite able to survive for up to two weeks on the micro-organisms and detritus in even the best-kept aquarium. If your plants have been nibbled, they will soon regrow. But if you prefer not to leave things to chance, then explain the feeding regime carefully to your

Q&A...

● *Should I leave an emergency medicine chest for my neighbour?*

Absolutely not; medications in inexperienced hands spell death for your fish! Emphasise the need to call on a dealer or an aquarist friend in emergencies; it is a good idea to introduce your stand-in to the experts before you leave.

● *Are there any restrictions on bringing fish back from my holiday?*

Consult your own government's guidelines on import licenses, health certificates, etc. Also check with the country you are visiting, as most require export permits. Finally, find out from the airline you are travelling with what conditions or restrictions it places on the transportation of livestock.

● *Can I use food bags to transport my fish?*

No – they are too thin and not sufficiently deep to trap enough air for the fish to survive. Special polythene bags are available from your local dealer.

● *I have a very large Snakehead and cannot find a bucket large enough to move it. What shall I do?*

Line a large plastic water tub or vat with a large, heavy bin liner and partially fill with water. Place the fish in the water and tie the liner closed. Pick up the rigid container – you'll probably need help – and move as required. Alternatively use a carp sack.

✔ PRE-HOLIDAY CHECKLIST

Run through this checklist two weeks before you leave to allow time for any changes you have made to settle in.

✔ **Heating** – Replace old or faulty heaters.

✔ **Lighting** – Ensure all is working well; if you are growing plants, it is worthwhile putting the lights on a time switch.

✔ **Trickle Filters** – Check free flow of water through the system. Clean pre-filters and check all pumps.

✔ **Canister Filters** – Clean filters and service motors; pay close attention to the impellers,

bearings, O-seals and pipework. Check the free flow of water through the system; unclog blocked spray bars and filter baskets.

✔ **Undergravel Filters** – Gently stir through the substrate and remove detritus.

✔ **Air Pumps** – Check diaphragms and filter pads, replacing if necessary.

✔ **Non-return Valves** – Check and replace if necessary.

✔ **Cables/plugs etc.** – Check that all wiring is safely connected and in good condition. If in doubt, consult an electrician.

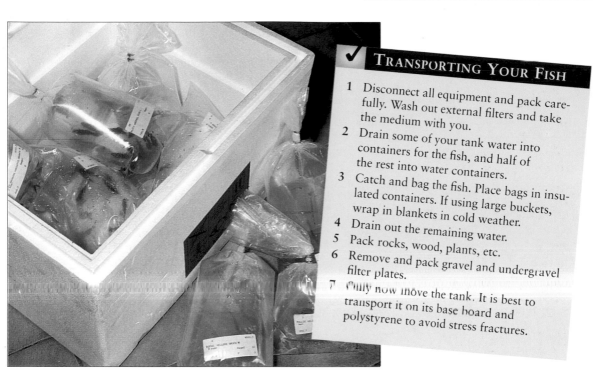

TRANSPORTING YOUR FISH

1 Disconnect all equipment and pack carefully. Wash out external filters and take the medium with you.

2 Drain some of your tank water into containers for the fish, and half of the rest into water containers.

3 Catch and bag the fish. Place bags in insulated containers. If using large buckets, wrap in blankets in cold weather.

4 Drain out the remaining water.

5 Pack rocks, wood, plants, etc.

6 Remove and pack gravel and undergravel filter plates.

7 Only now move the tank. It is best to transport it on its base board and polystyrene to avoid stress fractures.

▲ *Inflated bags of fish, clearly labelled, are placed inside a robust polystyrene box prior to moving. Such boxes protect and insulate the fish during transportation.*

stand-in. Prepare small packets of food and label them with the date and intended tank (if you have more than one). Leave the food in an airtight container near the relevant tank, or, if you are using frozen foods, store individual packets in the freezer in clearly labelled bags or boxes. During the two weeks before your holiday, it is a good idea gradually to cut down on the amount you feed, as this will ease the load on the filtration system.

Don't forget to ask your local dealer if he could be summoned in an emergency. Agree on a call-out charge in advance and pay any deposit required to cover replacement equipment.

Good forward planning can also make transporting fish a problem-free enterprise. Polythene bags are versatile fish carriers. Watch how your dealer bags them; enough water is put in to cover the fish, filling the bag to a quarter or third of its capacity, but leaving plenty of space above for air. If the fish are to be carried long distances, the bag is inflated with pure oxygen rather than air.

To carry spined fish, double-bag them, tying up each bag separately and taping its corners to prevent punctures. Piranha need an extra precaution – the gap between the two bags should be lined with several thicknesses of newspaper. If the fish bite through the first bag, this stops them piercing the outer bag. The inner bag will leak, but not deflate, and the piranha will survive. The best transportation method for spiny or aggressive fish is individually in plastic buckets with sealable lids. Again, follow the "quarter/third water, the rest air" principle. In extreme temperatures, put your bags of fish in either an insulated box (mostly available from dealers) or a picnic "cool box", to avoid chilling or overheating.

When moving house, only transport the fish you can't live without. To ensure the safe arrival of your tank and its stand, make sure that they are two of the first items to come off the removal van, or carry them in your own car. If possible, take about 50% of your water with you. Some will already be in with your fish, but fill a few containers as well. This tank water will enable you to reconstitute and restock your aquarium as soon as you arrive. Partially top up the tank and complete the filling a couple of days later.

Tropical Freshwater Fish

This section provides an overview of tropical freshwater fish commonly available to the domestic aquarist. Their origins, appearance, and habits (including compatibility with other fish) are outlined. In particular, the following profiles describe how to house and feed each species correctly – the paramount concern of every fish keeper. Many of the fish are peaceful, easy-care creatures ideally suited to life in a general community aquarium. For others, their exact water and/or decor requirements will mean reproducing a very specific biotope in the tank. Yet others, due to their size, demeanour or diet, are best confined to single-species aquaria, or not kept at home at all!

The fish have been organized into seven groups: Cichlids, Catfish, Cyprinids, Cyprinodonts, Characins, Anabantoids and Miscellaneous. Within each profile, a number of representative species are listed. The accent is on practicality rather than on academic questions of taxonomy. Thus, the reader can see at a glance the maximum size that his or her chosen fish will grow to in captivity. Each species is identified first by its scientific designation (incorporating the latest information on nomenclature changes), and then by its most common British and US names.

Whether you are a newcomer planning to stock your first tank, or a seasoned aquarist in search of detailed advice on breeding, the tips and facts offered here are an invaluable information resource.

▶ *Discus* (Symphysodon *spp.*) *see pages 78–79.*

What is a Tropical Freshwater Fish?

FISH ARE FOUND IN MANY DIFFERENT HABITATS and in widely divergent water conditions, which range from oceans and highly oxygenated, swift-flowing rivers to tiny, almost stagnant pools; and from soft, acidic forest streams to hard, alkaline lakes. Freshwater fish live in a less saline environment than marine fish, but it is not always absolutely salt-free, as certain freshwater species live in brackish conditions.

The definition of a tropical fish is less straightforward. In temperate northern climates it refers to a fish that has to be kept warm by artificial means in order to survive in a climate that is otherwise too cold for it. However, the same fish kept in an aquarium in Saudi Arabia might well need to be kept cooler than local conditions.

What is "tropical" depends on your point of reference, but fish must be maintained in conditions that reproduce their original habitat if they

▲ *The majority of aquarium fish come from rivers and lakes in the tropical regions of the world.*

● *Can I put brackish water fish into my freshwater aquarium?*

... Probably not. Some people try to acclimatize the fish by gradually adding freshwater to the brackish water to dilute the salts, so that the fish's metabolism can slowly adjust to the changes. Although some species that live in brackish water can tolerate periods of fresh water (due to ebbing and flowing tides, for example), this is totally different to living permanently in freshwater.

● *I have been told to add a teaspoon or two of salt to my community aquarium to help keep my mollies in good shape. Will my other fish be all right?*

It depends on what species you have. As a general rule, softwater fish do not like added salt, whereas hardwater species can tolerate it.

are to survive. They are less adaptable than land animals, which can migrate in search of clean air. Freshwater fish, in contrast, have evolved to fill certain niches, some of which are closed systems such as lakes, where they cannot escape if the water becomes polluted. In rivers and streams, their movement may be restricted by physical barriers such as waterfalls and rapids. River fish cannot cross the brackish water of an estuary, where the river meets the sea.

Fish, Water and Salt

The skin of fish, particularly that lining the gills, intestines and the inside of the mouth is a semipermeable membrane. It allows the free passage of water molecules while preventing the passage of other substances, such as salt molecules. The

▼ *The skin that covers the gills, intestines and inside the mouth of a freshwater fish allows fresh water to pass into the fish's body. The water is excreted as large quantities of dilute urine.*

movement of the water molecules is always from the weaker to the stronger salt solution, and this process is called osmosis.

The system used by either marine or freshwater fish to maintain an osmotic balance is known as osmoregulation. In the ocean, seawater has a greater salt concentration than that in the fish's blood, so marine fish lose water to the sea. To compensate for this water lost by osmosis, marine fish "drink" seawater; excess salt has to be excreted via the kidneys and gills. In freshwater fish, the reverse happens. The fish has a greater salt concentration than the surrounding water, so water molecules pass into the fish. Freshwater fish therefore do not "drink." In order to maintain their osmotic balance, they excrete copious amounts of very dilute urine via the kidneys.

If fish did not osmoregulate, the consequences would indeed be drastic. Freshwater fish would swell up and quite literally explode, while saltwater fish would shrivel up.

OSMOREGULATION IN TROPICAL FRESHWATER FISH

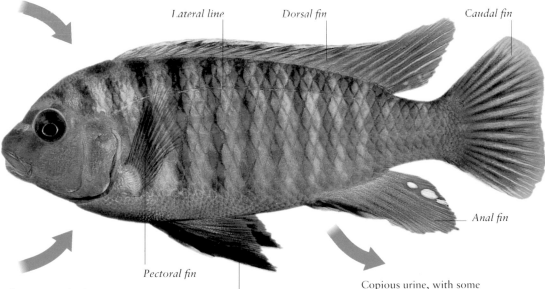

Freshwater in through gills and skin

Barbel

Lateral line   Dorsal fin   Caudal fin

Anal fin

Pectoral fin

Small amounts of salt taken up through gills

Pelvic fin

Copious urine, with some consequent loss of salt

Soft Water Dwarf Cichlids

FAMILY: CICHLIDAE

THESE SMALL SOUTH AMERICAN AND WEST African cichlids are often purchased for the community aquarium. Many are somewhat nervous fish and require the companionship of peaceful species. In order to instil some degree of confidence, "dither fish" are usually included in the set-up; these are small fish, usually characins, that swim about as a shoal, indicating to the cichlids that there are no predators nearby.

Furnish the aquarium with plenty of plants, caves and bogwood, which will not only provide suitable sanctuary for the adults but will also offer a selection of possible breeding sites. Caves are easily made from flowerpots with V-shapes cut out of the rim; the pot is then inverted. Another method is to lay the whole pot on its side, or to cut it in half from top to bottom and rest the halves on their cut edges.

Water conditions are crucial. These creatures prefer warm, soft, slightly acidic conditions – a pH of about 6.5 is usually ideal. For breeding, however, it may be necessary to acidify the water further. Use an efficient filtration system, as poor water conditions can lead to sick, or even dead,

Tank Conditions and Care

HABITAT: Planted community aquarium with other peaceful species. Provide caves. Use a tight-fitting cover glass for West African species.

Tank size 24x12x12in (61x30x30cm) for a pair – no other fish except dither fish.

pH	6.5
dH	0–6 check species requirements
Temperature	25–28°C (77–82°F)
Water changes	10–15% every week
Filtration	Any efficient, low-turnover system
Lighting	Type not critical

FEEDING: Small live foods and frozen foods. Flake only eaten as a last resort by a few species.

HEALTH: Susceptible to outbreaks of bacterial infections if kept in poor conditions.

Q&A

● *Can I keep West African and South American dwarfs together?*

... Yes, provided your aquarium is large enough. Remember, though they are peaceful, they can be territorial and need enough space for each pair to stake out and maintain a territory.

● *How can I breed my Cockatoo Dwarf Cichlids?*

Assemble a "harem" of females for a single male. Also, provide caves with small entrances so the females can wall themselves in until the fry are free-swimming.

● *I have a pair of* Nannacara anomala *that live (and breed) happily in hard water. Is this normal?*

For wild specimens, this would be distinctly abnormal behaviour, but several of the more popular species have been captive-bred for the trade for so long that they have become acclimatized to hard water.

▼ *A male Ram Cichlid (Microgeophagus ramirezi) guarding spawn. These fish are substrate spawners, and lay their eggs on flat pieces of rock or wood, which they clean thoroughly beforehand.*

Representative Species

South American species	max adult male size
Apistogramma agassizii Agassiz's Dwarf Cichlid	3in (7.5cm)
Apistogramma borellii Borelli's Dwarf Cichlid	3in (7.5cm)
Apistogramma cacatuoides Cockatoo Dwarf Cichlid	2.5in (6cm)
Apistogramma nijsseni Panda Dwarf Cichlid	3in (7.5cm)
Apistogramma steindachneri Steindachner's Dwarf Cichlid	3.5in (8.5cm)
Apistogramma trifasciata No common name	2.5in (6cm)
Dicrossus filamentosus Checkerboard Cichlid	3in (7.5cm)
Microgeophagus ramirezi Ram, Butterfly Cichlid	3in (7.5cm)
Nannacara anomala No common name	3.5in (8.5cm)
Cleithracara maronii Keyhole	4in (10cm)
West African species	
Nanochromis parilus No common name	3in (7.5cm)
Nanochromis transvestitus No common name	2in (5cm)
Anomalochromis thomasi African Butterfly Cichlid	4in (10cm)
Pelvicachromis pulcher Kribensis	4in (10cm)

NOTE: the figures given here are for adult males. Females of the species are approximately 1–1.5in smaller.

fish. A low-turnover system is important, as the fish cannot swim against a strong current.

As some species dig shallow pits with their mouths while breeding, make sure that you use a fine substrate; if you use large gravel, these small fish are unable to lift the pieces and are thus prevented from carrying out a natural and necessary part of their reproductive procedure. Most species are cave spawners, others open spawners. Although males are usually distinguished by their more flamboyant finnage and coloration, one particularly notable exception to this is *Nanochromis transvestitus*. The fry are sometimes very small and need infusoria as a first food, followed by newly hatched brine shrimp.

▶ *Kribs (Pelvicachromis pulcher) are easy to keep and breed, and fit well into the general community.*

East African Cichlids

THE CICHLIDS FROM EAST AFRICA THAT ARE encountered most frequently in the hobby come from Lakes Malawi and Tanganyika, which lie in the Rift Valley. Keeping these fish means reproducing in your aquarium the quite specific water conditions that exist in their natural habitats. Both lakes contain highly oxygenated water that is very clean, but the hardness and alkalinity varies: Lake Malawi has slightly hard and alkaline water (8–10°dH; 7.5–8.0pH), whereas Lake Tanganyika is harder and more alkaline (15–20°dH; 8.0–8.5pH). Lake Victoria fish are also sometimes available, and these require slightly hard, and neutral to slightly alkaline waters (8–10°dH; 7.0–7.5pH).

Within each lake there are several biotopes: rocky shore, sandy shore with *Vallisneria* beds, river estuaries with a silty substrate, and open water. The species you wish to keep will determine the type of environment you need to create in your aquarium. Exercise extreme caution if trying to mix species from different biotopes.

A typical Lake Tanganyika aquarium should be set up with a rock pile at each end of the tank and an open sandy area in the middle. This allows you to keep some of the rocky shore fish such as *Julidochromis* species, while still leaving space for a pair of shell dwellers (e.g. *Neolamprologus brevis*). If you are planning to keep the small goby cichlids, beware; they can be very territorial and aggressive. And note that you cannot stock Lake Tanganyika species to the same density as Lake Malawi fish because of their breeding methods. Substrate spawners (such as many Tanganyikan species) not only require space to spawn, they also need a larger safe area in which to rear their brood. To this end, they will defend their territory, even going as far as killing other fish. By contrast, Malawian mouthbrooders need only a small territory in which to spawn and do

Representative Species

Lake Tanganyika species	maximum adult size
Julidochromis dickfeldi	3in (7.5cm)
Julidochromis marlieri	6in (15cm)
Julidochromis regani	6in (15cm)
Julidochromis transcriptus	3in (7.5cm)
Chalinochromis brichardi	4–5in (10–12.5cm)
Cyprichromis leptosoma	4.5in (11.5cm)
Eretmodus cyanostictus	3in (7.5cm)
Telmatochromis bifrenatus	2.5in (6cm)
Tropheus duboisi	4.5in (11.5cm)
Tropheus moorii	4.5in (11.5cm)
Neolamprologus brevis	1.5in (4cm)
Neolamprologus leleupi Lemon Cichlid	3in (7.5cm)
Cyphotilapia frontosa Frontosa	8–12in (20–30cm)

NOTE: for the majority of these fish, just the species names are used as common names.

Lake Malawi species	
Dimidiochromis compressiceps Malawian Eye-biter	8in (20cm)
Melanochromis auratus Auratus	4.5in (11.5cm)
Melanochromis johannii	3in (7.5cm)
Aulonocara sp. "nyassae"	5in (12.5cm)
Aulonocara baenschi	4in (10cm)
Aulonocara stuartgranti	4in (10cm)
Nimbochromis livingstonii	8–10in (20–25cm)
Cyrtocara moorii	9in (23cm)
Nimbochromis polystigma	9in (23cm)
Labeotropheus trewavasae	4–5.5in (10–14cm)
Pseudotropheus lombardoi	5in (12.5cm)
Pseudotropheus zebra	4.5in (11.5cm)
Pseudotropheus tropheops	4–5in (10–12.5cm)
Cynotilapia afra	4.5in (11.5cm)
Placidochromis electra	6in (15cm)

▲ *A Lake Tanganyika community tank with its rocky decor and sandy substrate. The Cyphotilapia frontosa seen here (centre) is a small juvenile specimen. It grows much larger than its tankmates – two Lemon Cichlids (Neolamprologus leleupi) and a Chalinochromis brichardi – and should be removed well before there is any danger of it preying upon them.*

● *I have a Lake Tanganyika tank and would like to add some Malawian species. Would this be alright?*

No, not unless you are very experienced in keeping the lake cichlids. Fish from each of the Rift Valley lakes are incompatible as far as temperament and breeding strategies are concerned. Unless you are extremely adept, you will be unable to ensure that they live together peacefully.

● *Should I keep pairs of Lake Malawi Mbuna?*

Yes, but better still, have several females to each male. They breed readily, but single females have been known to be killed by an over-attentive male. Providing the male with two or more females solves the problem. Although some young will survive in the main aquarium, if you wish to raise a larger brood, carefully remove the brooding female after spawning.

● *Can I use Tufa rock in my tank, as I have heard that this will help maintain hard water?*

You can, indeed, use Tufa rock to harden the water, but its soft and crumbly consistency does not offer a suitable spawning surface to substrate-spawning species. For these, you should provide smooth, flat rocks. If you are only keeping mouthbrooding species, there is no problem. But it is generally easier to enhance water quality by adding limestone chippings to the filter system.

not need nursery space to raise their brood. Once they have taken the eggs into their mouths they, and the subsequent fry, are safe.

A specialized group of fish from Lake Malawi, the Mbuna (a Chitonga word meaning "rock fish") are some of the most popular species. These fish will live together in close proximity provided they have plenty of rockwork, stacked to simulate their natural rocky shore habitat. They are competitive, but keeping the tank densely populated seems to suppress some of their pugnacious instincts. Because of the numbers of fish being kept, the filtration needs to be efficient and frequent water changes are essential. Close attention to water chemistry and quality, and to diet, will help your Mbuna avoid contracting the disease known as Malawi Bloat (see Fish Health, page 51).

▼ *The Auratus* (Melanochromis auratus) *is a hardy, omnivorous Lake Malawi Mbuna. Here, a pair are engaged in a courtship ritual, with the male (left) driving and displaying at the female.*

Tank Conditions and Care

HABITAT: Abundant rocks for the Lake Malawi Mbuna. Open sandy area between rock piles for the Tanganyikan species.

Tank size	Min 24x18x18in (61x46x46cm) for substrate spawners; 36x18x18in (91x46x46cm) for mouthbrooders, depending on species.
pH	7.0–8.5 (see text for each lake)
dH	8–20° (see text for each lake)
Temperature	23–27°C (73–81°F)

Water changes 25–30% at least once a week, possibly twice, for crowded mouthbrooder tanks. 10–15% weekly for substrate spawners.

Filtration External canister filter. Water should be high in oxygen.

Lighting Type not critical

FEEDING: Many are specialist feeders, eating, for example, algae and micro-organisms. However, some will take normal commercial foods.

HEALTH: Incorrect water conditons and diet can cause Malawi Bloat. Occasional bitten fin.

Large "Amazonians"

THESE FISH ARE NATIVE TO THE BASINS OF THE Amazon and Paraguay rivers, and are also found in the river systems of the Guianas. They are a good food source for larger predators and therefore spend their time skulking among the roots, overhanging vegetation and fallen branches or trees along the quiet edges of rivers, lakes and streams rather than in open waters, where they would be easy prey for passing birds, other fish and reptiles.

They are seasonal breeders, and during the rainy season move into the flooded forest to feed and breed. Bearing this in mind, it may be necessary to use triggers to stimulate your fish into breeding. The usual triggers are large water changes (the water may sometimes be sprayed into the aquarium rather than poured), a rise in temperature and an increase in the amount of food offered.

During the dry season these fish congregate in shoals. You might automatically assume from this that you can keep tanks of mixed species in captivity, but beware. While some respond well to mixing, others do not; shoaling is also related to diet. Herbivores and omnivores shoal and are amenable to being kept together. On the other hand, piscivores (e.g. Oscars, *Cichla* and Pikes) don't shoal and should not be kept together. Problems can occur when any of the species start to stake out a breeding territory. At this time it may be necessary to consider partitioning the aquarium or, better still, to provide the pair with their own breeding tank.

As the fish are large, active and liable to undermine any rock or wood structures in the tank, ensure that such constructions are firmly seated on the base glass. If you are using piles of rock, it is worthwhile siliconing the smaller pieces together to prevent the fish from moving them

▼ *The Oscar* (Astronotus ocellatus) *is a popular fish, but newcomers to the hobby should bear in mind that it grows to a large size, and is a piscivore. This means that it should on no account be bought for a community tank.*

Representative Species

	maximum adult size		maximum adult size
Heros severus Severum	12in (30cm)	*Satanoperca jurupari* Jurupari, Devil Fish	10in (25cm)
Cichlasoma portalegrensis Brown Acara	6in (15cm)	*Uaru amphiacanthoides* Uaru, Triangle Cichlid	18in (46cm)
Astronotus ocellatus Oscar	15in (38cm)	*Hypselecara temporalis* Chocolate Cichlid	12in (30cm)
Cichla ocellaris Peacock Bass	36in (91cm)	*Mesonauta insignis* Festive Cichlid	8in (20cm)
Crenicichla lepidota Pike Cichlid	18in (46cm)	*Acarichthys heckelii* No common name	8in (20cm)
Geophagus brasiliensis Pearl Cichlid	12in (30cm)	*Gymnogeophagus balzanii* Paraguay Eartheater	5–6in (12.5–15cm)

With certain species, plants are fine – even desirable – but with others, the only way of improving their chances of survival is to place them in pots, with large pieces of rock around the base of the plant to prevent any excavating.

Breeding strategies vary among these cichlids, from substrate spawners to mouthbrooders. The substrate spawners can be very prolific, producing several hundred fry. You may well wonder how on earth you are going to raise this number of fry and, even if you do raise them, what you are going to do with them! Your best policy is to settle for raising 30 or 40 youngsters properly.

Feeding strategies also differ. Many are omnivorous, some are piscivorous and others are vegetarians; it is essential to research the particular species you wish to keep before you buy them. For example, an Uaru would be a disastrous choice for a beautifully planted aquarium. As an avid herbivore, it would first devastate your prized plants and then proceed to dig in the substrate in search of more plant matter to eat. Piscivores are best kept in a species aquarium, but make sure that their sizes do not differ too greatly, as the larger fish will devour the smaller ones. Males will even eat females!

Most will take prepared foods, flakes, pellets, frozen foods and the like, but do vary their diet.

Some fish become "hooked" on one particular food and develop dietary problems as a result. This is particularly true of fish, such as Oscars, that are fed predominantly on a diet of pellets. For the piscivores, notably the Pike Cichlids, it may be necessary to feed wild-caught fish initially on live foods, including small fish. If you are not prepared to do this, then you should not attempt to keep Pikes.

Tank Conditions and Care

HABITAT: Large aquarium with rocks and wood seated on the base glass and open areas of substrate to accommodate their digging.

Tank size	48x18x18in (122x46x46cm)
pH	5.5–7.5; check species requirements. If acclimatized to alkaline conditions, they will still require acid water to breed.
dH	To 12° depending on species
Temperature	22–26.5°C (72–80°F)
Water changes	25% every week
Filtration	External canister filter to cope with the amount of debris they can stir up. Gentle water flow.
Lighting	Subdued

FEEDING: Flake, pellets, live, frozen, or green foods depending on whether they are carnivorous, herbivorous or omnivorous. Check species requirements.

HEALTH: Few problems provided they have the correct diet.

▲ *A female Pike Cichlid* (Crenicichla lepidota). *These fish can spawn up to 1,000 eggs in a single clutch. Pike Cichlids must be kept in a species tank.*

● *Can I mix some of the eartheaters with my Central American species?*

... Although there are some cichlid species from northwestern South America that come from harder, more alkaline waters and are noted for their aggression (similar traits to your Central American species), they should only be mixed if extreme caution is exercised. However, the eartheaters are not among these, so they require a separate tank with the appropriate water conditions.

● *I have seen some very pretty Pike Cichlids for sale. Would they be suitable for my community aquarium?*

Absolutely not. They are voracious piscivores and will eat any fish they can fit into their mouths, including each other! They should never be kept with fish that are less than two-thirds their size. Because of the diversity of the group and the very specific requirements that many of them have, they need to be carefully researched before buying and are not recommended for beginners.

◀ *The Pearl Cichlid* (Geophagus brasiliensis) *is one of a group of South American fish collectively known as "eartheaters", from their habit of sucking up sand from the substrate while searching for food.*

● *How can I sex the Oscars in my community tank with an eye to breeding?*

In short, you can't. You would need to raise a small group of five or six, but this is not a wise move in your community aquarium. The Oscar is not a community fish, and tends to consume its smaller tank mates.

● *My Uaru died after eating the bogwood in my tank. Could the wood be the cause?*

Wood is a natural part of the Uaru's diet, and should be provided in the aquarium. It must be unvarnished, natural wood, and not one of the many artificial substitutes. If the wood you have used is varnished, this is almost certainly the cause of your fish's demise.

● *I put three small Severum in my community tank. They are 4in (10cm) long. Will they get much bigger?*

Yes – they can reach 12in (30cm) but, even at this size, are one of the more peaceful cichlids (but would not be averse to eating the odd small tetra). You will need to provide them with a larger tank as they grow.

● *I have a pair of Oscars and a Plec in my tank. The Oscars spawn regularly but the eggs disappear overnight. Who is the culprit?*

Not the Oscars; the Plec is a crepuscular feeder who will come out at twilight or at night and eat the eggs.

Discus
and Angels   FAMILIES: CICHLIDAE

THESE TWO VERY CLOSELY RELATED GENERA OF
fish come from the same type of habitat: shaded
bank zones with root and branch tangles providing abundant cover. Despite this basic simi-
larity, and the fact that angels (*Pterophyllum*)
are acknowledged as accommodating community fish, several myths persist about discus (*Symphysodon*). For example, they are reputed to be
very delicate and to require special conditions,
notably bare aquaria. Yet such unnatural conditions are likely to cause stress and ill-health; the
truth is that both discus and angels require
exactly the same type of set-up, and (to dispel
another myth) can successfully be kept together.

Bred by the thousand in the Far East and in
Florida, discus and angels are some of the most
popular aquarium fish and are often kept in
community tanks. The only drawback is that
they will eat small fish such as Neon Tetras.
Several colour and finnage variants of angels
have been bred, for example Marbled, Black,
Half Black and Veiltail. With discus, the number
of colour forms seems to increase almost by the

▼ *If you are keeping Discus – the stunning Turquoise
Discus* (Symphysodon aequifasciata *var.*) *is shown here
– excellent water conditions are essential, as the fish are
sensitive to pollutants, especially nitrites.*

week, with the result that the original species can now be rather difficult to obtain.

When setting up a tank specifically for angels and/or discus, bear in mind their body depth and length of finnage. The water should be 18–24in (46–61cm) deep, and must be in pristine condition. Wild-caught fish are the most demanding, but as long as you provide soft, acidic, warm water you should have no problems. Select your filtration system with care; neither angels nor discus can stand a raging torrent, so water movement should be very slow and gentle.

Sexing angels and discus is best done by looking at the shape of the genital papillae, which only becomes apparent during the spawning season. In both genera, it is pointed on the male and rounded on the female.

Angels are easy to care for, peaceful, and don't decimate the tank when breeding. However, they are notorious for eating their eggs. They spawn on a leaf or other vertical flat surface, which should then be removed to another tank for hatching the eggs and raising the fry. The best strategy for breeding them is to raise a group of youngsters and allow them to pair themselves, as they tend to stay with the same mate. The fry are easy to raise as they will take newly hatched brine shrimp from the very outset. Discus also eat their eggs but, unfortunately, these cannot be removed for artificial hatching, since the fry need to "glance" (feed) on the parental mucus.

Many problems arise from stress. This is usually caused by keeping them in the wrong tank conditions or with incompatible fish in a community aquarium. Avoid situations in which the discus or angels get bullied and are prevented from feeding, or have their fins nipped.

Representative Species

	maximum adult size
Pterophyllum scalare Angelfish	6in (15cm)
Pterophyllum altum Altum Angel	7in (18cm)
Symphysodon discus Heckel Blue Discus	6in (15cm)
Symphysodon aequifasciata var. Turquoise/Brown Discus	4.5in (11.5cm)

Tank Conditions and Care

HABITAT: Planted aquarium with other small, peaceful species or species tanks.

Tank size	30x18x18in (76x46x46cm) for a pair
pH	6.5; lower for breeding
dH	0–6 check species requirements
Temperature	25–28°C (77–82°F)
Water changes	10–15% every week
Filtration	Any efficient system with a slow flow
Lighting	Subdued

FEEDING: Will take flake, but prefer frozen and small live foods (latter essential for conditioning).

HEALTH: Prone to hole-in-the-head disease, brought on by stress and poor conditions.

● *I have some Altum Angels but they do not seem to be very happy in my tank. All the other fish are alright. What could be the matter?*

Possibly the water conditions. These fish, *Pterophyllum altum*, are usually wild-caught and have more exacting water requirements than *P. scalare*, which has been captive-bred for many generations. They need soft, acidic water at a temperature of around 25–28°C (77–82°F). They also benefit from being fed small live foods.

● *My discus spawned on a leaf, which I then removed to hatch the eggs. Only a few fry hatched and quickly died. Why did this happen?*

The first food of discus fry is the mucus on their parents' bodies. By removing the eggs for hatching, you deprived the fry of this vital sustenance. Next time they spawn, leave them to it and you should get a brood of a reasonable size.

● *How can I grow plants in my discus tank when the fish shun bright light?*

Pick species that will grow tall and provide shade. The ones that spring readily to mind are the smaller tropical water lilies, genus *Nymphaea*, which will produce floating lily pads and, if you are lucky, a flower or two, and provide cover for your fish. Alternatively, one or two *Cryptocorynes* will grow well at reduced light levels.

▶ OVERLEAF *The camouflage of the vertical stripe pattern on the bodies of Angelfish (Pterophyllum scalare) is seen to good effect in this aquarium with its subdued lighting.*

Large Neotropicals FAMILY: CICHLIDAE

OFTEN REFERRED TO AS CENTRAL AMERICAN cichlids, this group was, for a long time, grouped by ichthyologists within the genus *Cichlasoma*; certain species are, erroneously, still referred to as such. However, academic questions of nomenclature are far less important than keeping them alive and healthy!

The range of this group of fish extends from the southern USA, through Central America and northwestern South America, and even to some of the Caribbean islands. Their habitat is hard, alkaline rivers, streams and lakes. They are colourful creatures, and are often regarded by inexperienced aquarists as potential inmates for their community aquarium. Nothing could be further from the truth – these highly belligerent, territorial fish should never be kept in a general community set-up. As a general guide, the diameter of their territory will be 10 times the length of the male. With this in mind, it is better to keep breeding pairs in a tank of their own. Even so, care should be exercised, as the males of some species are not averse to seriously injuring or even killing their partner.

Provide areas of shelter as well as open areas of substrate. Like their "Amazonian" cousins, they dig in the substrate, uprooting plants and undermining the tank decor. Position rockwork, pieces of wood and other tank decoration securely so that they cannot be toppled. Any large plants, whether growing in the substrate or potted, should be surrounded by flat rocks to deter digging. The only alternative is to grow Java Fern on wood.

Representative Species

	maximum adult size
Archocentrus nigrofasciatus Convict	6in (15cm) males 3in (7.5 cm) females
"Cichlasoma" festae Red Terror	20in (51cm)
Parachromis managuensis Mannie, Jaguar Cichlid	12in (30cm)
Herichthys cyanoguttatus Texas Cichlid	12in (30cm)
Corpora nicaraguensis Nica	10in (25cm)
Thorichthys meeki Firemouth	6in (15cm)
Archocentrus sajica No common name	4.5in (11.5cm) males 3in (7.5cm) females
Archocentrus spilurus Blue-eyed or Jade-eyed Cichlid	4.5in (12cm) males 3in (8cm) females
Paratheraps synspilum Quetzal Cichlid	14in (36cm)
Amphilophus citrinellus Midas Cichlid, Yellow Devil	15in (38cm)
Aequidens rivulatus Green Terror	10in (25cm)
Herotilapia multispinosa Rainbow Cichlid	7in (18cm)
"Cichlasoma" octofasciatum Jack Dempsey	8in (20cm)

▶ *The Firemouth* (Thorichthys meeki) *is generally a nervous and peaceful fish, but becomes belligerent after spawning. Breeding them is easy.*

▲ *The Green Terror* (Aequidens rivulatus) *is a pugnacious creature that lives up to its common name.*

The food requirements of the neotropicals varies with species. Be sure you can provide the right foods for the species you are keeping.

Males are usually larger, more colourful and have longer finnage than females. They also develop nuchal humps. Spawning strategies vary from those that spawn in caves or in sheltered areas to those that are open spawners. Parental care is good and, provided you can supply copious amounts of brine shrimp, they will raise a brood without too much trouble.

Tank Conditions and Care

HABITAT: Large aquarium with rocks and wood seated on the base glass and open areas of substrate to accommodate their digging.

Tank size	48x12x12in (122x30x30cm)
pH	7.0–8.0
dH	Not critical
Temperature	24–27°C (75–81°F)
Water changes	25% every week
Filtration	External canister filter to cope with the amount of debris these fish stir up. Moderate current.
Lighting	Type not critical

FEEDING: Carnivores, omnivores, insectivores and herbivores. Flake, pellets, live, frozen, green foods. Check species requirements.

HEALTH: Few problems provided they have enough space to establish territories.

Q&A

● *Can I set up a Central American cichlid community aquarium?*

... In the short term, maybe, but you will never achieve harmony among the fish in such a tank. Even the smaller species are constantly staking their claim to territories – when they are not breeding. When sex enters the equation, the situation deteriorates and the tank can resemble a battle zone! At this stage, either place a divider in the tank or remove some of the fish for their own safety.

● *I have a breeding pair of Midas Cichlids in a large aquarium, but the male keeps attacking the female, even when they have eggs. What can I do?*

Males of some species are so highly defensive of their brood that they have to attack something, and if the female is the only fish around, she may bear the brunt of this aggression. Use a clear divider to create a separate compartment at one end of the aquarium, and place in it a "target fish", large enough to pose a genuine threat and thus distract the male. On no account, however, should target fish ever be exposed to actual physical attack.

● *Why do my Central American cichlids eat their young after raising them to a reasonable size?*

You must appreciate that you are breeding the fish under artificial conditions. In the confined space of the tank, the larger the fry become, the more they appear a threat to the parents, who may wish to breed again and regard the first batch of fry as a danger to the new brood. Ideally, you should remove the fry before they run the risk of being eaten and continue to grow them on in another tank.

Other Cichlids FAMILY: CICHLIDAE

OTHER, LESS FAMILIAR CICHLIDS FROM AFRICA and Asia provide an interesting alternative and challenge to the enterprising hobbyist. The chromides from the Indian subcontinent are becoming more widely available in the aquarium trade, while Madagascan cichlids, which are endangered in the wild, are still difficult to obtain.

Chromides

The chromides are a small group of cichlids that are native to southern India and Sri Lanka. Of these, two species are commonly represented in the aquarium trade. The small Orange Chromide (*Etroplus maculatus*) reaches 4in (10cm), while the Silver or Green Chromide (*Etroplus suratensis*) is considerably larger, growing to a length of 18in (46cm). Orange Chromides live in both fresh and brackish environments; in the aquarium they benefit from a little sea salt in the water (but do make certain that your other fish

Tank Conditions and Care
Chromides

HABITAT: Orange Chromide; planted community tank with other peaceful fish. Silver Chromide; brackish water and salt-tolerant plants.

Tank size Orange Chromide; 36x12x12in (91x 30x30cm). Silver Chromide; 48x18x18in (122x 46x46cm).

pH	7.0–7.5
dH	To 15°
Temperature	23–25°C (73–77°F)
Water changes	25% every week
Filtration	Not critical, provided it is efficient
Lighting	Type not critical

FEEDING: Orange Chromide; flake and/or frozen foods (e.g. bloodworm, mosquito larvae, *Daphnia*). Silver Chromide; scalded lettuce or spinach.

HEALTH: Sensitive to changing tank conditions.

will tolerate salt before adding it). For Silver Chromides, brackish conditions and spacious accommodation are absolutely essential.

Orange Chromides will breed in captivity; the pair form a strong bond and both parents exercise care over their brood for quite some time. While tending their young, they can be quite aggressive towards other fish. The breeding tank should have areas of open substrate with flat rocks and stones to provide a spawning site, as well as a thicket of plants and tangles of roots to give cover. The fry will initially feed, like discus, on parental body mucus. They can also be given newly hatched brine shrimp.

The fish are relatively easy to feed. The Silver Chromide is largely vegetarian. Along with commercially available foods, include plenty of vegetable matter in its diet. This has the additional benefit of dissuading it from eating your plants (plastic plants are another option). The Orange Chromide takes flakes, frozen and live foods, but has also been known to eat the eggs of the Silver Chromide and of neighbouring Orange pairs.

◀ *An Orange Chromide* (Etroplus maculatus) *guarding its clutch of eggs. These fish make excellent parents, but are not averse to cannibalizing the eggs and fry of other pairs of their own kind.*

● *Can I breed Silver Chromides in the aquarium?*

... Yes, but only so long as you maintain brackish conditions. Without salt, these fish rarely survive beyond 4in (10cm), so never grow large enough to breed. At about 6in (15cm) long, the fish are mature, and are prolific spawners. The fry hatch in about 36 hours but are not free-swimming for another week. Intriguingly, the parents' coloration changes when they are caring for the fry – they develop black throats and chests.

● *How can I get hold of Madagascan cichlids?*

At the time of writing, availability is very restricted. All species are endangered in the wild, so no collecting and export is permitted for the aquarium hobby. Some surplus young from captive breeding programs have been released to a few expert aquarists, and fry can occasionally be obtained from these amateur breeders. Expect to be thoroughly "vetted" before you are allowed any fish!

Tank Conditions and Care
Madagascan Cichlids

HABITAT: Large aquarium with rocks and bogwood for decor.

Tank size Min 48x15x15in (122x38x38cm), but the larger the better.	
pH	6.8–7.5
dH	4–10°
Temperature	27–28°C (81–82°F)
Water changes	20% every week
Filtration	Not critical, provided it is efficient
Lighting	Type not critical

FEEDING: Omnivores, flake, frozen foods, etc. but be sure to include vegetable matter.

HEALTH: No particular problems have come to light so far. These fish are too recently introduced to offer definitive health advice.

Madagascan Cichlids

One or two species of Madagascan cichlid are gradually appearing in the hobby; foremost among these are the Marakely (*Paratilapia polleni*) and *Paratilapia bleekeri*. Males of *P. polleni* customarily grow to 12in (30cm), and females to 9in (23cm); *P. bleekeri* uniformly reaches 7in (18cm) irrespective of sex. The comparative rarity and often striking coloration of these fish have made them much sought after.

Water conditions vary from region to region throughout Madagascar, and some species are found wild in a number of different water chemistries. In general, you should aim for fairly neutral pH and hardness. Fish bred in captivity are at present available only from a few hobbyists, who will doubtless supply details of the conditions that have suited their adults.

Madagascan cichlids appear to be tolerant of aquarium life, reasonably omnivorous (vegetable matter should be offered), but rather intolerant of each other. Males are usually larger than females, and possess a nuchal hump. A large aquarium is essential, which may be decorated with bogwood and rocks securely seated on the base glass. They are all substrate spawners with a digging habit. If you are fortunate enough to obtain these beautiful fish, you should resign yourself to your plants being vandalized!

Suckermouths

FAMILY: LORICARIIDAE

THE LORICARIIDAE ARE A SOUTH AMERICAN family of armoured catfish, characterized by three rows of bony plates along their flanks. In some regions, they are known as "armadillo del rio" (river armadillo). A few species have a wide range but most come from restricted localities. They can be found in a variety of habitats, from swift mountain streams to small pools and marshes. Thus some species require very soft, acidic water, while others prefer neutral to slightly alkaline conditions. The genera *Hypostomus* and *Ancistrus* contain some species that will inhabit brackish, estuarine conditions.

Although bottom-dwellers in the aquarium, in the wild they can be found at both the bottom and the top of rivers. Some species bury themselves in the sand, leaving just their eyes exposed.

▲ *Although large, the Royal Whiptail* (Sturisoma panamense) *is a peaceful fish, and makes a welcome addition to the larger community tank.*

Getting Around

Their sucker-like mouths allow these fish to hold station in swift-flowing streams. In order to breathe, they take water into the gill chamber before expelling it through the gill openings. Their rasping teeth enable them to feed on algae, detritus, small insect larvae and even (in some cases) flesh. The body of loricariids is usually depressed (as in *Loricaria* species) or triangular in cross-section (*Panaque* species); this allows water to pass easily over them while gently pressing them down, helping them retain their position on the substrate.

Q&A...

● *Why has my new Panaque begun to lose some of its large spines and cheek bristles?*

This is caused by stress, and is most noticeable on newly imported, mature fish or adult fish that have been moved from a well-established aquarium to a relatively new set-up. In severe cases, the fish may also shed some of its teeth.

● *How can I tell if I have a pair of Whiptails?*

Very young fish cannot be sexed. Adult males show bristles on their cheeks and, in some cases, heads; the amount and size of these depends on whether or not it is the spawning season. Also, females have a more pointed head. In sexually mature females, the eggs can sometimes be seen in the body cavity through the stomach skin. You can sex semi-adult fish by running your finger around the snout. If you can feel stubbly bristles, you probably have a male.

● *My local shop was selling "mixed Otocinclus"; some had the extra little fin on the back whereas on others it was missing. What causes this?*

The absence of an adipose fin is not caused by disease or fighting. Its presence or absence can help identify a particular species or, in this case, genus: *Parotocinclus* have an adipose fin, *Otocinclus* do not.

● *For several years my six Bristlenoses all lived together peacefully, each in its own cave or hollow. Why has one suddenly become aggressive?*

You probably have a male that is ready to breed. He will defend his chosen nest site, usually a cave or a hollow he has made in a piece of bogwood, from any other males and will only allow a female that is ready to spawn to enter the area. Remove the other fish.

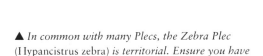

▲ *In common with many Plecs, the Zebra Plec (Hypancistrus zebra) is territorial. Ensure you have enough substrate area to accommodate them.*

● *I have seen several fish coded with "L" followed by a number. What does this mean?*

These codes are used for newly discovered species that have not yet been described by ichthyologists. They are an international standard in the trade that overcomes the problem of different common names being given to a particular fish in various countries. For example, the fish now known scientifically as *Hypancistrus zebra* was initially coded L46.

● *My Plec swims upside-down to take flake food from the surface. Is this normal?*

Loricariids make regular trips to the surface to take in air which is passed through their system and expelled through the gut. If they find food floating on the surface of the aquarium, many Plecs take advantage of it and come to no harm.

Tank Conditions and Care

HABITAT: Planted aquarium with sand or rounded gravel substrate.

Tank size Min 18x10x10in (46x25x25cm) depending on species.

pH	6.5–7.5
dH	To 15° depending on species
Temperature	22–26°C (72–79°F)
Water changes	15–20% every 10–14 days

Filtration Efficient filtration – if using undergravel make sure it is regularly maintained.

Lighting Fluorescent lighting sufficient to maintain plant growth.

FEEDING: Flake, tablet and frozen plus green food such as lettuce, spinach, slices of potato, courgettes (zucchini) and cucumber. For the species that require meaty foods, live foods such as *Daphnia*, *Tubifex* and bloodworm is beneficial, as well pieces of meat or fish. Some – notably the *Panaque* species – require wood in their diet.

HEALTH: Susceptible to bacterial infections if optimum conditions are not maintained. If water quality deteriorates, there may be some degeneration of the finnage and barbels. Remedy the situation with a water change.

For years the Common Plec (or Pleco) was considered a prime algae-eater for the community tank. Consequently, many small specimens were bought by unsuspecting aquarists, who only discovered their size potential when they had outgrown their home. Some smaller species, such as those of *Rineloricaria*, *Ancistrus* and *Otocinclus*, have also been imported and bred. In recent years, several new loricariids have appeared on the market, many of which remain undescribed by ichthyologists. They have proved a challenge to the trade and hobbyist alike.

The loricariids have always been considered vegetarians, but several have been found to eat flesh. Check with your dealer to see what the specimen you are interested in is eating. Most shops leave slices of potato or similar food in the tank with their fish and you will be able to see if this has been grazed on. Some species, notably those of *Panaque*, eat wood, so it is vital to provide them with driftwood (unvarnished) in the aquarium. When buying loricariids, avoid any specimen that has sunken eyes or a hollow belly.

Handling these fish can be difficult. They have stout spines on the dorsal and pectoral fins; some also have dermal denticles that make them feel rough to the touch; others (e.g. *Ancistrus*) have interopercular spines that can be raised and lowered at will – in short, a whole armoury of things to tangle in a mesh net! If this occurs, put the net and fish back in the tank and it will usually free itself. Unsurprisingly, many aquarists prefer to catch their loricariids by hand.

Loricariids can be challenging to breed because, although many species spawn readily in the community aquarium, raising the fry is fraught with difficulties. To help overcome them, special rearing tanks and foods are described in Breeding, pages 58–59.

◀ *The Goldy Pleco* (Scobinancistrus aureatus) *is one of a small number of loricariids that are carnivorous. They are partial to pieces of fish or prawn that they can rasp away at.*

Representative Species

	maximum adult size		maximum adult size
Ancistrus dolichopterus Bristlenose, Busynose	5in (12.5cm)	*Panaque nigrolineatus* Royal Plec	24in (61cm)
Chaetostoma thomsoni Bulldog Plec	4in (10cm)	*Panaque suttoni* Blue-eyed Plec	18in (46cm)
Farlowella spp. Twig Catfish	8in (20cm)	*Peckoltia pulcher* Pretty Peckoltia, Stripped Plec	4in (10cm)
Hypancistrus zebra Zebra Plec, Zebra Peckoltia	4in (10cm)	*Pterygoplichthys anisitsi* Snow King Plec	24in (61cm)
Hypostomus plecostomus Common Plec, Pleco	12in (30cm)	*Rineloricaria lanceolata* Whiptail Catfish	6in (15cm)
Leporacanthicus galaxias Tooth-nose, Vampire Plec	10in (25cm)	*Scobinancistrus aureatus* Goldy Pleco, Sunshine Pleco	12in (30cm)
Otocinclus vittatus Oto	2in (5cm)	*Sturisoma panamense* Royal Whiptail, Royal Farlowella	12in (30cm)

Mailed Catfish FAMILY: CALLICHTHYIDAE

THIS SOUTH AMERICAN FAMILY OF CATFISH, which includes the familiar *Corydoras* genus, is characterized by two overlapping rows of bony plates along its flanks. It is one of the most popular families in the hobby, with every fishkeeper having at an early stage kept a *Corydoras* or two to "clean up the tank". However, the family is not restricted to a single genus. It also includes, among others, *Aspidoras*, *Brochis*, *Callichthys*, *Hoplosternum* and *Dianema*, which are all readily available. Of all the catfish families, this is the one most studied by hobbyists with a view to breeding, and the success rate of aquarists around the world has been phenomenal.

Almost all species of mailed catfish are suited to community aquaria but the larger ones are boisterous and should be kept with companion fish of a similar size. Many are shoaling fish, and are best kept with a group of their own kind. They are able to survive in poorly oxygenated water by taking oxygen from the air at the surface; however, a common problem associated with poor water conditions in the tank is degeneration of the barbels. This becomes apparent when fish are kept in bare aquaria (as breeding

Tank Conditions and Care

HABITAT: Planted aquarium with sand or fine, rounded gravel substrate.

Tank size	Min 24x12x12in (61x30x30cm) depending on species. Smaller tanks may be used for breeding.
pH	6.5–7.0
dH	To 15° depending on species
Temperature	23–28°C (73–82°F)
Water changes	15–20% every 10–14 days
Filtration	Efficient filtration. If using under-gravel make sure it is regularly maintained.
Lighting	Fluorescent lighting sufficient to maintain plant growth.

FEEDING: Flake, tablet and frozen as staples. Live food such as *Daphnia*, *Tubifex* and bloodworm is beneficial, especially when conditioning the fish for breeding.

HEALTH: Susceptible to bacterial infections and whitespot if optimum conditions are not maintained in the aquarium. If water quality deteriorates, there may be some degeneration of the finnage and barbels. Rectify the situation with a water change.

▲ *The Armoured Catfish* (Callichthys callichthys) *is a bubble-nest builder, and is easy to breed. As it is somewhat boisterous, it is advisable to keep it with similar-sized fish.*

● *There is a reddish patch on the side of one of my new* Corydoras. *Is this harmful?*

The stress of transportation and differing water conditions can affect the immune system, exposing the fish to the risk of infection. If you have added the fish to a long-established tank, check the water conditions. It may have become too acidic or there may be a build-up of nitrates, which could harm a new fish. Change the water and check the filtration.

● *How can I tell the two species of* Dianema *apart?*

The Flagtail Catfish (*Dianema urostriata*) has a distinctive caudal fin with black-and-white stripes. This coloration is lacking in its close relative, the Porthole Catfish (*Dianema longibarbis*), which also tends to be somewhat smaller.

stock, or as youngsters being grown on). The barbels on *Corydoras* may also be cut or completely eroded by digging into sharp gravel for food. In the worst cases, the sores become infected by bacteria or fungus. Gravel with rounded grains or sand (again with rounded grains, such as filtration sand) are ideal tank substrates to provide for these fish.

Yet even in a well-balanced community tank with a fine substrate, it is not unknown for *Corydoras*, *Brochis* or *Aspidoras* to lose their barbels, as the result of a badly maintained undergravel filtration system. This allows bacteria to proliferate and infect the catfish's barbels.

Whatever the cause of the problem, it is vital that you rectify the situation in the aquarium, or move the fish to a more suitable home. Firstly, the fish use their barbels to find food; whereas, in the wild, barbel loss would be fatal, in captivity we can at least provide ample food for a fish without barbels to survive. Secondly – and far more importantly – males use their barbels to stimulate the female during breeding. If they are missing, no mating will take place.

Breeding Corydoras

Depending on the species, *Corydoras* can be bred with a pair, trio (two males to one female) or as a shoal. Some species are easier to spawn than others: *C. aeneus* or *C. paleatus*, for example, will spawn in a community tank without any help from the aquarist! Once you have got these to spawn and have raised the fry, you can try breeding a more challenging species, such as *C. panda*. First buy six young fish and grow them on – it may not be possible to sex juveniles. As they mature, the females become fuller in the body (easily spotted when viewed from above). You can also distinguish the sexes by the ventral fins: when extended, the male's fins are far more pointed than the female's.

For breeding, corys should be removed to a small, sparsely decorated breeding tank to avoid the danger of their eggs being eaten by other inmates. If the fish are initially reluctant to spawn, a partial water change can be undertaken to lower the temperature slightly; this replicates the corys' natural breeding time, at the onset of the rainy season.

Some species lay their eggs on a flat surface (leaves, aquarium glass) and tend the eggs; others stick them at random among plants or all over the glass and do not look after them. They hatch within 48 hours. The fry can be raised using *Artemia* (brine shrimp) as a first food, and then moving on to *Daphnia* and prepared foods.

◀ *The Bronze Catfish* (Corydoras aeneus) *is an accommodating fish, and makes an ideal starting point for anyone wishing to keep and/or breed* Corydoras.

● *How can I breed* Hoplosternum*?*

First ensure you have a pair! The male's pectoral fin spine is thick and stout, while the female's is much thinner and pointed at the tip. Feed the fish to bring them into spawning condition, then place the pair in a sparsely decorated breeding tank. Float a piece of polystyrene or a plastic lid on the surface, beneath which they will construct a bubble-nest. A water change usually triggers nest-building and spawning. The pair position their eggs in the foam. The male then guards the nest, and also repairs any damage to it. At this point, the female should be removed. As for the male, some aquarists prefer to remove him almost immediately, at the risk of damaging the nest, while others leave him until the fry are hatching. The eggs hatch in about a week and the fry can take freshly hatched brine shrimp.

● *Why have my new* Corydoras, *which were imported only two days ago, suddenly died?*

Importation is highly stressful to fish. Corys are packed several hundred to a bag; even after a long flight and customs clearance, they still have to be transported to the wholesaler. When they are unpacked (preferably in dim conditions to avoid shock) they are put into aquaria to recover. But if they are sold on too soon, they will succumb to the stress. In your case, the fish had three changes of water quality and three journeys in 48 hours. This was bound to prove fatal.

Representative Species

	maximum adult size		maximum adult size
Aspidoras pauciradiatus False Corydoras	1in (2.5cm)	*Corydoras pygmaeus* Pygmy or Dwarf Catfish	1in (2.5cm)
Brochis splendens Emerald Catfish	4in (10cm)	*Corydoras reticulatus* Network Catfish	2in (5cm)
Corydoras aeneus Bronze Catfish	3in (7.5cm)	*Corydoras treitlii* Hognosed Corydoras	3in (7.5cm)
Hoplosternum littorale No common name	8in (20cm)	*Corydoras trilineatus* Three-line Catfish	2in (5cm)
Corydoras habrosus Salt and Pepper Catfish	1in (2.5cm)	*Callichthys callichthys* Callichthys, Armoured Catfish	7in (18cm)
Corydoras metae Bandit Catfish	2in (5cm)	*Dianema longibarbis* Porthole Catfish	4in (10cm)
Corydoras paleatus Peppered Catfish	4in (10cm)	*Dianema urostriata* Flagtail Catfish	6in (15cm)
Corydoras panda Panda Catfish	2in (5cm)	*Megalechis thoracata* Bubble-nest Catfish	8in (20cm)

Talking Catfish
FAMILY: DORADIDAE

These popular south american catfish have a distinctive single series of bony plates running along the body from just behind the operculum to the caudal peduncle. Depending on species, these plates may be broad or narrow and possess one or more rows of backward projecting scutes ("thorns"). The number and size of these can aid species identification. Some species also have caudal fulcra, a series of bony plates on the top and bottom of the caudal peduncle.

Doradids are divided into two groups: broad-breasted, where the width between the base of the pectoral fin spines exceeds the length of the head; and narrow-breasted, where this ratio is smaller. The broad-breasted are easier to keep. Many narrow-breasted species have feathered barbels not seen in broad-breasted species. Both types are relatively peaceful.

Making Sounds

Newcomers to these fish are often surprised at the strange noises that come from the aquarium. The doradids have two methods of producing the sounds that give them their common name. The first is the "elastic spring mechanism", a muscle that attaches to the rear of the skull

● *My new Dolphin Cat, which was healthy when I bought it, is now listless, has lost its appetite and stays in a corner with its fins clamped. Can you help?*

Acclimatize it by putting it into a mature, planted aquarium with a fine substrate. Doradids like seclusion and do not adapt well to bare tanks. Remove any small fish that it might eat. Offer *Daphnia* and bloodworm.

● *Is it possible to breed any of the doradids?*

One or two species have been spawned in captivity. *Amblydoras affinis* builds a nest of leaves and practises parental care, while *Agamyxis* species are reputed to build nests but practise no parental care.

● *My Acanthodoras cataphractus produces a milky fluid when caught – is this dangerous?*

This is secreted by a gland at the base of the pectoral fin; its purpose is unknown. It can cause a burning sensation if it gets into any cuts or grazes on your hands.

● *My doradid is in good health but has a slight white coating on its eyes. Should I be worried about this?*

This condition, which is sometimes called "cloudy eyes", is caused by hard water. Gradually soften your water and remove any shells, limestone or earthenware pots. If it is not too far advanced, it should clear up.

Tank Conditions and Care

HABITAT: Aquarium with sand or fine gravel substrate. Avoid sharp-edged rocks that may damage their bodies. Java Fern attached to wood provides suitable cover.

Tank size	Min 36x12x12in (91x30x30cm)

pH Broad-breasted species require 6.5–7.5; narrow breasted species 6.5–7.0.

dH	To 15°

Temperature Broad-breasted 22–26°C (72–79°F); narrow-breasted 22–25°C (72–77°F).

Water changes	15–20% every 10–14 days

Filtration Broad-breasted need any efficient system. Narrow-breasted species require very efficient filtration, for example an external canister filter.

Lighting Fluorescent lighting sufficient to maintain plant growth.

FEEDING: Tablet foods, flakes, frozen foods, small shrimps, worms, small pieces of fish or meat, water snails, etc.

HEALTH: Broad-breasted species are not susceptible to disease if water quality is maintained and sharp objects are avoided. Narrow-breasted species are susceptible to disease if optimum conditions are not maintained. Poor water quality may cause some degeneration of the finnage and barbels. Rectify with a water change, and check on the efficiency of the filtration system.

▶ *The Humbug Catfish* (Platydoras costatus) *likes to squeeze into crevices. Avoid clay pipes, which can rub the tips of their fin spines and make them sore; wood makes a safer hiding place.*

▼ *Although potentially a large fish, the growth rate of the Mother of Snails Catfish* (Megalodoras irwini) *is slow and steady. It is most active at night and should be fed at this time.*

Representative Species

Broad-breasted species	maximum adult size
Platydoras costatus Humbug Catfish, Striped Raphael	8in (20cm)
Agamyxis pectinifrons Spotted Talking Catfish, Spotted Raphael	5in (12.5cm)
Megalodoras irwini Mother of Snails Catfish	24in (61cm)
Amblydoras affinis Hancock's Catfish, Talking Cat	4in (10cm)
Acanthodoras cataphractus No common name	4in (10cm)
Narrow-breasted species	
Opsodoras notospilus Black-finned Dorad	3in (7.5cm)
Opsodoras stubeli Feather Barbels Catfish	6in (15cm)
Oxydoras niger Dolphin Cat, Niger, Prehistoric Cat	33in (84cm)

and the anterior of the swimbladder. By rapidly contracting and relaxing this muscle, a fish can make its air-filled swimbladder resonate to produce a booming sound. The second sound is made by partially locking the fin spines in their sockets; when moved, they grate against the socket. A fish uses this sound to locate conspecifics in its home waters. In the aquarium it is made when fish are jostling for position in a hollow, being harassed or being caught.

Catching these fish can be difficult. When frightened, doradids lock their fin spines erect: their serrated edges are potent deterrents to predators. These can easily become entangled in a mesh net, so a heavyweight linen net that the scutes and spines cannot penetrate is an essential piece of equipment. If your fish does become entangled in a mesh net, leave the net and fish in the aquarium and it may release itself. Otherwise, remove the net and the fish, and carefully cut the net away. Avoid forcing the fin spines down, as this may damage the delicate musculature that supports them, and leaves you open to injury. Some aquarists prefer to catch these fish by hand, but injuries both to yourself and your fish may result – do this at your own risk. Doradids can exert great pressure with their fin spines and a finger trapped between their pectoral fin spine and the scutes on the body can be painful!

Upside-down Catfish
FAMILY: MOCHOKIDAE

NEWCOMERS TO FISHKEEPING OFTEN THINK that the mochokids consist of just a single genus – *Synodontis* – but in fact there are several other genera, such as *Hemisynodontis*, *Mochokiella*, *Chiloglanis* and *Brachysynodontis*. All these are native to Africa, and their natural habitats include lakes, rivers, swamps and streams. Most are suited to life in the community aquarium, so long as companion fish are large enough to avoid being eaten. Despite their common family name, very few regularly swim upside-down; two that do are *S. nigriventris* and *H. membranaceus*.

◀ *The Moustache Catfish* (Hemisynodontis membranaceus) *thrives on a meaty diet of bloodworm, mosquito larvae, etc. These may be fed live or frozen.*

Most of the mochokids possess a single pair of simple unbranched barbels (exceptions include *S. decorus* and *S. flavitaeniatus*) and two pairs of feathered (branched) barbels. These are used to search for food and guide it into the mouth. Their adipose fin can be quite large and fleshy. The body is naked, protected only by a thick skin, and the fin spines are stout. The head is covered with thick, bony plates; the shape and size of the backward, bony projection known as the humeral process can be used to determine species. The mouth is subterminal, indicating the catfish's method of feeding from a flat surface. Habitual inverted swimmers have a darker belly than their back, to avoid detection by predators.

The small species enjoy the company of their own kind but some of the larger species, such as *S. schall*, can be territorial to the point of real aggression. Give them plenty of space and hiding places to form territories, or keep single specimens with other large fish.

Representative Species

	maximum adult size		
Mochokiella paynei Payne's Catfish	3in (7.5cm)	*Hemisynodontis membranaceus* Moustache Catfish	12in (30cm)
Synodontis nigriventris Upside-down Catfish	4in (10cm)	*Synodontis multipunctatus* Many-spotted Catfish	8in (20cm) females 11in (28cm) males
Synodontis brichardi Brichard's Catfish	5in (12.5cm)	*Synodontis nigrita* False Upside-down Catfish, Dark-spotted Catfish	8in (20cm)
Synodontis alberti Albert's Catfish	6in (15cm)	*Synodontis flavitaeniatus* No common name	8in (20cm)
Synodontis eupterus Feather-fin Syno	6in (15cm)	*Brachysynodontis batensoda* Giant Upside-down Catfish	10in (25cm)
Synodontis njassae Malawi Catfish	6in (15cm)	*Synodontis decorus* Clown Catfish	12in (30cm)
Synodontis angelicus Polka-dot Catfish	8in (20cm)	*Synodontis schall* Grey Catfish	16in (41cm)

● *How can I prevent my catfish from hiding beneath the heater and burning itself?*

Plastic mesh cylinders can be fitted around the heater to stop the catfish coming into direct contact with it. If you are setting up a new tank, section off a back corner for the heater by siliconing a piece of glass across it. Leave a gap at the bottom to allow the water to flow freely, and if necessary use an airstone to circulate the water. Burns will normally heal of their own accord in good water conditions, but treat any resulting fungal infections with a fungicide.

● *How can I get my synos to come out so that I can see them?*

Synos are not fond of bright light. For those that invert, place some cork bark or floating plants on the surface. The fish will lurk beneath these much as they would in the wild. This cuts down the light to part of the aquarium yet still allows plant growth elsewhere.

● *Can I breed upside-down catfish?*

It is possible, but difficult. A few species have been bred in captivity, notably *S. multipunctatus* and *S. nigriventris*, but breeding reports are few.

▲ *The striking markings on the body of the Polka-dot Catfish* (Synodontis angelicus) *are unique to each individual fish. It is popular with hobbyists.*

Tank Conditions and Care

HABITAT: Equip aquarium with sand or fine gravel substrate. Avoid sharp-edged rocks that may damage their bodies but provide plenty of shelter such as Java Fern attached to wood, caves and floating bark.

Tank size depending on species.	Min 24x12x12in (61x30x30cm)
pH	Around 7.0
dH	To 15°
Temperature	22–25°C (72–77°F)
Water changes	15–20% every 10–14 days
Filtration	Any efficient system
Lighting	Fluorescent lighting

FEEDING: Small shrimps, worms, small pieces of fish or meat; some vegetable matter.

HEALTH: Not susceptible to disease provided water quality is maintained and fish do not injure themselves on sharp objects.

Naked Catfish

FAMILIES: PIMELODIDAE
AND BAGRIDAE

Representative Species

Pimelodid species	maximum adult size
Microglanis iheringi	
Bumblebee Catfish	4in (10cm)
Pimelodus pictus	
Polka-dot Catfish,	
Angelica Pim, Pictus Cat	6in (15cm)
Pimelodus ornatus	
Ornate Pim	8in (20cm)
Pimelodus albofasciatus	
White-striped Pim, 4-line Pim	10in (25cm)
Sorubim lima	
Shovel-nosed Catfish	18in (45cm)
Phractocephalus hemioliopterus	
Red-tail Catfish	39in (1m)
Pseudoplatystoma fasciatum	
Tiger Shovel-nose	80in (2m)
Bagrid species	
Pelteobagrus ornatus	
Dwarf Ornate Bagrid	1.5in (4cm)

Mystus armatus	
Pearl Catfish, One-spot Catfish	5in (12.5cm)
Mystus bimaculatus	
Two-spot Catfish	5in (12.5cm)
Leiocassis siamensis	
Bumblebee Catfish	6in (12cm)
Chrysichthys ornatus	
Ornate Catfish	8in (20cm)
Auchenoglanis occidentalis	
Giraffe-nosed Catfish	24in (61cm)
Mystus wykii	
Crystal-eyed Catfish	30in (76cm)
Mystus tengara	
No common name	9in (22.5cm)
Lophiobagrus cyclurus	
Tanganyikan Catfish	4in (10cm)
Mystus micracanthus	
No common name	6in (15cm)

ALTHOUGH PIMELODIDS ARE SOUTH AMERICAN in origin and bagrids come from Africa and Asia, in captivity they have similar habits and require similar conditions. They are called naked catfish because their bodies are covered with a thick skin that has a copious layer of mucus. In most, but not all, species the dorsal and pectoral fins have stout fin spines, which protect them against predators and can also inflict nasty scratches and cuts if any fights occur – take care when handling these creatures. If using plastic pipes or cut clay pots to provide cover, sand the cut edges to avoid damage to the fish.

Species of both families vary greatly in size, though the very largest are pimelodids. Many of the large species are commercially fished for food in their native lands. Generally, the smaller species are gregarious, whereas the larger species are loners. Some bagrids can make clicking and squeaking sounds, most often heard when the fish are shoaling, feeding or being caught.

● *Should I buy an adult or juvenile specimen of a Tiger Shovel-nose?*

... Without doubt, a juvenile. It will be easier to settle into the aquarium and will more readily accept food other than its natural diet of live fish.

● *What is making the barbels of my catfish curl at the ends and the fins look ragged?*

A slight build-up of nitrates will cause this, and bacterial infection may set in. Change the water, check on filtration and, if necessary, treat the infection.

● *My pimelodid seemed to be choking or trying to be sick. All the other fish in the tank then became listless and lost their appetite. What caused this?*

Sometimes pimelodids inexplicably evacuate their stomach contents. This can cause the aquarium's biological system to break down; the pH may suddenly change, ammonia levels rise, and filtration become less efficient. Any of these might result in the death of the fish. A water change helps; you should also cut down on feeding until the bacteria beds have recovered and monitor the tank for the next 7–10 days, doing another partial water change if need be.

▼ *Mystus micracanthus makes an ideal tank companion for a community of medium-sized fish. But be warned – it will eat smaller fish!*

Tank Conditions and Care

HABITAT: For smaller species, a planted aquarium; for larger species, a spacious aquarium big enough for them to swim and turn with ease. Avoid sharp-edged rocks that may damage their bodies; wood is preferable as decor.

Tank size 36x12x12in (91x30x30cm) for smaller species and juvenile large species but these will need rehousing at regular intervals.

pH	6.5–7.5
dH	To 15°
Temperature	22–25°C (72–77°F)
Water changes	15–20% every 10–14 days
Filtration	Any efficient system
Lighting	Fluorescent lighting

FEEDING: Tablets, flakes, small shrimps, worms, small pieces of fish or meat; adjust size of food offered to size of fish.

HEALTH: Not generally susceptible to disease.

These fish have characteristic barbels used for hunting prey. Pimelodids have three pairs of barbels; bagrids three to four, the extra pair being the nasal barbels. As they are predators, it is best to keep even the small species in aquaria with fish that are too big to be considered as food.

Good water conditions are vital. The pimelodids are particularly susceptible to poor water quality, so ensure reliable filtration. As they are mainly carnivorous, they produce high-protein waste that can quickly pollute the closed system of an aquarium. External canister filters are ideal, especially if coupled with trickle filters.

Captive breeding reports are mostly sketchy. *Mystus tengara* lays cream-coloured eggs in the mulm among plant thickets; *Sorubim lima* have spawned in a pit in the substrate under some wood, but no young resulted. The breeding of *Lophiobagrus cyclurus* is better documented: this catfish from Lake Tanganyika digs beneath an overhang and lays 30–40 eggs. Parental care is practised and the fry thrive on brine shrimp and commercial foods. *Mystus armatus* and *M. micracanthus* are best spawned with one male and several females (males are smaller and more slender than the females) in a specially set-up tank with plants, no substrate and cool water. Development of the fry is rapid.

Other Catfish

THERE ARE SEVERAL OTHER CATFISH FAMILIES, some quite large, of which only a few species are regularly imported for the aquarium trade. Take care in choosing them, as not all are of a suitable size or temperament for the community tank.

The Siluridae

A Eurasian family of some 50–60 species, relatively few are imported. They are naked catfish with compressed bodies and a long anal fin, which they undulate while swimming. The maxillary barbels are usually long, and there may also be one or two pairs of mandibular barbels. The best known tropical species is the Glass Catfish (*Kryptopterus bicirrhis*); the novelty of being able to see the silvery sac containing its internal organs and its bones makes this fish popular.

All glass catfish are best kept in shoals in an aquarium with plenty of open swimming space. Feed them on a diet of small aquatic invertebrates such as *Daphnia*, bloodworm and mosquito larvae (both live and frozen). They will also accept flake foods.

Not all of the silurids, however, are small and suited to the home aquarium. For example, although *Wallago attu* has appeared in the trade, this large and highly predatory fish is really only appropriate for public aquaria. In its home territory, it is highly prized as a food and sport fish.

▼ *The Glass Catfish* (Kryptopterus bicirrhis) *from Southeast Asia is favoured for its striking transparent body. It requires excellent water conditions if it is to avoid bacterial infection.*

Driftwoods: The Auchenipteridae

This fairly small South American family is closely related to the Doradidae. The family contains about fifteen genera, the most commonly kept of which are *Parauchenipterus* and *Liosomadoras*. *Tatia*, *Auchenipterichthys*, *Entomocorus* and *Trachelyichthys* are less widely available. All of these naked catfish have a broken lateral line that appears to zig-zag along the flanks, and three pairs of barbels. The Auchenipterids practice internal fertilization; in most species, the males have a modified anal fin which allows them to accomplish this.

They are relatively easy to keep and several species may be bred in the aquarium. They are mostly nocturnal and require hiding places such as dense thickets of plants and tangles of roots or small hollows in which they can wedge themselves. If these are lacking, they may hide behind or beneath the heater, and suffer burns.

Driftwoods can be difficult to acclimatize to the aquarium. They require a mature, planted and very peaceful tank. Feed them on a diet of *Daphnia*, shrimp and bloodworm, chopped up if necessary.

Banjos: The Aspredinidae

These small catfish are not a common import to the aquarium trade. Although they make ideal additions to the community tank – so long as it doesn't contain very small fish that may get eaten – they tend to spend much of their time down on the bottom, only venturing out during twilight

Q&A

● *Why is it, when my Glass Catfish died, that its body became opaque?*

... The reason for this transformation is unknown, but it may have to do with the fish's metabolism. This phenomenon also occurs in other transparent fish.

● *My Glass Catfish seem to spend much of the day almost static with their heads up in the aquarium. Is this behaviour any cause for alarm?*

No, don't worry. Glass catfish are crepuscular – undertaking most of their activity at dawn and dusk – and it is quite normal for them to rest during the day. When they emerge to feed you will see that they are swimming normally.

● *I saw a driftwood with a hideously deformed dorsal fin. Is this normal?*

Yes – male specimens of *Parauchenipterus fisheri* have a "deformed" dorsal fin spine. They also have a long bony base to their barbels. When spawning, the male wraps himself around the female in a similar manner to the gouramis; he maintains this position, using his dorsal fin spine and bony barbels to keep a grip on his mate.

Tank Conditions and Care
Silurids, Driftwoods and Banjos

Silurids
As for Naked Catfish; see page 97

Driftwoods
As for Talking Catfish; see page 92

Banjos
As for Mailed Catfish; see page 89

Representative Species

Silurids	maximum adult size
Kryptopterus bicirrhis Glass Catfish	5in (12.5cm)
Kryptopterus macrocephalus Malaysian Glass Catfish	8in (20cm)
Wallago attu No common name	79in (2m)
Driftwoods	
Auchenipterichthys thoracatus Midnight Catfish, Zamora Cat	4in (10cm)
Liosomadoras oncinus Jaguar Catfish	6in (15cm)

Parauchenipterus galeatus Driftwood Catfish	8in (20cm)
Trachelyichthys exilis No common name	3in (7.5cm)
Tatia creutzbergi No common name	1.75in (4.5cm)
Banjos	
Bunocephalichthys verrucosus Craggy-headed Banjo	3in (7.5cm)
Dysichthys knerri Banjo Catfish	3in (7.5cm)

Tank Conditions and Care
Clariids

HABITAT: An aquarium with a few pieces of wood to provide shelter. Avoid sharp-edged objects, as these can damage the body of the fish. Provide a good cover glass to stop the fish from jumping out.

Tank size:	Min 36x12x12in (91x30x30cm); be ready to provide a large aquarium as the fish grow.
pH	7.0–9.0
dH	15–40°
Temperature	22–28°C (72–82°F)
Water changes	15–20% every 10 days

Filtration A canister filter to cope with these messy feeders. Undergravel systems are inappropriate, as these fish are constantly stirring up the substrate.

Lighting	Fluorescent lighting

FEEDING: Flake, tablet and frozen plus green foods and pieces of meat or fish of a suitable size for the catfish to eat.

HEALTH: Generally extremely robust, they are occasionally prone to heater burns.

hours to feed. In the wild they are found among leaf litter and dead wood, which blends with their cryptic coloration to conceal them. Dead oak leaves added to the aquarium provide a suitable substrate.

The Clariidae
Members of this family are native to Africa and Asia but have also been introduced, by irresponsible aquarists who wanted to get rid of them, into various other waters around the world, for example Florida and Hawaii in the US. In their native countries, Clariids are farmed commercially as a valuable food fish.

The genus *Clarias* is most commonly kept by aquarists, even though these long, eel-like creatures are not particularly attractive. Their body is naked, the dorsal and anal fins are usually

▲ *The Clarias Catfish* (Clarias batrachus) *– seen here in an albino form – is a highly voracious and frequently predatory fish. Take great care when handling it!*

long, and the caudal fin is rounded. Their pectoral fins have a stout spine, and they have four pairs of barbels.

In the aquarium environment, Clariids tend to be boisterous and aggressive, and should only be kept with other large fish that are capable of looking after themselves. They are also accomplished escape artists, so the cover glass on your tank should be heavily weighted down. Extreme care is needed when handling these fish or even just when servicing the aquarium – they think nothing of attacking their owner's hands, and the bite from even a small specimen can draw blood. If one of their pectoral spines punctures your arm, the resulting wound may swell up and become very painful. You should immediately consult a doctor, specifying what type of fish caused the wound.

Representative Species

Clariids	maximum adult size
Clarias angolensis Angola Walking Catfish	14in (36cm)
Clarias batrachus Clarias Catfish	20in (51cm)
Clarias gareipinus African Walking Catfish	31in (79cm)
Pangasiids	
Pangasius sutchi Pangasius, Iridescent Shark	18in (46cm)
Pangasius sanitwongsei No common name	8–10ft (2.5–3m)

Because they possess an accessory breathing organ, Clariids can live in the most foul conditions and, when their native streams dry up, will survive out of water for a long time so long as they remain wet. In such circumstances, they migrate across land at night in search of another river or stream.

The Pangasiidae

This Asian family of naked catfish contains some of the largest catfish. *Pangasiodon gigas* from the Mekong River in Vietnam can grow to just over 6ft (2m), while *Pangasius sanitwongsei* can attain 8–10ft (2.5–3m).

The species most commonly available to the aquarist is the Pangasius (*Pangasius sutchi*), a relatively hardy creature in the right conditions. Although they are nervous and constantly on the move, they may be kept with other species provided these fish can tolerate them. Avoid any sudden movements or noises, as they easily take fright and may harm themselves by colliding with rocks or wood or by leaping out of the water. If the water quality is maintained, they are highly resistant to the usual ailments.

Recently, *P. sanitwongsei* has become available in the trade. Bearing in mind their potential size and the fact that they are not solitary fish, you should not attempt to keep them unless you have a suitably large tank and filtration system.

● *I would like to show my banjo catfish. How can I tell the genus* Dysichthys *from* Bunocephalichthys?

The easiest way of telling these two genera apart is by the much higher and craggier head of *Bunochephalichthys*. In *Dysichthys* the head is much flatter.

● *Is it possible to breed Clariids in captivity?*

Yes, *C. batrachus* has spawned in a tank. The parents made a gravel nest in the corner. They then began a courtship ritual, which involved nudging one another in the genital region. After chasing around the nest, the male wrapped himself around the female; repeated copulation produced several batches of eggs. One parent stayed guarding the nest. The eggs were 0.5mm in diameter, hatched in about 24 hours, and the fry were free-swimming in three days.

● *I have a single Pangasius in my community tank, but it hides in a corner. What is wrong?*

Pangasius are gregarious fish, and should be kept in a group of at least four or five.

▼ Pangasius sanitwongsei *can reach a considerable size, even when kept under aquarium conditions. Before buying it, think carefully whether you will be able to accommodate it as a fully grown adult.*

Tank Conditions and Care
Pangasiids

HABITAT: Long and spacious aquarium decorated with a few plants and pieces of wood. Ensure that your tank is equipped with a tightly fitting cover to prevent the fish from jumping out. Robust tank companions are recommended.

Tank size:	Min 48x12x12in (122x30x30cm). Be prepared to provide a larger aquarium as the fish grow.
pH	6.5–7.5
dH	To 15° depending on species
Temperature	22–26°C (72–79°F)
Water changes	15–20% every 10–14 days
Filtration	Efficient filtration; a canister filter will also create a good water flow for the fish to swim against.

Lighting Fluorescent lighting sufficient to maintain plant growth.

FEEDING: Pangasiids are extremely voracious eaters. Flake, tablet and frozen plus green foods and pieces of meat or fish of a suitable size.

HEALTH: Very healthy provided they are kept as a group and water conditions are maintained.

Barbs FAMILY: CYPRINIDAE

BARBS ARE FOUND IN AFRICA, SOUTHEAST ASIA, and the Indian subcontinent. They are some of the most popular and accommodating tropical aquarium fish. Many species are bred commercially throughout the world and escapees are common in, for example, Florida. Several long-finned and colour varieties have also been bred.

Know Your Fish

Keeping the smaller species usually presents no problems as they are commercially bred; if you are offered wild-caught fish, you will need to research the needs of the species concerned and then provide them. Barbs are active shoaling fish, and so need plenty of room. Although the water conditions in a mature community aquarium are fine, the fish do benefit from being kept in a planted tank rather than one with no plants, or plastic "plants". The larger species need large aquaria and associated filtration systems. The tank will need a tight-fitting, heavy cover glass as they are prone to jumping, especially if alarmed.

Sexing in some species is easy, with males more colourful than females, but in others it can be difficult if not impossible to differentiate the

Representative Species

	maximum adult size		maximum adult size
Barbus arulius Arulius Barb	4in (10cm)	Barbus lateristriga Spanner Barb	7in (18cm)
Barbus conchonius Rosy Barb	4in (10cm)	Barbus nigrofasciatus Black Ruby Barb	2.5in (6.5cm)
Barbus cumingi Cuming's Barb	2in (5cm)	Barbus oligolepis Chequer Barb	6in (15cm)
Barbus eugrammus Zebra Barb, Striped Barb	4in (10cm)	Barbus orphoides No common name	10in (25cm)
Barbus everetti Clown Barb	4in (10cm)	Barbus schwanefeldi Tinfoil Barb	13in (33cm)
Barbus filamentosus Black–spot Barb, Filament Barb	6in (15cm)	Barbus tetrazona Tiger Barb	3in (7.5cm)
Barbus gelius Dwarf Barb, Golden Dwarf Barb	1.5in (4cm)	Barbus titteya Cherry Barb	2in (5cm)

▼ *These Tiger Barbs* (Barbus tetrazona) *display the standard coloration of the species. There are also green and albino Tiger varieties available. The albino may or may not have gill covers.*

sexes, except at breeding time when colour may intensify. Males of some commonly kept aquarium species (notably the larger ones) may develop small white or pearly tubercules on the snout and anal fin.

Barbs are egg-layers, or more precisely egg-scatterers. The eggs are either laid among plants to which they stick, or are allowed to fall to the bottom. The parents do not tend the eggs and should be removed before they eat them. Water conditions and temperature requirements vary with species. Some, for example *Barbus nigrofasciatus*, need to be overwintered in cooler conditions prior to spawning in the spring. Others, such as *B. everetti*, take time to mature and older males should be set up with young females.

Barbs can be very prolific, with some species producing 300 or more eggs at a single spawning. Hatching time is between 24–48 hours depending on species and water temperature. The fry will accept small live foods such as newly hatched brine shrimp.

Tank Conditions and Care

HABITAT: Peaceful, planted, mature community aquarium with plenty of open water for smaller species; for larger species roots and rounded rocks with a few large, hardy specimen plants.

Tank size	24x12x12in (61x30x30cm) for the smaller species; 48x18x18in (121x46x46cm) minimum for larger ones.
pH	6.0–7.0; check species requirements
dH	To 10°
Temperature	14–26°C (57–79°F) but check individual species requirements.
Water changes	10% every week
Filtration	External filters are preferable as larger species grub in the substrate, disrupting undergravel systems.
Lighting	Sufficient for plant growth

FEEDING: Omnivores. Flake and pelleted foods plus some vegetable matter (lettuce, peas, algae) and live or frozen foods (bloodworm, mysis shrimp, mosquito larvae).

HEALTH: No particular problems provided good water conditions are maintained; some species, such as Tiger Barbs, appear to be susceptible to whitespot.

● *I have two Tiger Barbs that keep chasing and nipping other fish. Would they be best kept in a species tank?*

A species tank is certainly one solution to this common problem. Another is to keep a shoal of 8–10 in your tank so that they are too busy checking on each other to harass the other fish.

● *How can I stop my barbs eating my plants?*

Some of the worst offenders are the larger species, such as Tinfoil Barbs (*B. schwanefeldi*) and *Barbus orphoides*. Feeding them plenty of green foods helps. Barbs will eat fine-leaved species such as *Cabomba*, *Ambulia* and *Wysteria* whereas they are less fond of broad-leaved species, so try growing *Cryptocorynes*, Amazon Swordplants or Java Fern.

Danios and White Clouds
FAMILY: CYPRINIDAE

COLLECTIVELY KNOWN AS DANIOS, THE GENERA *Danio* and *Brachydanio* are native to Burma, the Malay peninsula, Sumatra and India (except for the northern part of the country). They are found in rivers, streams and pools and have also established themselves in artificial paddy fields. *Tanichthys albonubes* (the White Cloud Mountain Minnow) comes from the gorges of the White Cloud Mountains of China. White Clouds and danios are fairly similar (apart from the coloration), but danios have two pairs of barbels.

Excellent Community Fish

These small, slim-bodied, active, shoaling fish are ideal for the community aquarium provided they are given plenty of space. Avoid keeping them in ones and twos as they tend to skulk away in among plants. Companion fish should be peaceful.

▲ *Given good conditions, the Bengal Danio (Danio devario) is a magnificent fish. Sadly, because it never exhibits its true coloration in dealers' tanks, it is often overlooked by aquarists.*

A long, rather than deep, community aquarium is required to give the necessary swimming space. They are not fussy about water conditions, provided extremes are avoided.

These fish are best bred in a specially set-up tank using a female and two males. For the smaller species, an 18x10x10in (46x25x25cm) tank is ideal. Introduce the female first and the males 24–36 hours later. If possible, site the tank where sunlight falls on it, as this triggers spawning. They are egg scatterers. For danios, the eggs hatch in about 24 hours, for White Clouds 48 hours. First foods should be fine – newly hatched brine shrimp and finely crumbled flake.

▶ *White Cloud Mountain Minnows* (Tanichthys albonubes) *are small, attractive and hardy fish, which are easy to care for and breed.*

● *I have seen some long-finned danios for sale. Are they suitable for my community tank?*

Yes, they are – long-finned varieties of various danios and the White Cloud have been bred for the trade. However, they are not as robust as the true species, requiring slightly warmer conditions and care when choosing tank companions – their long, trailing fins are just too much of a temptation to certain fin-nipping fish. They require the same foods and conditions as the true species, and can be bred using the same methods.

● *Should I keep a small shoal of a single species or can I mix them up?*

It depends on what you want to do with them. If they are just for show in your community tank, then it is perfectly acceptable to mix species, provided they all have a similar adult size (e.g. zebras, pearls, and White Clouds). However, if you wish to breed them, then a single species shoal is for you. Danios will interbreed although the fry are not usually viable.

● *How can I tell the difference between species of* Danio *and* Brachydanio?

The easiest method is to look at the lateral line; in *Brachydanio* it is incomplete, whereas in *Danio* it is complete. There are also differences in the number of soft fin rays on each genus: *Danio* has 8–18 in the dorsal fin and 13–20 in the anal; *Brachydanio* has 6–7 dorsal and 9–14 anal fin soft rays.

Representative Species

	maximum adult size
Brachydanio albolineatus Pearl Danio	2.3in (6cm)
Brachydanio kerri No common name	2in (5cm)
Brachydanio nigrofasciatus Spotted Danio	2in (5cm)
Brachydanio rerio Zebra Danio, Zebra Fish	2.3in (6cm)
Danio aequipinnatus Giant Danio	4in (10cm)
Danio devario Bengal Danio	6in (15cm)
Tanichthys albonubes White Cloud Mountain Minnow	1.5in (4cm)

Tank Conditions and Care

HABITAT: Planted community aquarium with plenty of open water.

Tank size	24x12x12in (61x30x30cm) for the smaller species; 36x12x12in (91x30x30cm) for larger ones.
pH	Not critical, around 7.0 is fine
dH	Max 10°
Temperature	22–24°C (72–75°F): 18–21°C (64–70°F) in winter.
Water changes	10–15% every week
Filtration	Type not critical

Lighting   Type not critical

FEEDING: Omnivores that will survive on flake foods but should have their diet supplemented with live and frozen foods. Especially important if trying to breed them or to retain their subtle colours.

HEALTH: Can suffer from bacterial infections, usually brought on by poor water conditions. Long-finned varieties are more prone to these, especially if kept in too cool conditions. Will also suffer stress if they are constantly chased and harassed by unsuitable companion fish.

Rasboras FAMILY: CYPRINIDAE

RASBORAS ARE FOUND OVER A BROAD AREA, extending from East Africa, throughout Southeast Asia, and into Australia. They are shoaling fish, and occur in large schools in the upper levels of both still and flowing waters. Often overlooked by aquarists, this group contains both species that are colourful and easy to keep in a well-matured, community aquarium, and others that are more challenging.

Among those suited to the mature community aquarium are *Rasbora trilineata* (Scissortail), *R. elegans* (Elegant Rasbora), *R. pauciperforata* (Red-line Rasbora) and *R. borapetensis* (Red-tailed Rasbora). Pick companion fish with care, ensuring that they will not consider the *Rasbora* species as a potential meal! The larger species are prone to jumping, especially when frightened.

Tank Conditions and Care

HABITAT: Peaceful, planted, mature community aquarium with plenty of open water.

Tank size	24x12x12in (61x30x30cm) for smaller species; 36x12x12 (91x30x30cm) for larger ones.
pH	6.5–7.0, but some species are more critical; check for those you are keeping.
dH	To 10°; check species requirements
Temperature	22–26°C (72–79°F)
Water changes	10–15% every 10–14 days
Filtration	Type of filter is not critical provided it is working efficiently. For those species that prefer water movement (such as *R. trilineata*), this can be provided by the return flow from an external canister filter or from an internal power filter.
Lighting	Type not critical

FEEDING: Omnivores. Most will survive on flake foods but one or two species (e.g. *R. vaterifloris*) require small live foods and/or frozen foods such as *Daphnia* and mosquito larvae.

HEALTH: These fish can suffer from bacterial infections usually caused by poor water conditions or incorrect water conditions.

This reaction can be lessened by the addition of some floating plants but this on its own will not suffice, so make sure your tank is also equipped with a closely fitting cover glass.

There are a few species which are more difficult, either because they are sensitive to water conditions or are very small fish best kept in a species tank or with other like-sized, peaceful fish. These species include *R. maculata* (Pygmy Rasbora), *R. espei* (Espes Rasbora), *R. kalochroma* (Clown Rasbora), and *R. vaterifloris* (Pearly Rasbora). Check the individual requirements before keeping them.

Several species have been bred. Sexing them varies; generally speaking, if the fish are ready to spawn, females have a more rounded body than males. Most prefer shallow water and spawn among fine-leaved plants (see Breeding, pages 54–57 for suitable set-ups). The parents should be removed after spawning, as they will eat the eggs. Harlequins spawn differently, placing their eggs on the underside of broad-leaved plants.

If you fail to get a successful spawning, it may be because the parents are the wrong age: Elegant Rasboras spawn best with older parents, whereas for Harlequins you need a young female and an older male. Most Harlequin breeders recommend using a two-year old male.

Representative Species

	maximum adult size
Rasbora heteromorpha Harlequin, Red Rasbora	1.75in (4.5cm)
Rasbora vaterifloris Pearly Rasbora	1.5in (4cm)
Rasbora maculata Pygmy Rasbora, Spotted Rasbora, Dwarf Rasbora	1in (2.5cm)
Rasbora dorsiocellata Eye-spot Rasbora	2.5in (6cm)
Rasbora pauciperforata Red-line Rasbora	3in (7.5cm)

▲ *Harlequins* (Rasbora heteromorpha) *are lively, shoaling fish for the established community tank, and are best kept in groups of eight or more.*

Rasbora trilineata Scissortail, Three-line Rasbora	6in (15cm)
Rasbora borapetensis Red-tailed Rasbora	2in (5cm)
Rasbora elegans Elegant Rasbora, Two-spot Rasbora	8in (20cm)
Rasbora kalochroma Clown Rasbora	4in (10cm)
Rasbora espei Espes Rasbora	1.75in (4.5cm)

Q&A

● *Do you have any tips for catching my Scissortails?*

... These fish are noted for their speed and their propensity for jumping. Using two fairly large nets, hold one still while gently steering the fish into it with the other. Once the fish is in the net, bring both nets together to prevent the fish from jumping out as you remove it from the water. Do not bring the net up under the fish, as this will alarm it and cause it to jump.

● *I have a small shoal of* Rasbora kalochroma *that are dying off one by one. What is causing this?*

This species doesn't shoal. Each individual stakes out a small territory, so your fish may be killing each other in territorial disputes. Alternatively, your water may be too soft; they like a hardness of 9–10°. Adding a little salt (1 level teaspoon per 10 litres of water) is beneficial.

Sharks FAMILY: CYPRINIDAE

Tank Conditions and Care

HABITAT:	Mature, planted community tank.
Tank size	Min 36x12x12in (91x30x30cm)
pH	6.0–7.5
dH	To 15°
Temperature	22–28°C (72–82°F)
Water changes	15% every week

Filtration External canister filter with spray bar return, and/or trickle system to provide well-oxygenated water.

Lighting Sufficient lighting to promote the steady growth of plants.

FEEDING: Omnivores: small live foods, algae, lettuce, tablet foods, flake foods.

HEALTH: Any stress – poor water conditions, harassment from other incompatible fish – may lead to outbreaks of disease.

ORIGINALLY, ONLY FRESHWATER FISH OF THE genus *Labeo* were referred to by the trade as "sharks". After studying this group more closely, ichthyologists have subdivided it into several genera. The common name derives from dealers and aquarists noticing the superficial resemblance between fish of this group and the marine sharks, but this is as far as the relationship goes. The name appealed to children, who were keen to have a "shark" in their tank!

With the sole exception of the Black Shark (*Labeo chrysophekadion*), sharks may be kept in a planted tank. They are easy to feed, taking live, frozen, flake and tablet foods. Some nibble at plants, others graze on algae; careful choice of plants and feeding plenty of green foods such as peas and lettuce will limit damage. The Diamond Shark is also partial to Java Moss and will keep a large clump in check.

Q&A

● *Is it possible to breed Red-tailed Black Sharks?*

... Maybe. First sex your fish! It is said that on males the dorsal fin is more pointed and on females the back edge forms a right-angle. They are believed to spawn in hollows and the eggs hatch in about 48 hours. However, their first instinct will be to fight rather than to reproduce! In order to overcome this, you will need to provide an aquarium that has plenty of hiding places such as caves or thickets of plants, if the fish are not to damage, or even kill, one another.

● *Have you any tips on keeping Diamond Sharks?*

Because the term "sharks" encompasses such a wide range of species, it is important that you should check each species' individual requirements carefully before buying them. Diamond Sharks (*Labeobarbus festivus*) prefer a pH of 6.0−6.5 and a hardness of up to 10°; they will not tolerate harder, more alkaline conditions. A peaceful fish despite their size, they require a large aquarium with plenty of plant cover. However, avoid fine-leaved, tender vegetation or the fish will eat it. The filtration system should be efficient; an external power filter is ideal, providing them with a reasonable flow of clear, clean water. Regular water changes are also essential.

◀ *The only suitable tank companions for the quarrelsome Red-tailed Black Shark (*Epalzeorhynchos bicolor*) are robust fish such as medium-sized barbs or catfish.*

Representative Species

	maximum adult size
Epalzeorhynchos bicolor Red-tailed Black Shark, Red-tailed Labeo	4.75in (12cm)
Epalzeorhynchos frenatus Ruby Shark, Red-finned Shark, Rainbow Shark	6in (15cm)
Labeo chrysophekadion Black Shark, Black Labeo	24in (61cm)
Balanteocheilus melanopterus Silver Shark, Bala Shark 14in (35cm)	
Labeo variegatus Harlequin Shark, Variegated Shark	12in (30cm)
Labeobarbus festivus Diamond Shark, Festive Apollo Shark	8in (20cm)

Companions for Sharks

The size range within the group is great. Smaller specimens are often recommended for community aquaria, but they should be accompanied by a hazard warning. Both *Epalzeorhynchos frenatus* and *E. bicolor* have a reputation for belligerence, picking on smaller, peaceful species and driving them away from food until they starve. You should only attempt to keep them if you have enough space and companion fish of a similar size that can take care of themselves. Avoid keeping them with any species that have very long, flowing fins, such as Lace Gouramis (*Trichogaster leeri*), as they will prove too great a temptation to nipping.

The larger species need spacious aquaria. They are active fish and need plenty of swimming space. A typical tank should have rocks, wood and large plants such as Amazon Swordplants, *Cryptocoryne* species and Java Fern – avoid soft-leaved plants as these are prone to being nibbled. Companion fish should again be of a similar size and capable of defending themselves.

The Black Shark, however, is boisterous, quarrelsome and best kept alone or with, say, a large *Hypostomus* species of catfish in a sparsely decorated, unplanted aquarium. It will jump, especially if frightened. Even a small specimen is powerful enough to dislodge a standard cover glass, so you must provide a heavyweight cover glass, and if necessary weigh it down with a brick or two. Heaters, thermostats and filter pipes should also be protected, as it may knock into these and dislodge them.

▲ *The Silver Shark (*Balanteocheilus melanopterus*). This large cyprinid has a mild demeanour.*

Flying Foxes   FAMILY: CYPRINIDAE

▲ *The Siamese Algae Eater* (Crossocheilus siamensis). *Members of this genus differ from* Epalzeorhynchos *in having nasal lobes.*

NATIVE TO SOUTHEAST ASIA, TWO SPECIES OF flying fox are available in the aquatic trade – *Epalzeorhynchos kalopterus* and *Crossocheilus siamensis*. They eat algae, but are often over-looked for this role in favour of the Algae Eater, or Sucking Loach (*Gyrinocheilus aymonieri*). This is a shame, as the flying foxes are smaller, growing respectively to 6in (15cm) and 5.5in (13cm), are more efficient algae eaters, and are far better suited to a community aquarium.

Their main drawback is their sensitivity to water quality. Soft, slightly acidic conditions are preferred by *E. kalopterus*; *C. siamensis* can be kept in slightly harder, alkaline conditions. Well-oxygenated water is essential for both. If you fail to maintain these conditions *E. kalopterus*, in particular, becomes prone to a range of stress-related ailments, from whitespot to bacterial infections. Another common error is to intro-duce *E. kalopterus* to a newly set-up system; it is better to wait five or six months.

When planting your tank, be sure to include some broad-leaved plants and wood, as both fish have the endearing habit of resting on leaves, supporting themselves on their pectoral fins.

● *My flying foxes are always chasing each other, and sometimes damage each other's fins. Is this normal behaviour?*

Although these fish are community creatures and like the company of their own kind, they also need their own territory. It could be that you are keeping too many in too confined a space. Two specimens in a 24x12ix12in (61x30x30cm) aquarium is fine; three or four would need a 36in (91cm) tank, or larger. They are rarely aggressive towards other species.

● *I have thread algae in my aquarium and, although I can remove most of it, I wondered if there is a fish that eats it.*

There is one, the Siamese Algae Eater, *C. siamensis*, but you should not expect it to live on thread algae alone. Include some small live foods such as bloodworm, whiteworm (in small amounts) and *Daphnia* (or their frozen equivalent) in its diet. Siamese Algae Eaters are also useful fish in as much as they will eat Planarium worms.

Tank Conditions and Care

HABITAT:	Mature, planted community tank
Tank size	24x12x12in (61x30x30cm)
pH	6.5 for *Epalzeorhynchos kalopterus*; 6.5–8.0 for *Crossocheilus siamensis*.
dH	To 8° for *Epalzeorhynchos kalopterus*; to 15° for *Crossocheilus siamensis*.
Temperature	24–26°C (75–79°F)
Water changes	15% every week

Filtration External canister filter with spray bar return, and/or trickle system to provide well-oxygenated water.

Lighting Sufficient to promote the abundant growth of plants.

FEEDING: Omnivores: small live foods, algae, lettuce, tablet foods, flake foods.

HEALTH: Any stress – poor water conditions, harassment from incompatible fish, etc. – may lead to outbreaks of disease.

Algae Eater

FAMILY: GYRINOCHEILIDAE

THERE ARE SEVERAL MEMBERS OF THE GENUS *Gyrinocheilus*. The Algae Eater (*Gyrinocheilus aymonieri*) is native to China, Laos, Thailand and Cambodia. Its common name makes it a popular fish with newcomers to the hobby. Virtually every aquarist has at some stage acquired one or more of these creatures for the sole purpose of eating algae, only to discover that they are not all that they are cracked up to be!

Trouble in Store

There is no denying that young specimens of the Algae Eater – which is also known as the Sucking Loach – are endearing characters. Their appealing antics include clinging to the glass like living thermometers, rasping away at bits of algae, and darting rapidly around the tank from hiding place to hiding place. So furious are their chases that they will often leap out of the water, so make sure your tank's cover glass fits tightly.

Small Algae Eaters are initially welcome additions to the community aquarium, but problems arise as they begin to grow; with the potential to reach 8in (20cm) in length, they may swiftly become a nuisance. They develop their habit of hanging on the aquarium glass into clinging on to the sides of other fish such as angels (*Pterophyllum* spp.), causing great distress to the fish concerned. They also become very territorial and

Tank Conditions and Care	
HABITAT:	Planted community aquarium
Tank size	Min 24x12x12in (61x30x30cm); most fish seen in the hobby are small specimens.
pH	Not critical; around 7.0 is fine
dH	To 12° maximum
Temperature	20–28°C (69–82°F)
Water changes	10–15% every two weeks
Filtration	Type of filter is not critical provided the one chosen is working efficiently,
Lighting	Type not critical

FEEDING: Herbivores when young but they will also take flake and live foods.

HEALTH: Robust fish. May suffer heater burn if tank is at too low a temperature.

will fight both with each other and with other fish in the tank. This not only causes physical damage to fins and bodies, but also leads to considerable stress and stress-related ailments. Adult specimens are best kept either alone or in a large aquarium with other species capable of looking after themselves.

▼ *This is the standard coloration for the Algae Eater* (Gyrinocheilus aymonieri) *but it is also available in an albino variety.*

● *Can I breed Algae Eaters?*

Q&A ... Sexing them is easy, but as for breeding them – you could be the first! The fish become sexually mature when they are about 5in (12cm) in length. Both sexes develop little "thorns" around the mouth which may, or may not, be larger and more prolific on males.

● *I run my aquarium fairly cool, at 20–21°C (68–70°F). Can I keep a Sucking Loach at these temperatures?*

Yes, but this is about as cool as they can endure. At low temperatures, the fish tend not to feed on algae, but they may be tempted to eat flake foods.

Botias and Other Loaches

FAMILY: COBITIDAE

▼ *Coolie Loaches* (Pangio kuhli) *have a habit of disappearing up filter pipes. You should put a basket over the end of the pipes to prevent this.*

LOACHES ARE VERY WIDELY DISTRIBUTED, BEING found in Europe, North Africa, Asia and the Malay Archipelago (where some of the larger species, such as *Botia macracanthus*, are caught for food). Only the tropical species encountered by aquarists are dealt with here.

As a rule, the bottom-dwelling loaches are small, measuring less than 12in (30cm). Their bodies, which may be completely or partially covered in small scales, are generally elongated and cylindrical, although some species have a flattened belly. Their small mouth is surrounded by 3–6 pairs of barbels depending on species.

Some loaches have two spines beneath the eyes (bifid spines). These are used for defence, shredding the fins or lacerating the flanks of other fish. They will even slash the fingers of unwary aquarists! The spines also make a clicking sound when raised and lowered; this can be heard when the fish are feeding, terrorizing a tank mate or being caught. To transport the fish, put them in a bucket or tape the corners of plastic bags so that they cannot wedge themselves in and pierce the bag.

A fine sand or fine gravel (provided it has rounded grains to prevent damage to the fish's body) is most suitable for loaches to burrow in. Any rocks or wood should be placed directly on the bottom glass of the tank, since loaches

Representative Species

	maximum adult size
Pangio kuhli Coolie Loach, Prickly Eye	4in (10cm)
Pangio semicinctus Half-banded Loach	3in (7.5cm)
Acanthopsis choirorhynchus Horse-faced Loach, Long-nosed Loach	8in (20cm)
Botia berdmorei No common name	5in (12.5cm)
Botia morleti Hora's Loach, Skunk Botia	4in (10cm)
Botia lohachata Pakistan Loach	3in (7.5cm)
Botia macracanthus Clown Loach, Tiger Loach	6in (15cm)
Botia modesta Orange-finned Loach, Redtail Botia	9in (23cm)
Botia sidthimunki Pygmy Chain Loach, Dwarf Loach	2.25in (5.5cm)
Botia striata Zebra Loach	2.5in (6cm)
Lepidocephalus thermalis Indian Stonebiter, Lesser Loach	3in (7.5cm)
Misgurnus anguillicaudatus Weather Loach, Chinese Weatherfish	20in (51cm)

▼ *The Weather Loach* (Misgurnus anguillicaudatus) *is apt to stir up soft substrates.*

▶ *The Clown Loach* (Botia macracanthus) *is one of the few species of cobitid that is active during the day. It grows to double its tank length in the wild*

can undermine such structures with disastrous consequences. Plants should be well-established in the substrate or potted.

Check individual species requirements for pH, hardness and temperature. All need good water conditions but some (e.g. *Botia berdmorei*) are sensitive to nitrate build-ups and benefit from water filtered through peat. In general, loaches may be kept in groups but be sure to check a particular species' temperament, as some can be belligerent and require plenty of space.

Feeding is rarely a problem. Loaches are partial to small live and frozen foods and will also forage for flake. Some species are nocturnal feeders, others feed at dawn and dusk and yet others seem to eat anything at any time. When you get your fish, observe it when you put food in and alter your feeding times accordingly. If it still doesn't feed, try offering different types of food, making sure that they are chopped into small enough pieces for its mouth.

Q&A

● *My Weather Loach makes rapid darts up to the surface. Why?*

... The Weather Loach has developed the ability to "breathe" air and so survive in oxygen-depleted waters. The fish take in air from the surface and pass it into their intestine, where oxygen is absorbed. They tend to do this more frequently during periods of hot, humid weather.

● *Have Coolie Loaches been bred?*

Yes they have, but only with some difficulty. Soft, acidic water conditions are required. The fish spawn among floating plants, sticking their bright green eggs onto the roots and stems.

Hill-stream Balitorids
FAMILY: BALITORIDAE

THE BALITORIDS ARE A GROUP OF HILL-STREAM fish from China and Southeast Asia. Their natural habitat is rapidly flowing and relatively shallow clear water. They can be found clinging to the rocks of the stream bed against the flow of the current, grazing on algae and small invertebrates. At present, the best-known examples come from the genera *Homaloptera*, *Gastromyzon* and *Pseudogastromyzon*. But more genera are constantly finding their way into the hobby.

The balitorids may be loosely divided into two types. The loach-like species, such as those of *Homaloptera*, have an elongated body with a flattened underside and broad expanded paired fins. These features cause the fish to be pressed down onto the substrate by the swift water current, in much the same way as the aerodynamic "wings" of a racing car improve its downforce and road grip. The flattened underside is usually devoid of scales or has only a sparse distribution, as scales in this region would quickly become dislodged. The broad fins and flat ventral surface also aid stability when lying on the substrate.

The second group of balitorids, which includes species such as those of *Gastromyzon*,

Representative Species

	maximum adult size
Gastromyzon punctulatus Spotted Hill-stream Fish	2in (5cm)
Homaloptera orthogoniata Saddle-backed Hill-stream Fish	4.5in (11.5cm)
Homaloptera zollingeri No common name	4in (10cm)
Pseudogastromyzon cheni Chinese Hill-stream Fish	2in (5cm)

▲ Homaloptera zollingeri *requires well-oxygenated, fast-flowing, cool clean water.*

Tank Conditions and Care

HABITAT: Fast-flowing, clear, well-oxygenated water. Ensure the water movement is not confined just to the upper levels of water, but also the substrate. Substrate with large smooth pebbles or rocks, with sandy infill.

Tank size	36x12x12in (91x30x30cm): water conditions are difficult to recreate in a smaller tank. Water depth should be minimal, 10–12in (25–30cm).
pH	6.5–7.0
dH	To 15°
Temperature	22–25°C (72–77°F)
Water changes	10–15% every 10–14 days

Filtration Mechanical filtration from a power filter. Undergravel filters, are mostly unsuitable on their own, as water current is not substantial enough. Internal power filters can provide both supplementary filtration and boost water movement. Ensure good water flow at all strata in the aquarium.

Lighting Two full-length strip lights can be used to promote a little algal growth.

FEEDING: Small aquatic invertebrates (*Daphnia*, bloodworm, etc.) and whiteworm. Also include vegetables in their diet.

HEALTH: Water quality and temperatures that are too high, and not disease, are the most common causes of death. Excellent water is critical and, once provided and maintained, ensures a long and healthy life.

have taken hydrodynamics a stage further and are very much flatter. Representatives of this group have such large expanded paired fins that the pectoral and ventral (or pelvic) fins almost join, or actually overlap. When viewed dorsally, these paired fins look like a large fringe skirting most of the depressed body. With these expanded fins, and with the ability to distend the underside of their body, they are able to create a partial suction with the rock on which they are seated in a limpet-like manner, to avoid being swept away by the strong current.

While rapidly flowing waters might seem too hostile an environment to support aquatic lifeforms, they do have the attraction of being free of most aquatic predators (fish), this role being taken on by certain specialized fish eating birds and mammals. They also offer the fish an abundance of food, since the clear, shallow water readily transmits the light that promotes the growth of algae, plants and "aufwuchs" (microorganisms that grow on submerged objects and that form an important part of their diet).

▼ *The Saddled-backed Hill-stream Fish* (Homaloptera orthogoniata) *may tussle with one another, especially when feeding, but no damage is done. These rheophilic creatures leave companion fish alone.*

● *What is the secret of keeping hill-stream balitorids?*

... Try to understand their natural habitat and reproduce it as far as possible in your tank. Apart from ensuring a fast flow of well-oxygenated water, balitorids are fairly easy to keep.

● *What fish would you recommend keeping with balitorids?*

Hill-stream balitorids are very peaceful. Select fish from similar environments, such as danios, White Cloud Mountain Minnows, or some of the smaller rasboras.

● *What should I feed hill-stream balitorids?*

Balitorids are omnivorous, and their diet must contain both small invertebrates and vegetable matter. If insufficient algae are present in the tank, provide them with small amounts of chopped spinach, the outer leaf of a lettuce, or the inner two halves of a pea. Flake food will be taken if other food is not provided. Make a small amount of paste of the flake food and attach it to a small pebble. If the water conditions are right, there is rarely any problem in getting balitorids to eat.

● *I have seen these fish sold as "Hong-Kong Plecos". Are these catfish?*

No. Balitorids are closely related to loaches (*Cobitidae*) and cyprinids (*Cyprinidae*). Those sold as Hong-Kong Plecos look like a catfish but are in fact a species of *Pseudogastromyzon*.

Guppies and Mollies

FAMILY: POECILIIDAE

GUPPIES AND MOLLIES ARE THE BEST-KNOWN members of a subgroup of fish known as "live-bearing toothcarps". The first part of this designation is self-evident, distinguishing this type of cyprinodont from the egglaying killifish, while the term "toothcarp" refers to the fact that they have teeth in their jaws. Guppies and Mollies are often the first fish owned by new aquarists.

Guppies

The original range of the wild guppy (*Poecilia reticulata*) was northern South America, Barbados and Trinidad. Nowadays, following deliberate introduction for "biological" mosquito control and release from home aquaria, they are far more widespread, being found, for example, in Australia, New Zealand, and the US.

These hardy fish can tolerate a wide range of water conditions and will even adapt to seawater provided they are acclimatized properly. Males of *P. reticulata* reach a length of 1.2in (3cm), while females grow to 2in (5cm). Yet the guppies most commonly available to the modern aquarist are fancy varieties with long, flowing fins, a far cry from the wild form. They are considerably larger and are best kept in harder conditions. A small amount of salt added to the water (5ml/4.5l) is recommended.

Commercial guppy farming grew as breeders learned to exploit the differing characteristics already evident among the many wild populations. Line-breeding produced a wide variety of colour forms and of caudal-fin shapes in males. So huge is the range that specialist guppy societies around the world now set their own showing and breeding standards. Popular fancy varieties include the Triangle, Fantail, Veiltail,

◀ *A pair of Blue Variegated Delta Guppies* (Poecilia reticulata *var.*) *display the flamboyant finnage and coloration for which cultivated Guppies are renowned, and which has made them one of the most widely kept tropical aquarium fish.*

▲ *Line-breeding is essential if you wish to maintain colour strains such as this Golden Snakeskin Delta Guppy* (Poecilia reticulata *var.*).

● My guppies keep nipping at my tank plants; will they damage them?

... No, not substantially. Although guppies browse almost constantly on vegetation, they prefer to eat algae off the plants rather than rip the leaves.

● How can I stop my Tiger Barbs constantly biting my guppies' fins and intimidating them?

This is a common problem for the novice. Tiger Barbs (*Barbus tetrazona*) are considered a community fish, but are notorious fin-nippers (especially if kept in ones and twos). Your options are either to get rid of the barbs or to add some more; kept in a shoal of 6–10 they are too busy checking on each other to worry the other fish. If you do this, your guppies suffer less stress and will come out into the open again.

● When she was ready to drop her young, I placed my molly in a breeding trap. Within two days she was dead and had not produced any fry. What went wrong?

Female mollies are large fish, and commercial breeding traps are small. Being in a confined space at this time creates a lot of stress on the fish and it is not uncommon for them to die. It is better to employ a larger set-up as shown in Breeding, page 58.

● My Black Mollies hang listlessly at the surface of the water, and won't eat. Sometimes a few white flecks appear on them. What causes this?

This sounds like a water problem – maybe it is too soft or too acidic. Check and rectify as necessary. Black Mollies prefer hard, alkaline conditions with some salt added. Also check that the water temperature isn't too high or too low.

Tank Conditions and Care
Guppies

HABITAT: Planted, mature community aquarium with plenty of cover. Avoid fin-nipping tankmates.

Tank size	24x12x12in (61x30x30cm)
pH	7.0
dH	To 15°
Temperature	21–25°C (70–77°F)
Water changes	10% every week

Filtration Any efficient system. Avoid fast-flowing water, as fish with long fins cannot easily swim in it.

Lighting	Sufficient for plant growth

FEEDING: Omnivores – will take flake and pelleted foods, green foods and small live or frozen foods (e.g. *Daphnia*, mosquito larvae).

HEALTH: No particular problems provided good water conditions are maintained. May suffer from stress-related ailments if harassed by other tankmates.

Lyretail, Speartail, Roundtail, Topsword, Bottomsword, Doublesword, Coffer- or Spadetail, and Bannertail.

Sexing guppies is easy: males have a gonopodium and are more colourful, while females have a standard-shaped anal fin and a drab grey-brown body with some colour apparent in the caudal fin. Guppies are prolific, producing broods every 4–6 weeks. They will reproduce in a community aquarium but tankmates tend to treat the young fish as live food. Therefore, if you wish to raise more fry, you should use one of the methods described in Breeding, pages 58–59.

Mollies

Mollies have a very wide distribution, from the southern US, through Central America and into northern South America. There are also populations of escapees and released specimens elsewhere around the world. Their natural habitats include estuaries, mangrove swamps and similar regions and they are commercially produced by the million in saline conditions.

Contrary to popular belief, mollies are not straightforward community fish. They have very specific water requirements that must be met if you are to achieve any degree of success with them. Also, in order to keep and breed them in prime condition, a regular supply of vegetable matter in their diet is essential.

A particularly striking member of the family is the Sailfin Molly, of which two species commonly appear in the aquarium trade (*Poecilia latipinna* and *P. velifera*). Male specimens of these fish have a spectacularly large dorsal fin that they raise during courtship displays or territorial

Representative Species of Mollies

	maximum adult male size
Poecilia sphenops Sphenops Molly, Green Molly, Black Molly, Liberty Molly, Mexican Molly	2.5in (6cm)
Poecilia velifera Sailfin Molly, Yucatán Molly	6in (15cm)
Poecilia caucana South American Molly	1.5in (4cm)
Poecilia latipinna Sailfin Molly	4in (10cm)
Cultivated forms Albino, Lyretail Molly, Gold Sailfins, etc.	

NOTE: the figures given here are for adult males. Females of the species are 0.5–1in larger.

▶ A male *Sailfin Molly* (Poecilia velifera) *displays to a subordinate male (partially hidden). Above, a female fish is seen following the dominant male. The front of the male's fin has been damaged but has regenerated.*

challenges. Crossing of *P. latipinna* with other species has produced some of the many strains that are available today. They are prolific breeders, and broods of up to 140 are not uncommon from large females. Broods can be produced every 8–10 weeks.

Black Mollies (*P. sphenops*) are one result of cross-breeding. They are renowned for tolerating a wide range of water conditions, from brackish to marine. Indeed, marine fishkeepers often use these freshwater fish to mature their tanks. They breed readily, dropping young every 5–7 weeks.

Tank Conditions and Care
Mollies

HABITAT: Mature, planted community tank with plenty of cover. Avoid fin-nipping companion fish.	**Water changes** 10% every week
Tank size 24x12x12in (61x30x30cm)	**Filtration** Type not critical, provided it is efficient
pH 7.0–8.0; prefer brackish water but can be acclimatized to hard, alkaline freshwater. If using hard water, the addition of salt (5ml/4.5l) is beneficial.	**Lighting** Sufficient for plant growth
dH To 15°	**FEEDING:** Omnivores. Flake and pelleted foods, green foods (lettuce, peas, algae) and live or frozen foods (bloodworm, mysis, mosquito larvae).
Temperature 20–28°C (68–82°F); check individual species requirements.	**HEALTH:** No particular problems provided correct water conditions are maintained.

Platies, Swordtails and Other Poeciliids

FAMILY: POECILIIDAE

A NUMBER OF OTHER SPECIES OF POECILIID ARE common in the aquarium trade. Principal among these in popularity are two species of the genus *Xiphophorus*, the platies (*X. maculatus*) and the larger swordtails (*X. helleri*). In addition, hobbyists can obtain a number of other species.

Platies and Swordtails

Although the various species of swordtails and platies are widely distributed from Mexico to Belize, Honduras and Guatemala, the fish seen in the trade are mostly farmed specimens. Different-coloured populations of the same species can occur, making them ideal for exploitation by breeders producing new forms. In general, the commercially produced varieties are larger than the wild species.

Platies and swordtails are generally suitable for a community aquarium. The fancy varieties should be treated with some caution, as those with trailing fins, such as Hi-fin Platies and Swords and Lyretail Swords, can suffer harassment and injury from fin-nippers. Male swordtails can be aggressive towards each other and also to companion fish, so you should either keep a single male and several females or keep them in a good-sized shoal. Platies, on the other

▶ *This well-planted community aquarium includes a selection of platy varieties. All these varieties cross easily, producing many different colour forms.*

● *I have crossed a female platy with a male swordtail. Is this normal?*

... The Platy (*Xiphophorus maculatus*) is a very fecund species, mature females producing up to 80 fry every four to six weeks. It will also hybridize with other *Xiphophorus* species such as *X. helleri* and *X. variatus*, a fact that has been exploited by commercial breeders to produce new colour forms and different fin shapes.

● *I recently bought some Swordtail Platies, which the dealer told me were* X. xiphidium. *Could you please advise me on keeping them?*

This species is a little more of a challenge to keep and breed, as it requires far more precise water conditions: pH 7.0–7.5 and a water temperature of about 25°C (77°F). It produces small broods of about 25 every five to seven weeks and is ideally suited to a well-planted species aquarium.

● *I have some Dwarf Swordtails. Some of the males have swords and others do not. Is this normal?*

For this species, yes. The males without swords are still viable as broodstock.

Representative Species of Platies and Swordtails

	maximum adult male size
Xiphophorus maculatus Platy, Moonfish	1.5in (4cm)
Xiphophorus maculatus var. Black Platies, Hi-fin Platies, Rainbow Sword Variatus, etc.	1.5in (4cm)
Xiphophorus variatus Sunset Platy, Variegated Platy, Variatus Platy	2.25in (5.5cm)
Xiphophorus xiphidium Swordtail Platy	1.5in (4cm)
Xiphophorus helleri Swordtail	5.5in (14cm) but usually smaller

	maximum adult male size
Xiphophorus helleri var. Lyretail Swordtails, Black Marble Swords, Hi-fin Swords, Red Wag Swords, Half Black Swords, Black Swords, Tuxedo Hi-fin Swords, Hi-fin Wag Pintail Swords, etc.	5.5in (14cm)
Xiphophorus montezumae Montezuma Swordtail	2.25in (5.5cm)
Xiphophorus pygmaeus Pygmy Swordtail, Dwarf Helleri	1.5in (4cm)

NOTE: the figures given here are for the adult male body length and exclude the sword. Females are 0.25–1in larger.

hand, seem to be far more tolerant of each other. There are, however, some species that are best kept in species tanks (for example, *X. xiphidium* and *X. pygmaeus*).

Platies and swordtails will produce broods in the community tank but, to maintain colour strains or species (they hybridize easily), it is better to set them up for breeding in their own aquaria. The fry are easy to raise and grow on provided you have sufficiently large rearing tanks. Fry are easily stunted and the swords start to grow on males when they are around 2in (5cm) in body length.

When buying swordtails, it is best to avoid small specimens with long swords, and to look instead for young males that have not yet developed their swords. They are easy to identify because they have a gonopodium, a sexual organ formed by the fusion of the third, fourth and fifth rays of the anal fin. These will make stronger and healthier fish for you to breed from.

Tank Conditions and Care
Platies and Swordtails

HABITAT: Peaceful, planted, community tank.

Tank size	24x12x12in (61x30x30cm)
pH	7.0–7.5; check species requirements
dH	6–8°; check species requirements
Temperature	15–27°C (59–81°F); check species requirements.
Water changes	10% every week
Filtration	Type not critical
Lighting	Sufficient for plant growth

FEEDING: Omnivores. Flake and pelleted foods plus some vegetable matter (lettuce, peas and algae) and live or frozen foods (bloodworm, mysis shrimp and mosquito larvae).

HEALTH: No particular problems provided good water conditions are maintained. If conditions deteriorate then these fish become susceptible to whitespot and bacterial infections.

▲ *Red Hi-fin Swordtails* (Xiphophorus helleri *var.*) *can become victims of fin-nipping. Good quality water in your tank will help deter secondary infections.*

Q&A...

● *Could I keep a pair of Knife Livebearers in my community aquarium and breed them?*

These are shy, nervous fish, but may be kept with other mild-mannered species. But if you are intending to breed them, a species tank is advised. You should be able to keep six in a well-planted 24x12x 12in (61x30x30cm) tank. Provide plants that reach the surface or a few floating plants with trailing roots as hiding places. They like a good water flow and parents and fry alike are sensitive to poor water conditions and susceptible to bacterial infections. The water should be soft with a neutral pH. Temperature: 25°C (77°F) for general maintenance, up to 28°C (82°F) for breeding.

● *I am having problems raising my* Brachyrhaphis episcopi *fry. Have you any suggestions?*

The fry need tiny foods such as "aufwuchs" (micro-organisms that live in algae) that are difficult to provide at home. In the summer you can put stones in shallow water-filled containers outside to grow algae, then place them in the breeding tank. Brine shrimp nauplii will do as a first food but it is not always taken.

There have been some reports of sex reversal in swordtails (*X. helleri*) but these are thought to be erroneous. Female swordtails were supposedly observed giving birth and then changing into males. However, closer investigation revealed that the individuals in question had been kept in a group with females that had not changed sex (with which they had been confused) and that they were probably just late-developing males.

Other Poeciliids

This group of livebearers is distinct from the platies and swordtails in not being "cultivated" fish bred for their finnage. They are found in the southern USA, Central America and South America, and also on some Caribbean islands. Many species have been introduced into other countries to eat mosquito larvae and curb malaria. If you are buying wild specimens, check their origin, as some have an incredible range of habitat. For example, *Heterandria bimaculata* live in mountain streams at 2,500m (8,200ft) yet are also found in brackish coastal waters.

Sexing them is simple: males have a gonopodium and are usually smaller than females. Most females also exhibit a gravid patch (a darkened area near the vent) especially when ready to drop their young. The gestation period varies with species. Broods may be small (five or six) or large (60 or more), again depending on species. Many eat their young, so females are best placed in breeding tanks for birthing if you wish to raise a reasonable brood. Yet even this cannot guarantee success, as the fry of some species prey on each other! Provide clumps of Java Moss as cover.

Although they are regarded as omnivores, they really need live or frozen foods (e.g. *Daphnia*, mosquito larvae) in their diet. Indeed, some will not breed unless conditioned on live foods.

In common with swordtails and platies without elongated finnage, these fish are generally ideal for the novice aquarist. Of the other poeciliids, *Limia melanogaster* and *Gambusia affinis* are well suited to community life. Others, however, such as *Brachyrhaphis episcopi*, are much more difficult to keep in captivity. They have very specific water requirements, will only accept flake and frozen food reluctantly, and are susceptible to bacterial infections. As a result, they are best placed in a species tank. Provide a cover glass, as certain species jump. It cannot be stressed too greatly that you should check each species' particular requirements before you purchase them.

Tank Conditions and Care
Other Poeciliids

HABITAT:	Planted, mature community tank with fine-leaved plants to provide cover for fry.
Tank size	Min 18x12x12in (46x30x30cm); check species requirements.
pH	5.0–8.0; check species requirements
dH	To 20°; check species requirements
Temperature	18–30°C (64–86°F); check species requirements.
Water changes	20% every two weeks. Some species may need more frequent and larger water changes.
Filtration	Type not critical
Lighting	Sufficient for plant growth

FEEDING AND HEALTH: See Platies and Swordtails, page 121.

▼ *The Pike Livebearer* (Belonesox belizanus) *is one poeciliid that is wholly unsuited to the community tank. It is a highly predatory creature that ambushes other fish from behind vegetation, and is even cannibalistic towards its own kind.*

Representative Species of Other Poeciliids

	maximum adult size		maximum adult size
Belonesox belizanus Pike Livebearer, Piketop Minnow	4.5in (11.5cm) males; 8in (20cm) females	*Limia melanogaster* Black-bellied Limia	1.5in (4cm) males
Gambusia affinis Mosquito Fish	1.75in (4.5cm) males	*Limia nigrofasciata* Black-barred Limia	2in (5cm) males
Girardinus metallicus Girardinus	2in (5cm) males	*Poecilia vivipara* No common name	2in (5cm) males
Heterandria bimaculata Spotted Tailed Mosquito Fish	2.75in (7cm) males; 6in (15cm) females	*Priapella intermedia* No common name	1.75in (4.5cm) males
Heterandria formosa Mosquito Fish, Dwarf Livebearer, Dwarf Top Minnow	0.75in (2cm) males	*Priapella compressa* Slap-sided Blue-eye	1.25in (3cm) males
Phallichthys amates Merry Widow	1in (2.5cm) males	*Alfaro cultratus* Knife Livebearer	3.5in (8.5cm) males; but usually smaller
Phalloceros caudimaculatus Spotted Livebearer	1in (2.5cm) males	*Brachyrhaphis episcopi* Bishop	1.5in (4cm) males

NOTE: where female sizes are not given they are 1–1.5in larger.

Four-eyed Fish FAMILY: ANABLEPIDAE

▶ *A close-up showing the distinctive divided eye of* Anableps anableps.

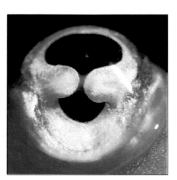

● *Can I breed Anableps anableps?*

A... Yes, but with difficulty. First, make sure you have a pair: the male has a gonopodium, while the female does not. Next, check that they are compatible. Males can move their gonopodium only to the right or to the left. Females, similarly, have either a right-handed or left-handed genital opening, so you need to pair a right-handed male with a left-handed female, or vice versa. Buy several of each sex and let them pair off themselves, or try to select one compatible pair in the shop – not an easy task! Two broods of 2–3 large fry are normally produced each year. Put the fry in a separate tank to prevent cannibalism by the adults. Finally, make sure the fry tank is ready in advance.

Tank Conditions and Care

HABITAT: Species aquarium set up with shallow water (8–12in/20–30cm deep) and a "beach" or platform and a good, heavy cover glass. .

Tank size Min 36x15x15in (91x38x38cm), but provide larger quarters as the fish grow.

pH 7.0–8.0; the addition of a small amount of salt (5ml/4.5l) is beneficial.

dH	To 15°
Temperature	22–30°C (72–86°F)
Water changes	15% every week

Filtration Efficient system; external power filters with spray-bar return.

Lighting Sufficient for plant growth

FEEDING: Carnivores. Frozen meaty foods such as mussels, shrimps and pieces of lance fish. Live foods such as worms and shrimps. Will sometimes accept floating pelleted foods.

HEALTH: Damage to eyes may occur if the tank decor has sharp edges. Treat bacterial or fungal infections with appropriate aquarium remedy.

THE MOST WIDELY IMPORTED species of this family is *Anableps anableps*, which lives in both fresh and brackish waters from southern Mexico to northern South America. Males of this species can grow to 6in (15cm) and females up to 12in (30cm). Other species, which inhabit the coastal regions of Central America, are less familiar: *A. dowi* is found on the Pacific side and *A. microlepis* on the Atlantic side of the isthmus. These have similar requirements and characteristics to *A. anableps*.

Divided Eyes

The most striking feature of these fish is their eyes, which are divided in two, so that the fish can see equally well above and below the water at the same time (hence their common name).

Four-eyed fish are best kept in a large species tank with plenty of open swimming space. Make sure that any rocks are rounded. The substrate is immaterial, as these are surface-dwellers, but if you construct a "beach" area where your fish can rest, use fine sand or gravel so that they do not scratch themselves. Alternatively, suspend a platform at the water surface as a resting place. A tight cover glass maintains high humidity and prevents the fish from jumping out of the tank.

Once the fish have settled in they will eat floating pellets, but these should only form part of their diet. They take anything that falls on the surface (e.g. flies and spiders) or anything swimming near the surface, including other fish! Fortunately, they also eat dead foods. You can drop these into the tank (they will be ignored if they reach the bottom), but they are best placed just above the water surface for the fish to jump at. External canister filters, sometimes combined with trickle filters, are necessary for removing the high-protein waste of these carnivores.

Goodeids FAMILY: GOODEIDAE

THIS FAMILY DIVIDES INTO TWO SUBFAMILIES: the egglaying Empetrichthyinae from the southwestern US and the livebearing Goodeinae from Mexico. Only the livebearers are dealt with here.

Goodeids are normally thought of as coming solely from the central Mexican highlands, but one popular genus, *Ilyodon*, is found in the lowlands. They have a wide range of habitats, from temperate to tropical, and even live in desert regions where the temperature can fluctuate by 20°C over a 24-hour period. All prefer water that is neutral to alkaline and medium to hard, but it is vital that you check the needs of each species. Many dwell in fast-flowing waters and usually have streamlined bodies as a result; others prefer pools and lakes and have deeper bodies. Yet other species live on the bottom and are somewhat loach-like in their body form.

One feature that distinguishes the Goodeids from other livebearers is that males have a notched anal fin (spermatopodium) instead of a gonopodium. Another is that the embryos are fed by means of trophotaenia, small structures produced from the vent of an embryo that enable it to absorb nutrients from the ovarian fluid surrounding it in its mother's body. Brood size and gestation period varies with species.

Some Goodeids, such as *Ameca splendens*, are fine for a community tank containing similar-sized fish. Others definitely need a species tank; *Goodea atripinnis*, for example, is both large and a fin-nipper.

▲ *Young specimens of the Red-tailed Goodeid* (Xenotoca eiseni) *are well suited to a community tank, but they become fin-nippers with age.*

Representative Species

	maximum adult size
Ameca splendens Butterfly Goodeid, Ameca	3in (7.5cm) males
Xenotoca eiseni Red-tailed Goodeid, Orange-tailed Goodeid	2.5in (6cm) males
Ilyodon whitei No common name	2.5in (6cm) males
Goodea atripinnis Black-fin Goodeid	4.7in (12cm) males 8in (20cm) females
Chapalichthys pardalis No common name	2.5in (6cm) males

NOTE: where female sizes are not given they are 0.25–0.75in larger than males.

Tank Conditions and Care

HABITAT: Planted, mature community aquarium. Thickets of plants, and floating plants, for the fry to hide in. Some species are best kept in a species tank.

Tank size	24x12x12in (61x30x30cm)
pH	7.5; check species requirements
dH	To 10°; check species requirements
Temperature	15–30°C (59–86°F); check individual species requirements.

Water changes	10–15% every week
Filtration	Type not critical
Lighting	Sufficient for plant growth

FEEDING: Omnivores. Flake, green foods (lettuce, peas, algae) and live or frozen foods (bloodworm, mysis, mosquito larvae).

HEALTH: No particular problems.

Killifish

KILLIFISH ARE WIDESPREAD THROUGHOUT the tropics and a few species extend into the temperate zones. There are 450 or more species but many are severely restricted in their habitat, being confined to a single pool. Several of these are now extinct, or threatened with extinction, in the wild. Through the efforts of dedicated aquarists, some species have been maintained in captivity. However, it is doubtful whether it will ever be possible to reintroduce any of them back into the wild, as their original habitat has in many cases been obliterated by development or contaminated by mining activities. Changing climatic patterns also threaten the survival of these fish.

Nevertheless, a number of species are still commonly available through the aquatic trade and it is those that are covered here. They are tropical, freshwater species. Some are suited to

▲ *The Five-lined Killi* (Aphyosemion striatum) *is native to Gabon in West Africa. It is a challenging fish to breed in captivity.*

keeping in community aquaria, while others are more specialized fish that are best kept in a species tank. The avid enthusiast and breeder may well keep killifish in a large number of small tanks, each containing a pair or trio of fish, with other, slightly larger tanks used for growing on the fry. Yet this need not be the case.

For instance, a trio (a male and two females) of one of the various species of *Aplocheilus* is ideal

Representative Species of Egg Hangers

	maximum adult size		maximum adult size
Aplocheilus panchax Blue Panchax	3in (7.5cm)	*Lamprichthys tanganicanus* No common name	6in (15cm)
Aplocheilus lineatus Sparkling Panchax, Lineatus	4in (10cm)	*Pachypanchax playfairi* Playfair's Panchax	4in (10cm)
Epiplatys dageti Red-chinned Panchax	3in (7.5cm)	*Epiplatys sexfasciatus* Six-barred Epiplatys	4in (10cm)
Aplocheilus dayi Ceylon Killifish	4in (10cm)	*Pseudepiplatys annulatus* Rocket Panchax	1.5in (4cm)
Aplocheilichthys macrophthalmus Lampeye	1.5in (4cm)	*Aphyosemion striatum* Five-lined Killifish	2in (5cm)
Aplocheilichthys pumilis No common name	2in (5cm)	*Aphyosemion cognatum* No common name	2.25in (5.5cm)
Procatopus aberrans Green Lampeye	2in (5cm)	*Aphyosemion gardneri* Steel-blue Aphyosemion	3in (7.5cm)
Procatopus similis Nigerian Lampeye	2.75in (7cm)	*Aphyosemion australe* Cape Lopez Lyretail, Lyretail	2.25in (5.5cm)
Rivulus cylindraceus Green Rivulus, Cuban Rivulus	2in (5cm)	*Jordanella floridae* American Flagfish	2.5in (6cm)

● *The scales on my Playfair's Panchax are standing out from its body. Is this a cause for alarm?*

Not at all. This feature, which is sometimes mistaken for dropsy, is peculiar to this species, and quite normal. It is particularly pronounced at breeding time.

● *I have some Sparkling Panchax that keep jumping and cutting themselves on the supports for the cover glass. How can I prevent this?*

Create a thick tangle of floating plant – say, *Riccia* or Indian Fern – as a sanctuary for these fish. Being surface-dwellers, their natural reaction when frightened is to jump to avoid a possible predator from below.

● *Should I introduce a Ceylon Killifish to my community tank?*

Yes, but do take special care with your choice of companion fish. You should have no small fish in your tank, as *Aplocheilus dayi* can be very pugnacious towards them. Alternatively, keep the Ceylon Killifish in a species aquarium.

◀ *The Blue Panchax* (Aplocheilus panchax) *is a Southeast Asian killi. It is a firm favourite with aquarists, and is one of the oldest species to have regularly been kept in captivity.*

for the community tank. As surface-dwelling fish, they occupy a region that is normally devoid of livestock except at feeding time. Just make sure that you keep a cover glass on the tank as the fish will jump. Provide them with a spawning mop and they will reward you with a clutch of eggs to hatch and rear elsewhere.

In the main, though, killis are kept in a species tank in pairs or trios and are usually sold as such. Trios are best, as otherwise the male becomes dominant and may kill a single female. Needless to say, it is important to provide clumps of plants as retreats for the females. At times, even the females can become hostile to one another.

There are certain species that need to be kept in a shoal – those of *Aplocheilichthys* and *Procatopus*, for instance – and they should be provided with plenty of open water to swim in. Although they can be kept with other peaceful fish of a similar size, they should be housed in a species tank for breeding.

Peat spawners must be kept in species tanks as they need a dark substrate, subdued lighting and softer, more acidic water than is the norm for the community tank. Fresh peat is recommended; although regarded as messy and difficult to deal with, it can help problem fish spawn by adding certain chemical compounds to the water and preventing bacterial infections. A coarse, fibrous type is easiest to handle; to prepare it, soak for a period of several days or even weeks, or speed up the process by boiling it (do this when no-one else is home, as it smells awful!).

Although many killis are found in very soft, rather acidic waters that are rich in organic matter and stained the colour of tea, if they are kept in similar conditions in captivity for any length of time, they are prone to attack by mycobacteriosis. (The bacillus that causes this is absent from their native waters.) Adult fish thus need to be acclimatized to slightly harder and neutral conditions if they are to avoid infection.

Sexing killis is usually quite straightforward: males are far more colourful and have more flamboyant finnage than females. Indeed, the females of, say, various species of *Aphyosemion* all appear similar. To avoid cross-breeding, only keep one species of a particular genus per aquarium (although they can be mixed with other genera provided you can tell them apart). Also, some species have a very wide range and are found in distinct populations distinguished by colour patterns. Although it is easy to tell the males apart, it is not so with the females, so make sure that you do not interbreed. It is also possible to get albino forms, for example of *Cynolebias whitei*; again keep the forms true.

In the wild, killifish are primarily insectivores, but also eat small aquatic invertebrates. In day-to-day feeding, frozen and flake foods can be substituted. For breeding, however, live foods are vital to condition some of the fish, so you will have to culture your own (see Foods and Feeding, pages 61–62). Conditioning is especially crucial with killifish, as spawning can be a protracted business, with batches of eggs being laid over a period of a week or more.

◀ *The Cape Lopez Lyretail* (Aphyosemion australe) *is a particularly beautiful fish in its shape and coloration and has long been popular in the hobby.*

▶ Lamprichthys tanganicanus *is a hardwater killifish native to Lake Tanganyika. It can be kept and bred successfully in a Tanganyika community tank, in the company of peaceful cichlids from the same region.*

Tank Conditions and Care

HABITAT: Planted, mature tank. Egg-hangers require an aquarium with fine-leaved plants and mops. Peat-spawners need a species aquarium with a dark peat substrate.

Tank size Min 10x8x8in (25x20x20cm) for species tanks depending on size of adult fish.

pH	5.5–7.5 check species requirements
dH	To 12° check species requirements

Temperature 18–26°C (64–79°F); check species requirements – normally higher for breeding.

Water changes 10% every week – with the amount of high-protein foods being fed, some species may need more frequent water changes.

Filtration Type not critical on a community aquarium provided it is efficient, although peat filtration is beneficial. If keeping them in species tanks an air-operated sponge filter is beneficial, but many enthusiasts do not use aeration at all on their killi tanks.

Lighting   Sufficient for plant growth

FEEDING: Insectivores. Mainly small live foods. Frozen foods are taken but take care when feeding, as small tanks are easily polluted with uneaten foods. Flake should be used sparingly. Some species are very particular in their requirements.

HEALTH: Soft, acidic conditions can cause Velvet (*Oodinium* sp.) and mycobacterial attacks.

Breeding Egg Hangers

Sometimes, killifish breed quite successfully in the harder, more alkaline conditions of the tank. On the other hand, they may produce eggs that fail to hatch. If this occurs, take a few of the eggs off the plants or spawning mop and put them in a shallow dish with some of the water from the parents' tank. Add a few drops of methylene blue; if, after 24 hours, the eggs have absorbed the dye you can be sure your fish require softer, more acidic conditions for spawning. Either the egg membrane is affected by the hard water or the sperm cannot survive in it. Fish can tolerate a change from soft to hard conditions fairly well, but the reverse process poses more problems and

can result in heavy losses. All changes should be conducted gradually, over 24–48 hours. Likewise, pH adjustment should be gradual.

It is usual to use a trio of fish (one male to two females), which deposit their eggs among roots and fine-leaved plants. The eggs have long filaments attached that anchor them to the roots. Spawning mops are a handy alternative; harvest the eggs from these at regular intervals for hatching in other containers. In community tanks, mops can also be introduced for the use of killis – *Rivulus cylindraceus* and *Pachypanchax playfairi* can both be spawned easily by this method.

One species of killifish, *Lamprichthys tanganicanus*, deposits its eggs in cracks and crevices in

Representative Species of Peat Spawners

	maximum adult size		
Nothobranchius rachovi Rachow's Nothobranch	2in (5cm)	*Cynolebias whitei* No common name	3in (7.5cm) males 2in (5cm) females
Nothobranchius palmqvisti Palmqvist's Nothobranch	2in (5cm)	*Aphyosemion occidentale* Red Aphyosemion	3.5in (8.5cm)
Nothobranchius kirki Kirk's Nothobranch	2in (5cm)	*Aphyosemion filamentosum* Plumed Lyretail	2in (5cm)
Nothobranchius korthausae Korthaus' Nothobranch	2.5in (6cm)	*Aphyosemion gulare* No common name	3.25in (8cm)
Nothobranchius guentheri Guenther's Nothobranch	1.75in (4.5cm)	*Aphyosemion sjoestedti* Golden Pheasant, Red Aphyosemion	4.5in (11.5cm)
Cynolebias nigripinnis Dwarf Argentine Pearl, Black-finned Pearl	2in (5cm)	*Pterolebias peruensis* No common name	4in (10cm)
Cynolebias bellottii Argentine Pearl	2.75in (7cm)	*Pterolebias longipinnis* Longfin Killifish	4in (10cm)

rocks. If you have no rocks, place one earthenware flower pot inside another, slightly larger one and the fish will use the gap between them. This species also spawns as a group on mops.

Some *Aphyosemion* species (e.g. *A. australe*) hang their eggs on plants and mops to hatch in the normal way, but the eggs can be treated like those of annuals and stored in damp peat. Other species – for example *Aplocheilus panchax* – lay their eggs both on plants and on the substrate, but these hatch in the normal manner and do not need to be stored.

Brood sizes can vary from 10–12 up to 100 or more. Eggs laid over a period of time also develop over a lengthy period, so the fry need to be moved on if some are not to become stunted, or the larger fry eat the smaller ones. Fry grow best on a diet of small live foods which you will need to collect or culture. Infusoria (beware, some species are sensitive to this), and brine shrimp nauplii make excellent first foods.

Breeding Peat Spawners

The annual killifish are very fecund and will spawn almost daily from the time they mature until they die if given the chance. If you are keeping a male and two females, it is better to condition them separately, place them in the breeding tank to spawn and then separate them again. In order to keep up this level of procreation, their intake of live foods is phenomenal. Live foods are preferable, since they do not pollute the substrate as uneaten frozen or dried foods would.

During breeding, the male displays to the female, encouraging her down to the substrate to spawn. He then comes beside her, wraps his dorsal and anal fin around her and presses her into the substrate. The African species tend to deposit their eggs on or just below the surface, whereas the South American species dive right into the substrate and may bury themselves completely.

▼ *The Dwarf Argentine Pearl* (Cynolebias nigripinnis) *tends to be skittish, and should be provided with plenty of hiding places if kept in a larger tank.*

▼ *A male Rachow's Notho (Nothobranchius rachovi) shows its striking coloration. It is still relatively rare in aquaria, as it is hard to care for.*

Once spawning is complete, remove the parents. The peat should be drained through a sieve and placed on some old newspaper to partially dry out. When ready to store it is like crumbly pipe-tobacco. It can then be packed into an airtight plastic bag or jar, labelled with the species and the storage date, and placed in a warm place for the minimum incubation period for that particular species. Check the length of time carefully; it can range from 4–6 weeks for some African species to a year for some of the South American species.

When you want to hatch the fry, put the peat containing the eggs in a shallow tank, add cool water – about 18°C (64°F) – and agitate the mixture to ensure that the peat is thoroughly wet. You need at least enough water to make the peat float. If the fry are unwilling to hatch, try adding a tiny amount of dry food. After a few days, when the peat has settled to the bottom, you can carefully remove the fry for growing on elsewhere. Their requirements are similar to those for the egg hangers.

Do not discard the peat from the hatching tank but repeat the drying out, storage and labelling process up to twice more (this time write "2nd drying", "3rd drying" or a similar comment on the label so that you know what is going on). You should get larger hatching from the second and third batches.

Q&A...

● *Which peat-spawning killis are to be recommended for the novice hobbyist?*

Korthaus', Guenther's or Palmqvist's nothobranches would all make ideal choices. These fish are hardy and relatively easy to care for. By contrast, Rachow's Notho and the Dwarf Argentine Pearl are difficult fish and thus only suitable for the more experienced aquarist.

● *I didn't get a very good hatch from a batch of* Nothobranchius *eggs, maybe a dozen fry. I'm sure the fish produced far more. Could the eggs be infertile?*

Probably not, as you have had some hatch. Dry the peat, store it again, and then wet it. You should get a second batch of fry and, if you repeat the process again, perhaps even a third. In the wild, some killis inhabit tiny pools and watering holes and, in order to ensure their survival, the eggs hatch at differing rates. The development (diapause) of some is arrested, so that if, when the rains come, they turn out to be light, only some of the eggs will be ready to hatch. Thereafter, although the pools dry out within hours or days, there will still be eggs in the mud waiting for the next, more substantial rains (or, if these fail, a third rainfall).

● *I am having trouble keeping my* Aphyosemions *alive for longer than about a year. Is this usual?*

In all likelihood, you are keeping them at too high a tank temperature. Although a slight increase in warmth helps initiate spawning, prolonged exposure to high temperatures tends to reduce their longevity.

Tetras FAMILIES: CHARACIDAE

THE TERM "TETRA" COVERS A MULTITUDE OF small characins from both Africa and South America. They are some of the most popular fish in the hobby, and those treated here represent a very small selection of those available to the aquarist, and only a tiny fraction of all species known to science.

In the wild, they are found in both black-water and white-water streams, but are more populous in the former conditions, where the food supply is more plentiful. The streams that form the tetras' habitat are usually shallow, but they will also inhabit larger rivers where there are tangles of roots and plants for them to live among. Many of these fish are carnivores, feeding in open waters on insects or mosquito larvae from the surface or on small aquatic invertebrates.

● *Are Neon Tetras difficult to breed?*

No; Neon Tetras have an undeserved reputation among aquarists for being difficult to breed. In fact, spawning them is fairly straightforward, so long as you take care to prepare the water conditions carefully (make it softer, and increase its acidity by filtering it through peat). Also, it is especially important when breeding Neon Tetras to keep all the materials in the rearing tank clean.

● *I would like to keep some Ulrey's Tetras. What particular conditions would you advise?*

You should provide this species of tetra with a large tank, plenty of swimming space, a current from the filter system, and soft, slightly acidic water. Small live and frozen foods are preferred.

Others are limnivores (literally "mud-eaters"), which feed on small micro-organisms and algae. A few also require plant matter in their diet.

In the aquarium, allow tetras ample space; they are active fish and, if kept in too confined a space, become stressed and prone to infection. Position tall plants at the rear and sides of the aquarium and use low-growing species for the middle section, thus allowing plenty of open water for the fish to shoal in. More delicate, fine-leaved plants will thrive in these conditions.

◀ *The Bleeding Heart Tetra* (Hyphesso-brycon erythrostigma) *is a peaceful species for the community aquarium.*

▶ *The Emperor Tetra (Nematobrycon palmeri) prefers a quiet, densely planted aquarium.*

The water conditions are also critical; a high oxygen content is essential for all species. Most require soft, slightly acidic conditions and it is a good idea to filter through peat for newly imported, wild-caught fish. Other species have very specific requirements, which it is essential to investigate before buying the fish and setting up a species aquarium for them. Any tank should have been established for

Representative South American Species

	maximum adult size		maximum adult size
Aphyocharax anisitsi Bloodfin	2in (5cm)	*Hyphessobrycon erythrostigma* Bleeding Heart Tetra	2.5in (6cm)
Corynopoma riisei Swordtail Characin	2.5in (6cm)	*Hyphessobrycon flammeus* Flame Tetra	1.5in (4cm)
Prionobrama filigera Glass Bloodfin	2.5in (6cm)	*Hyphessobrycon herbertaxelrodi* Black Neon	1.5in (4cm)
Boehlkea fredcochui Blue Tetra	2in (5cm)	*Hyphessobrycon pulchripinnis* Lemon Tetra	1.75in (4.5cm)
Paracheirodon axelrodi Cardinal Tetra	2in (5cm)	*Paracheirodon simulans* No common name	1in (2.5cm)
Gymnocorymbus ternetzi Black Widow, Black Tetra	2.25in (5.5cm)	*Paracheirodon innesi* Neon Tetra	1.5in (4cm)
Hasemania nana Silver-tipped Tetra	2in (5cm)	*Megalamphodus megalopterus* Black Phantom Tetra	1.75in (4.5cm)
Hemigrammus erythrozona Glowlight Tetra	1.5in (4cm)	*Megalamphodus sweglesi* Red Phantom Tetra	1.5in (4cm)
Hemigrammus ocellifer Head and Tail Light Tetra	2in (5cm)	*Moenkhausia pittieri* Diamond Tetra	2.5in (6cm)
Hemigrammus pulcher Pretty Tetra, Black Wedge Tetra	2in (5cm)	*Moenkhausia sanctaefilomenae* Yellow-banded Moenkhausia	2.75in (7cm)
Hemigrammus bleheri Rummy-nose Tetra, Red-nose Tetra	2in (5cm)	*Nematobrycon palmeri* Emperor Tetra	2in (5cm)
Hemigrammus ulreyi Ulrey's Tetra	2in (5cm)	*Thayeria obliqua* Penguin Fish	3in (7.5cm)
Hyphessobrycon callistus No common name	1.5in (4cm)	*Poecilocharax weitzmani* No common name	1.25in (3.25cm)

3 months or more, so that the system is mature; for the more difficult fish, an older tank with plants that are growing well is beneficial.

Feeding the more common species is simple. Many have been bred in captivity and will take flake foods. If, however, you have wild-caught fish, you may need to offer them live foods, such as *Daphnia*, micro-worms and white worms, all of which can be cultivated (see Foods and Feeding, pages 60–61). Live and frozen foods are also essential in maintaining colours. Additionally, you can collect mosquito larvae. Whatever you are feeding the fish, make sure that it is small enough for them to eat without choking.

Choose their companion fish with care, avoiding anything that is too large or boisterous, otherwise your tetras may be driven to hide away in the darker recesses of the tank. A good-sized shoal (i.e. 10 or more) in a large aquarium has a special strategy for dealing with threats. Whenever they are under stress, the fish release their fright chemical and the shoal tightens, making them feel safer. Once the threat has receded, the shoal breaks up and the tetras resume their normal behaviour.

Some of the more delicate species, for example *Poecilocharax weitzmani*, will require extremely careful acclimatization. Even transporting them home from the dealer's can result in one or two deaths. For such fish, a species tank is the only option, at least initially. Characins are prone to stress and some fish, especially wild-caught ones, have been known to die just from the shock of being netted. It is therefore important to keep stress levels to an absolute minimum, avoiding

Tank Conditions and Care

HABITAT: For the majority, a planted community aquarium with peaceful companion fish of a similar size. Some should be kept in a species tank owing to size or very specific water conditions.

Tank size	24x12x12in (61x30x30cm) for a community tank; 18x10x10in (46x25x25cm) for a species tank.
pH	5.0–7.5; check species requirements
dH	To 15°; check species requirements
Temperature	22–28°C (72–82°F); check individual species requirements.

Water changes	10–15% every week
Filtration	Type of filter is not critical provided the one chosen works efficiently.
Lighting	Type not critical

FEEDING: Carnivores that require small foods such as flake and tiny live and/or frozen foods such as mosquito larvae and *Daphnia*.

HEALTH: No particular problems if good water conditions are maintained and they are not kept with fish that harass them and nip their fins.

 ● *I set up a tank a couple of months ago, and recently bought a shoal of Cardinal Tetras to add to it. Sadly, they have all died; what have I done wrong?*

Cardinal Tetras are delicate fish, and are extremely demanding of water quality. A mature aquarium is essential for keeping them, so, to be on the safe side, allow three months' maturation time at the very least (though six months is preferable) before adding them. Most failures with this highly popular fish are caused by inexperienced aquarists providing them with unsuitable water conditions.

▲ *Cardinal Tetras* (Paracheirodon axelrodi) *are some of the most popular aquarium fish. Most of those offered for sale are wild-caught fish.*

● *My community tank is neutral to slightly alkaline and the water is hard. Is there a tetra suited to these conditions?*

One of the penguin fish, *Thayeria boehlkei*, would be suited to your tank. Ensure that your existing fish are not likely to harass them, or even eat them, and that you provide some plant cover. A word to the wise: penguin fish are sensitive to any build-up of nitrites or nitrates, so do check for these regularly.

▲ *The flanks of the Blue Tetra* (Boehlkea fredcochui) *become intensified in slightly acidic water. Feeding small, live foods will also help maintain the colour.*

troublesome companion fish, unnecessary meddling with the tank, or any violent fluctuations in temperature, pH, etc. Stress can cause newly imported fish to contract whitespot and bacterial infections, and they may not always respond to treatment. However, dealers are becoming far more adept at handling them and will happily advise you on optimum conditions – don't be too proud to ask!

Breeding certain species is a challenge, while others will spawn quite easily in one of the set-ups using fine-leaved plants (see Breeding, pages 56–57). The critical factors are water conditions and correct feeding of the parents. Live foods (sometimes quite specific, e.g. black mosquito larvae) form an essential part of the diet to bring the parents into spawning condition. Fortunately, the frozen equivalents are an acceptable alternative in most (if not all) cases.

Tetras scatter their eggs through plants; a large clump of Java Moss placed in the aquarium is ideal for the purpose. The eggs hatch relatively quickly, in 24–36 hours, but the fry do not

◀ *The Lemon Tetra* (Hyphessobrycon pulchripinnis) *will lose much of its striking colour if it is kept in hard water conditions.*

● *Can I breed my Diamond Tetras?*

Yes; this can be achieved in a small, 18x10x10in (46x25x25cm) tank with soft (4°dH), acidic water which should be filtered through peat. Add a large clump of Java Moss or equivalent synthetic spawning fibre. Feed the adults (males have much longer and more resplendent finnage than females) on mosquito larvae and keep the tank darkened at first, gradually increasing the light. The pair display to each other prior to spawning and will deposit their eggs among the moss. The fry need very small foods at first, but after a week should take newly hatched brine shrimp.

● *Can I keep Sierra Leone Dwarf Characins in my community aquarium?*

Only if you have other small, very peaceful species in a planted, well-established tank. They are demanding of both water quality and food, although they will eventually take flake. Small, live foods are preferred. They are skittish fish and jump at the slightest provocation.

● *My African Red-eyed Characins spend a lot of the time hidden. What can I do to make them come out?*

First determine the cause. Have you any larger fish or territorial fish which are preventing the Red-eyes from coming out? If so, either move the Red-eyes to another tank or remove the threat. Is the lighting too bright? This can be controlled by the addition of some floating plants. Are there too many fish in too small a tank? Red-eyes need swimming space, which means open water. If conditions are crowded, the Red-eyes will retreat to a quiet corner and stay there.

● *My Glowlight Tetras always look washed out. How can I get them to assume their full colour?*

This is a common problem, especially if you have a light-coloured substrate. Over large areas of sand or pale gravel, the fish lose their colour. Add some low-growing plants to tone down the glare from the substrate. Feeding also helps enhance coloration; if you are not doing so already, add live or frozen *Daphnia*, bloodworm or mosquito larvae to their diet.

become free-swimming until several days later. After spawning, it is advisable to remove the parents before they eat their eggs.

Make sure you have a production line of infusoria and, later, newly hatched brine shrimp to feed the fry. The rearing tanks must be kept scrupulously clean if you are not to lose the fry to fungal or bacterial infections; make small water changes and siphon off uneaten food each time you feed them. You will also need to provide a larger tank for growing the fry on.

Finally, a word of warning. In shipments of wild-caught fish (and this applies not only to characins), it is not uncommon to find "contaminants". These are species that have not been ordered by the wholesaler but are shipped, usually in error with the species that was ordered. Thus, in a box of Cardinal Tetras, you may find a handful of other small characins. These unidentified fish may turn out to be fry of a much larger, and perhaps aggressive, species. As a general rule, then, the purchase of contaminants should be left to the experienced aquarist.

Representative African Species

	maximum adult size
Arnoldichthys spilopterus African Red-eyed Characin	3in (7.5cm)
Brycinus imberi No common name	4in (10cm)
Brycinus longipinnis Long-finned Characin	4.5in (11.5cm)
Lepidarchus adonis Adonis Characin, Jelly Bean Tetra	1in (2.5cm)
Phenacogrammus interruptus Congo Tetra	3in (7.5cm)
Micralestes acutidens No common name	2.5in (6cm)
Ladigesia roloffi Sierra Leone Dwarf Characin	1.5in (4cm)

▼ *A shoal of Congo Tetras* (Phenacogrammus interruptus). *The extremely light coloration of these fish is due to the fact that they have not yet become acclimatized to the aquarium conditions.*

Pencilfish
FAMILY: LEBIASINIDAE

THESE SMALL SOUTH AMERICAN CHARACINS, native to Suriname, Guyana, Brazil and Colombia, are widely imported but often overlooked by new aquarists, presumably because they tend not to show their beautiful, delicate colours in dealers' tanks.

Pencilfish have a reputation for needing very specific water conditions. While this is the case during breeding, most are generally quite happy living in a community tank occupied by other small, quiet species. They do not like very bright conditions, so a few floating plants may be used to create a darker area without affecting growth elsewhere. Regular water changes are essential.

Something that often needlessly worries new aquarists is the pencilfish's change of body patterning at night. During the day, they have longitudinal lines along their bodies; at night, these become almost invisible and the fish develops dominant vertical bars that are barely visible during the day. Their general body and finnage colours also become less distinct, allowing the fish to blend into their surroundings. Some species of pencilfish have an adipose fin, while others do not. Most confusingly, this variation can even occur among fish of the same species!

▲ *These Hockey-stick Pencilfish* (Nannobrycon eques) *are seen in their characteristic oblique posture – they sometimes even swim vertically!*

Representative Species

	maximum adult size
Nannobrycon eques Hockey-stick Pencilfish, Three-striped Pencilfish	2in (5cm)
Nannobrycon unifasciatus One-lined Pencilfish	2.5in (6cm)
Nannostomus beckfordi Golden Pencilfish	2.5in (6cm)
Nannostomus bifasciatus Two-lined Pencilfish	1.5in (4cm)
Nannostomus espei Espe's Pencilfish	1.25in (3cm)
Nannostomus harrisoni Harrison's Pencilfish	2.5in (6cm)
Nannostomus marginatus Dwarf Pencilfish	1.25in (3cm)
Nannostomus trifasciatus Three-lined Pencilfish	2in (5cm)

▼ *The Dwarf Pencilfish* (Nannostomus marginatus) *is the smallest of the pencilfish. If kept with other small, peaceful species, it poses no real problems either to keep or to breed.*

Pencilfish may be bred: *Nannostomus* species are easier to breed than *Nannobrycon*. Use pairs of fish and condition them well before placing them in the breeding aquarium. They are egg scatterers, and eat their spawn; set up a breeding tank with a 3–4mm mesh that allows the eggs through but not the parents (see Breeding, pages 56–57). If this method is impractical, spawn them over fine-leaved plants or Java Moss and remove the parents as soon as spawning is complete. The tank should have a dark bottom. Water conditions are critical: soft, about 2–3°, acidic, about 6.0pH and at the warmer end of the fishes' temperature range. Once they have spawned, feed them well and they should spawn again in about three to four days.

The fry hatch in 24–72 hours and, although they are tiny, are not too difficult to raise, as long as you provide a steady supply of infusoria and rotifers followed by brine shrimp nauplii.

● *I feed my fish flake food each morning but have never seen my pencilfish feed. Is there anything else I can offer them?*

Your pencilfish should take flake, but being timid creatures will not compete with their tankmates for it. Try feeding the rest of the fish until they are sated, then feed the pencilfish separately in the area where they normally rest. Or try the same method, but in the evening rather than the morning; this is the time they normally eat. Pencilfish also feed avidly on small black mosquito larvae and *Daphnia*, both live and frozen, which they take from near the surface.

● *I have tried breeding my pencilfish, but without success. My tank has the right water conditions, and the female seems full of eggs. What's going wrong?*

The reason could be the foods you are using to condition the fish. Try black mosquito larvae, live for preference, or frozen if you cannot collect or culture your own. Alternatively, use *Drosophila* (fruit flies), which can also be cultured. These bring the fish into breeding condition far better than anything else because they contain the required amino acids.

● *The pencilfish in my tank spawn and the eggs hatch successfully, but after a couple of days I lose all the fry. Why is this happening?*

It is probably due to your supplying foods that are too large for the fry to eat or not feeding them often enough. As well as feeding them, it is a good idea to have a mature, air-operated sponge filter in the tank, so that the fry will be able to pick away at the micro-organisms on the sponge.

Tank Conditions and Care

HABITAT: Planted community aquarium with other peaceful species.

Tank size	24x12x12in (61x30x30cm)
pH	6.0–7.5
dH	To 8°
Temperature	22–28°C (72–82°F)
Water changes	10–15% every week
Filtration	Type not critical if efficient
Lighting	Type not critical

FEEDING: Flake and tiny live and/or frozen foods such as mosquito larvae and *Daphnia*.

HEALTH: No particular problems provided they are not kept with fish that harass them.

Splash Tetras FAMILY: LEBIASINIDAE

Representative Species

	maximum adult size
Copeina guttata	6in (15cm), but
Red-spotted Characin	usually smaller
Copella arnoldi	
Splash Tetra,	3.5in (8cm) males
Jumping Characin	2.5in (6cm) females
Copella metae	
No common name	2.5in (6cm)
Copella nattereri	
Beautiful Scaled Characin	2in (5cm)
Copella nigrofasciata	
Black-banded Pyrrhulina	2.5in (6cm)
Pyrrhulina filamentosa	
No common name	4.5in (12cm)
Pyrrhulina vittata	
Striped Pyrrhulina	2.5in (6cm)

THESE SMALL, ELONGATE FISH FROM SOUTH America inhabit the upper layers of the water and customarily feed from the surface. They require soft, slightly acidic water and benefit from peat filtration. This is particularly important if you are attempting to breed them. Good plant growth also helps maintain healthy water conditions. They jump at the slightest provocation, so a cover glass is essential.

All but one species spawn on large leaves or, if these are not available, in a pit in the substrate. The male cleans the spawning site prior to courting the female, whom he shepherds to the site with gentle prods and bites. After spawning is completed, he guards and tends the eggs. The fry hatch in 24–36 hours and need small live foods.

The sole exception is the Splash Tetra (*Copella arnoldi*), which spawns above the water. After courtship, the pair leap from the water, turn belly-up, and deposit their eggs on the underside of a broad leaf near the surface. They do this several times. When spawning is finished, the male remains beneath the eggs, occasionally splashing water over them with his caudal fin. They hatch in 36 hours and the young drop into the water. In captivity, if there is no suitable leaf, the pair will spawn on the underside of the cover glass.

◀ *The Splash Tetra* (Copella arnoldi), *although not very brightly coloured, is worth keeping for its unusual method of reproduction.*

Tank Conditions and Care

HABITAT: Planted community aquarium with some floating plants (to deter jumping) and other peaceful species.

Tank size	24x12x12in (61x30x30cm)
pH	6.0–7.5
dH	To 8°
Temperature	22–28°C (72–82°F)
Water changes	10–15% every week

Filtration   Type of filter is not critical so long as the one chosen is working efficiently.

Lighting	Type not critical

FEEDING: Flake and tiny live and/or frozen foods such as mosquito larvae and *Daphnia*. Live foods will increase your chances of spawning them.

HEALTH: No particular problems provided they are not kept with fish that harass them.

Hatchetfish FAMILY: GASTEROPELECIDAE

● *I have two Silver Hatchetfish in my community aquarium, but they spend most of their time skulking in a corner. What is wrong?*

Check your water conditions are right for them and adjust as necessary, having first ascertained that any change will suit the other inmates. Next consider their companion fish – are they nipping and chasing the hatchetfish? If so, transfer the hatchetfish to a more suitable aquarium. Finally, it may simply be that there are not enough hatchetfish in your tank – they are shoaling fish and should be kept as such.

▲ *The Marbled Hatchetfish* (Carnegiella strigata) *is hard to acclimatize to the tank, but well worth the effort.*

HATCHETFISH ARE WIDESPREAD THROUGHOUT northern South America. They are irregular imports into Europe as they do not travel well; the genera most seen in the trade are *Gasteropelecus* and *Carnegiella* (smaller, with no adipose fin).

Their shape is distinctive – the straight dorsal profile, with the fins set well back, is characteristic of surface-dwellers, while their deep, compressed body allows them to cut through the water easily. They are popular additions to the community aquarium, not least because they occupy an area of the tank that is notoriously difficult to fill. Leave them plenty of room to jump without hitting the cover glass and injuring themselves. Silver Hatchetfish (*Thoracocharax securis*) have been known to "fly" more than 4ft, flapping their pectoral fins like a bird's wings.

The Marbled Hatchetfish (*C. strigata*) has been bred, and requires water conditions similar to pencilfish. Use a breeding tank so the adults can be removed before they eat the spawn. In courtship, the fish dart around the surface, then lay their eggs on the roots of floating plants or let them fall to the substrate. The eggs hatch in 24–36 hours but it is five days before the fry become free-swimming. First foods are infusoria, rotifers (tiny pond creatures) and other small organisms.

Tank Conditions and Care

HABITAT: Planted tank with other placid species. Some floating plants. A tightly fitting cover glass.

Tank size	24x12x12in (61x30x30cm)
pH	5.5–7.5; check species requirements
dH	To 15°; check species requirements
Temperature	23–27°C (73–81°F)
Water changes	10–15% every week

Filtration External canister filter with spray bar return. Water well-oxygenated and with current.

Lighting Type not critical

FEEDING: Flake plus live and/or frozen foods such as mosquito larvae and *Daphnia*. Ensure there is enough open surface for them to feed.

HEALTH: Prone to whitespot. Good water quality prevents bacterial infections and appetite loss.

Representative Species

	maximum adult size
Carnegiella marthae Black-winged Hatchetfish	1.5in (4cm)
Carnegiella strigata Marbled Hatchetfish	1.5in (4cm)
Gasteropelecus sternicla Common Hatchetfish	2.5in (6cm)
Thoracocharax securis Silver Hatchetfish	3.5in (8.5cm)

Other Small Characins
ORDER: CHARACIFORMES

WHENEVER PEOPLE THINK OF CHARACINS, THE tetras are the first that spring to mind. However, there are several other small characins – namely, under 6in (15cm) in length – that are equally at home in a furnished community tank, as well as one or two that are not! The latter, despite their "awkward" personalities and particular requirements, nevertheless deserve a mention and are well worth the challenge of keeping.

As with any of the characins, maintaining good water quality is of the utmost importance. Listless fish with clamped fins are a sure sign of a problem – the tank may be too warm or too cold, or simply in need of a water change. Particularly prone to poor water are *Characidium fasciatum*, *Chilodus punctatus* and *Neolebias ansorgei*. However, if your water management is good, you should otherwise have no trouble keeping these fish. Feeding is reasonably easy, as most species will eat the usual commercial fresh, frozen or flake foods, with the herbivores needing some vegetable matter in their diet. Check the individual species' particular requirements.

Breeding techniques vary from egg scattering to egg depositing. Some spawn readily in the community aquarium but don't expect to raise any fry, as the other inmates will feed avidly on this free supply of protein. For all species, live foods and/or algae (or their equivalent) are necessary to raise good quality youngsters.

Some fish display particular characteristics, not all of them appealing. For example, *Anostomus anostomus* and *A. ternetzi* are often bought for their striking coloration and are a welcome addition to the medium-sized or large community aquarium. Yet they should never be kept in ones and twos; *A. anostomus* in particular can become almost as much of a bully and a nuisance as a lone Tiger Barb, nipping at fish with flowing finnage! Keep a group of five or six and they will pick on each other rather than on their companions. Another common problem associated with these fish, which they share with *Abramites hypselonotus* and *Distichodus affinis*, is their voracious appetite for aquarium plants. To curb this, a lettuce leaf (or several) "planted"

▶ *A group of Striped Anostomus* (Anostomus anostomus) *feeding on a lettuce leaf. This species of Amazonian characin has a bad reputation for territorial behaviour and fin-nipping, and should be kept in a group in a large aquarium.*

Representative Species

	maximum adult size
Distichodus affinis Silver Distichodus	4.5in (11.5cm)
Nannaethiops unitaeniatus One-striped African Characin	2.5in (6cm)
Nannocharax fasciatus No common name	2.75in (7cm)
Neolebias ansorgei Ansorge's Neolebias	1.5in (4cm)
Abramites hypselonotus High-backed Headstander	4.5in (11.5cm)
Anostomus anostomus Striped Anostomus	7in (18cm)
Anostomus ternetzi No common name	6in (15cm)
Exodon paradoxus Bucktoothed Tetra	6in (15cm)
Characidium fasciatum Banded Characidium, Banded Darter	3.5in (8.5cm)
Crenuchus spilurus Sailfin Characin	2.5in (6cm)
Chilodus punctatus Spotted Headstander	3.5in (8.5cm)
Astyanax fasciatus mexicanus Blind Cavefish	3.5in (8.5cm)

● *I cannot get my* Nannocharax
fasciatus *to feed. They swim around
and go as if to take flake but never
actually eat it. What can I do?*

Newly imported specimens of this African fish are
notoriously difficult to get to feed. At least yours seem
hungry and willing to eat. Your best approach is to offer
a variety of small live foods such as *Daphnia, Cyclops*
and mosquito larvae. Once you have got them to
accept these, try offering the frozen equivalent and,
later on, graduate to flake foods.

● *How can I tell the difference between* Anostomus
anostomus *and* Anostomus ternetzi?

Although the slender body shape and striped markings
of these two species are extremely similar, *A. ternetzi*
has none of the prominent red coloration in the dorsal,
caudal and anal fins that characterizes *A. anostomus.*
Also, *A. ternetzi* is a slightly smaller fish. For the
fishkeeper, one of the benefits of owning *A. ternetzi* as
opposed to *A. anostomus* is that it has a slightly more
agreeable nature. Even so, you would be well advised
to keep them as a group.

▲ *The Sailfin Characin* (Crenuchus spilurus) *is a sensitive fish that requires soft, acidic conditions. It is best kept in a densely planted tank in the company of its own kind and provided with a variety of hiding places. Males can be rather territorial.*

◄ *Despite its pronounced head-down swimming attitude, the Spotted Headstander* (Chilodus punctatus) *is not an anastomid like the other "headstanders", but is a member of the family Chilodontidae. It benefits from a varied diet.*

Tank Conditions and Care

HABITAT: Planted community aquarium with other peaceful, similarly sized species or a planted species aquarium.

Tank size	Min 24x12x12in (61x30x30cm)
pH	6.0–7.8; check species requirements
dH	To 25°; check species requirements
Temperature	20–28°C (68–82°F) check individual species requirements
Water changes	10–15% every week

Filtration Type of filter is not critical so long as it is efficient and provides a good supply of well-oxygenated water.

Lighting   Type not critical

FEEDING: Varies according to species. Carnivores: mosquito larvae, *Daphnia*, bloodworm, etc., either live or frozen; many will also take flake. Herbivores: plentiful supply of green foods such as lettuce, peas. Omnivores: combination of the above, plus flakes.

HEALTH: No particular problems so long as good water conditions are maintained. It is essential that you check the special requirements of the fish you wish to keep.

in the substrate, or anchored with a stone, will tempt the fish away from the harder-leaved aquarium plants. The lettuce must be held down – if it is allowed to float they will ignore it.

A noteworthy trait of *A. hypselonotus* is their intolerance of their own kind as they mature. Young fish live together in harmony but, once they have reached a length of about 4in (10cm), become extremely territorial, especially if kept in confined quarters. Be prepared to provide a larger aquarium or split them up into several tanks. If you already have some of the smaller, more peaceful catfish and cichlids in your community tank, *D. affinis* makes an ideal tankmate.

The Blind Cavefish (*Astyanax fasciatus mexicanus*) is popular in the hobby and is far more readily available than its pigmented, normally sighted counterpart. It is an easy fish to keep in a community aquarium despite its tendency to boisterousness. For preference, keep them with similar-sized fish rather than with the smaller tetras. Breeding can be problematic, as they require cooler conditions for spawning; the water temperature should be about 18–20°C (64–68°F). They spawn through plants, but the eggs usually fall to the bottom and will hatch in about 48 hours, the fry becoming free-swimming a few days later. The young are small and require fine foods. Interestingly, when these fish are young they have eyes, but these regress as they grow. If you have specimens of both the Blind Cavefish and its pigmented form in your aquarium, they will cross-breed, as they are the same species.

Q&A...

● *I have seen some Sailfin Characins for sale. Are they suitable for my community aquarium?*

These fish are best kept in a species tank. Despite being carnivorous, they are very timid and will often hide away if kept with more boisterous species. A pair (the male has a longer, pointed, red dorsal fin; the female's dorsal is much smaller and less colourful) can be housed in an 18x10x10in (46x25x25cm) planted tank. Use soft, slightly acidic water at 24–28°C (75–82°F).

● *Every so often my Spotted Headstanders lose their spots and a couple of dark patches appear on their head and back. What causes this? Have they damaged themselves?*

This phenomenon has been reported when the fish are spawning. If they are in a community aquarium, try setting up a separate, large breeding tank for them. Provide a sand substrate with some algae-covered pebbles, clear, soft, slightly acidic, warm water and clumps of fine-leaved plants. Peat filtration also helps trigger spawning. Feed ample small, live foods and algae or similar green foods. Remove the parents after spawning. Raise the fry on brine shrimp and algae.

● *I put a dozen small* Neolebias ansorgei *in a sunlit species tank with soft, slightly acidic water and fine-leaved plants. But with each water change, a fish or two dies; now only five are left. What am I doing wrong?*

Neolebias ansorgei are very sensitive to an excess of fresh water and it is best to use well-aged water (using a water conditioner if need be) to carry out small water changes. Set up another tank with an airstone to turn the water over so that you always have a ready supply of "good" water for them. They only require shallow water; 8–10in (20–25cm) deep is fine.

● *Can I breed* Neolebias ansorgei *?*

Yes, you can; treat them as you would a killifish. These fish reach maturity at about seven months old. Use peat fibre as an aquarium substrate and a pair will produce 250 or so eggs that fall to the bottom of the tank and hatch in 24 hours. Supply the fry with infusoria as a first food and progress to newly hatched brine shrimp when they are large enough to take it.

◀ *The Blind Cavefish (*Astyanax fasciatus mexicanus*) comes from subterranean caves in central Mexico, and should be kept in hard water conditions.*

Piranha FAMILY: CHARACIDAE

PIRANHA HAVE A REPUTATION FOR FEROCITY. A shoal can strip the flesh from bones in seconds. Sadly, their notoriety has led some unscrupulous dealers to sell single specimens as unusual items for community tanks. This is most irresponsible; firstly, fish should never be sold for their novelty value, and secondly, even a well-fed piranha can launch unprovoked attacks and seriously injure its tank companions, however large.

However, if they are properly housed – as a shoal in a large species tank – piranha are very easy fish to keep. The key point that you should always bear in mind is that they demand respect. They are nervous fish that will attack an owner's fingers if alarmed. Siting of the tank is also crucial; avoid main thoroughfares and provide a heavy cover glass and a good hood to prevent children from putting their hands in the water.

Young piranha are attractive fish. For example, Red Piranha (*Pygocentrus nattereri*) have red gill covers, pectoral fins and anal fin, and bodies with black spots on a silver background. As they mature, the colouring changes to a silvery grey body with a red throat and belly (hence their common name). For preference, buy young fish, as these will adapt to captivity far more readily than adults.

Sexing piranha is relatively easy. Males of the *P. nattereri* species are silvery with a pronounced red throat, while females are more yellow; in *Serrasalmus rhombeus*, the leading edge of the male's anal fin is extended, whereas in females it is straight; and in *S. spilopleura*, the caudal is deeply indented on males and less so on females. All three species may be bred in captivity provided the aquarium is large enough. Soft, slightly acidic, warm water is required and spawning can sometimes be triggered by a water change. Either pairs or a shoal may be used.

Red Piranha deposit up to 1,000 eggs in a nest which is guarded by the female. The male may defend it for about a day before being chased off by the female. The eggs may be removed for hatching elsewhere or, if they have spawned in the tank with the shoal, it can be partitioned off. After a few weeks, the fry become cannibalistic and you will need a series of rearing tanks so they can be sorted according to size.

◀ *The Red Piranha* (Pygocentrus nattereri) *possesses a fearsome set of teeth. The import of piranha is banned in some countries to avoid the risk of release into the wild and the subsequent decimation of native species.*

● *What is the best method of transporting piranha?*

... If possible, put a single fish in each bucket. If not, then double-bag them, taping the corners of the inner bag to make a square base and lining the space between the bags with layers of newspaper to stop them puncturing the outer bag.

● *My piranha have spawned in the aquarium. What should I feed the young fish?*

After the fry have absorbed their yolk sac, usually in about 4–8 days depending on the species, offer brine shrimp. As they grow you will need a constant supply of ever larger live foods – e.g. *Daphnia* and then bloodworm. Also try them on ox heart and fish, finely chopped, as the fry can easily choke on large pieces.

● *My piranha often have damaged fins. Is this a cause for concern?*

This is a natural hazard of keeping these fish! If the water conditons are good, the fins heal. In poor water, the fish may develop a bacterial or fungal infection, which should be treated with the appropriate remedy. Check that the medication is suitable for use on piranha – some are not.

Representative Species

	maximum adult size
Pygocentrus nattereri Red Piranha	11in (28cm)
Serrasalmus rhombeus Spotted Piranha, Black Piranha, Red-Eye Piranha	15in (38cm)
Serrasalmus spilopleura Dark-banded Piranha, Diamond Piranha, Red-Throat Piranha	10in (25cm)

Tank Conditions and Care

HABITAT: Spacious planted aquarium decorated with roots which may have Java Fern (*Microsorium pteropus*) attached and dense thickets of plants.

Tank size 48x18x18in (122x46x46cm) for youngsters but much larger for a shoal of adult fish.

pH	5.5–7.5; check species requirements
dH	To 20°; check species requirements
Temperature	23–27°C (73–81°F)
Water changes	15–20% every week
Filtration	External canister filter combined with

trickle system to provide highly oxygenated, clean water, with a good flow.

Lighting Diffused; just sufficient for plant growth.

FEEDING: Carnivores, will take anything meaty (e.g. fish fillets, sprats and whitebait as well as larger aquatic invertebrates); avoid overfeeding. Remove any scraps of uneaten food to prevent decomposition and fouling of the tank.

HEALTH: Can be susceptible to bacterial infections, especially if the water quality deteriorates.

Metynnis and Myleus

FAMILY: CHARACIDAE

MEMBERS OF THE SAME FAMILY AS THE PIRANHA, the Metynnis and Myleus have none of their relative's malevolence. They are peaceful, shoaling herbivores that require plenty of free swimming space. There is no reason why they should not be kept in a community aquarium with fish of a similar size and temperament.

One of the main problems people have with these fish is supplying them with enough green food to prevent them from eating the aquarium greenery. If you are growing soft-leaved aquatic plants, then forget about keeping these fish. The only suitable plants are those with harder leaves, such as Java Fern, Amazon Swordplants and *Cryptocorynes* – you may even have to resort to plastic plants! Adequate and regular feeding also helps curb their appetite for plants. For a small specimen, a lettuce leaf once a day is fine, but don't forget to increase the number of leaves offered over a 24-hour period as the fish grows.

Representative Species

	maximum adult size
Metynnis argenteus Silver Dollar	5in (12.5cm)
Metynnis hypsauchen Metynnis	6in (15cm)
Metynnis lippincottianus No common name	4.75in (12cm)
Myleus rubripinnis Redhook Metynnis	4in (10cm) in aquarium 10in (25cm) in wild

▶ *The Redhook Metynnis* (Myleus rubripinnis) *is particularly sensitive to water conditions in the tank, requiring very clear, well-oxygenated water.*

If you are keeping a shoal, vary the amount given accordingly. Because they are vegetarians, they tend to eat little and often, nibbling at morsels all day rather than taking a single large meal as a carnivorous fish would. You can also include vegetable flakes in their diet, and certain species appreciate *Daphnia*.

Some species have been bred, for example *Metynnis hypsauchen*. The fish can usually be sexed by the length of the anal fin, which is longer in males and edged in red and/or black. They may spawn in pairs or shoal spawn. Use soft, slightly acidic, warm water filtered over peat. The fish spawn among plants, so be sure to provide thickets of fine-leaved plants that reach up to the surface. If this is not practical, float some bunches of plants on the surface or use floating plants such as Water Lettuce (*Pistia stratiodes*) that have tangles of roots trailing down into the water. The eggs fall to the bottom and are ignored by the parents. They take about three days to hatch and the fry become free-swimming within a week. After hatching you will see the fry hanging from the plants or sides of the tank, at which time they require very tiny first foods. Gradually increase the food size as the fry grow.

Tank Conditions and Care

HABITAT: Spacious aquarium with a dark substrate and decorated with roots and Java Fern (*Microsorium pteropus*). However, because these fish are herbivorous, plastic plants are favoured by many aquarists.

Tank size	48x18x18in (122x46x46cm) for youngsters; adults 72x20x20in (183x51x51cm).
pH	5.0–7.5; check species requirements
dH	To 22°; check species requirements
Temperature	23–28°C (73–82°F)
Water changes	15–20% every week
Filtration	External canister filter combined with trickle system to provide highly oxygenated, clean water.
Lighting	Diffused lighting

FEEDING: Herbivorous, provide plenty of green foods in the form of lettuce, peas, etc.

HEALTH: Can be susceptible to bacterial infections especially if the water quality deteriorates.

● *My Redhook Metynnis has developed some very small spots on its sides that look like tiny air-bubbles but they do not float off the fish. What are they?*

These tiny blisters are the symptoms of a disease that has not yet been identified by ichthyologists. They do look somewhat unsightly, but fortunately are not fatal; indeed, they do not seem to affect the fish adversely at all. Note that this disease is not exclusive to the Redhook Metynnis.

● *My Silver Dollars spend most of the day hiding at the back of the tank, and only come out to eat when the lights go off. Why is this?*

Your aquarium may be too brightly lit. In nature, the fish live in forest streams full of plants; to imitate this in the aquarium you should use diffused lighting, sufficient to grow plants but not enough to scare the fish. Alternatively, floating plants will cut down the light to parts of the tank but leave other areas well-lit. There is a third option; you could reduce the lighting further and use plastic plants in your tank.

Pacu FAMILIES: CHARACIDAE

THESE LARGE, PEACEFUL SOUTH AMERICAN characins are ideally suited to large display tanks in public aquaria. Indeed, it is here that they are most often seen, as their potential size makes them rare imports for the aquarium trade. Any large fish of this sort is described as a Pacu – even *Mylossoma* species are covered by this term. There are two species loosely recognized in the trade, the Pacu or Black Pacu (*Piaractus brachypomum*), which grows to 40in (102cm), and the Black-finned Pacu, or Black-finned Colossoma (*Colossoma macropomum*), which reaches similar proportions.

Pacu are heavily built fish with a deep body, so the aquarium not only needs to be long, it must also be deep and wide. For example, a couple of 12in (30cm) specimens would require a 72x 24x24in (183x61x61cm) aquarium with, perhaps, a bottom-dwelling peaceful catfish as a companion. Because of the size and depth of the aquarium, it is probably best lit by spotlights, in which case one or two large specimen Amazon Swordplants may be grown. Although pacu are herbivores, they will leave the plants relatively unscathed so long as you supply them with sufficient alternatives.

Mainly vegetarian (though the stomach contents of some specimens caught in the wild have been found to include insect larvae and aquatic invertebrates), they are inefficient feeders and produce copious amounts of nutrient-rich waste. Although the detritus-sifting catfish, *Oxydoras niger*, will eat much of this, it cannot deal with all the pacu's waste! In addition, an efficient mechanical filtration system is vital, plus a trickle filter with its series of filter beds, to break down the waste products effectively. Healthy plants also help in the conversion of waste material.

Little is known of the breeding habits of pacu and the likelihood of them breeding in the confines of the home aquarium is remote. In the wild, large shoals have been known to make migratory spawning runs.

● *I've just acquired a very small pacu. It won't feed, but rests on the bottom at the back of the tank all the time twitching occasionally. What can I do?*

Young, newly imported fish can be very nervous and, at worst, will hide in a corner of the aquarium and refuse to feed. This is particularly the case if only a single specimen is being kept. Pacu are shoaling fish and, if space permits, it is advisable to keep them this way. If this is not practical, then one or two other peaceful shoaling fish, such as barbs, will help them settle in. Sometimes new fish seem to learn by example; the pacu may take its cue from the barbs and decide that it is safe to come out and eat pieces of food falling through the water. Also ensure that the water parameters are acceptable. If they are not, slowly adjust as necessary.

◀ *Young species of pacu are virtually impossible to identify to species level. Their dentition, body shape, and colour all change before they reach adulthood.*

● *I have been feeding my young pacu on a diet of lettuce, spinach and peas and it seems to be growing well, but could you suggest some different foods to supplement its diet with?*

In the wild, they are known to eat fruits and seeds and congregate in large shoals beneath fruiting trees to eat any that falls into the water; fishermen even use citrus fruits as bait to catch them! So, in addition to what you are already feeding them, you might like to try pieces of banana, figs, small cherry tomatoes and the like.

● *I am having problems with my pacu eating my plants. Is there any easy way to prevent this?*

The easiest way, if you have the space, is to cheat and grow your plants in pots. Have two or three in your show tank and in another tank grow on six or eight more so that you can rotate them. If you have a deep tank, swim in the plants when you do a water change, otherwise you will need a snorkel to reach the bottom! Also check that you are providing enough of the right foods. If their dentition changes, so does their diet; mature fish will eat such things as unsalted almonds!

Tank Conditions and Care

HABITAT: Spacious aquarium decorated with roots which may have Java Fern (*Microsorium pteropus*) attached as cover for young fish.

Tank size 48x18x18in (122x46x46cm) for a juvenile specimen. Much more spacious accommodation will need to be provided as it grows to adulthood.	
pH	5.0–7.8
dH	To 20°
Temperature	22–26°C (72–79°F)
Water changes	15–20% every week
Filtration External canister filter combined with trickle system.	
Lighting	Type not critical

FEEDING: Provide them with plentiful quantities of green foods – lettuce, peas, spinach, etc. are ideal.

HEALTH: No particular problems so long as good water conditions are maintained and they have plenty of space.

◀ *The Black-finned Pacu (Colossoma macropomum) is bred in Florida for the aquarium trade. They are sold under a number of common names, including (confusingly) the "Red-finned Pacu".*

Other Large Characins ORDER: CHARACIFORMES

AFRICA AND SOUTH AMERICA ARE HOME TO A number of larger characins that are popular in the hobby. This loose category of fish includes both harmless herbivores, which make excellent additions to large community display tanks, and out-and-out predators, which require far more thought and care to keep. It is essential, therefore, that you investigate each individual species' habits and requirements before you buy them.

Naturally, the main requirement for keeping these fish is a large aquarium. For the peaceful species, such as *Semaprochilodus taeniurus* and *Citharinus citharinus*, this should be a well-planted tank with open areas for them to swim. Both are jumpers, especially when frightened,

▲ *If you are thinking of keeping Pike Characins* (Boulengerella maculata), *site your tank in a quiet spot – these timid fish can seriously injure themselves by dashing their snouts against the glass.*

and the plants will provide a degree of security. However, the tank should also be equipped with a heavy cover glass – large, powerful specimens can easily dislodge lightweight plastic or perspex covers. Many owners like to keep these fish in aquaria lit by spotlights, which create shady, secluded areas while still providing enough light for plant growth. In captivity, these fish are omnivorous, accepting flake, frozen and tablet foods. Their feeding habits in the wild vary; for

Q & A... ● *I have a planted 4ft tank housing several loricariid catfish. I would like to add a* Distichodus lusosso *to provide some movement. Would this be alright?*

If you value your plants, don't! The appetite of young specimens can be stilled by a plentiful supply of vegetable foods, but as they grow they tend to devour everything. The fish would also outgrow your aquarium before long.

● *I have several specimens of Slant-nosed Gar in a 6ft tank. I would like to try and breed them. Can you give me any pointers?*

First check that you have a pair! Males are generally smaller than females and their ventral fin has a ragged edge, owing to the fact that the central rays are longer than the outer ones. Females have a straight edge to their ventral fin. These fish have been bred using either pairs or a trio of two males and one female. They are prolific, producing 1,000 or more eggs. Large amounts of space are needed to separate and raise the cannibalistic fry. Use brine

shrimp as first foods and then progressively larger live foods. Spawning can sometimes be triggered by an increase in the water temperature.

● *My Pike Characin keeps banging its snout and now there is fungus growing on it. I have treated the tank but it doesn't seem to have killed the fungus. What else can I do?*

Firstly, ensure that you have treated the tank at the correct strength. Secondly, if you have activated carbon in the filter, remove it (but don't stop the filter!), as it will draw the medicament out of the water. Don't be tempted to mix remedies (i.e. use a different fungal treatment), as the resultant cocktail may kill the fish. If you wish to use another treatment, it is essential that you carry out a thorough water change first. As a last resort, catch the fish and paint the proprietary remedy directly onto the fungus. It should stain the fungus and eventually kill it. Most importantly, once you have cured the infection, try to ascertain what caused the fish to keep banging itself and rectify it. It may simply have been frightened by people passing; adding some floating plants will give it security.

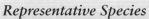

▶ *The Flagtail Characin* (Semaprochilodus taeniurus) *is a long-lived species, but is especially prone to leaping from the aquarium*

Representative Species

Carnivorous Species	maximum adult size
Boulengerella maculata Pike Characin	13in (33cm)
Chalceus macrolepidotus Pink-tailed Characin, Pink-tailed Chalceus	10in (25cm)
Erythrinus erythrinus Wolf Fish	10in (25cm)
Hoplias malabaricus Tiger Fish, Wolf Fish	18in (46cm)
Acestrorhynchus falcirostris No common name	16in (41cm)
Ctenolucius hujeta Hujet Pike Characin, Slant-nosed Gar	26in (66cm)
Hydrocynus goliath African Tiger Fish, Wolf Fish	16in (41cm)
Hepsetus odoe African Pike	13in (33cm)

Herbivorous Species	
Distichodus lusosso Long-nosed Distichodus	16in (41cm)
Distichodus sexfasciatus No common name	10in (25cm)
Leporinus affinis Striped Leporinus	10in (25cm)
Leporinus fasciatus Black-banded Leporinus	12in (30cm)
Semaprochilodus taeniurus Flagtail Characin	10in (25cm)
Citharinus citharinus No common name	20in (51cm)

example, *C. citharinus* feeds by sifting through muddy substrates to extract small worms. To approximate such conditions in the aquarium without the water becoming too cloudy, a fine sand substrate should be used.

Other large, herbivorous characins include fish of the African genus *Distichodus* and the South American genus *Leporinus*. They graze continually on algae and plant matter, but offerings of vegetables such as peas and lettuce should prevent them from consuming all your tank plants. Although they are not predators, their disposition means that they can become troublesome in a community aquarium by fighting among themselves and bullying other fish.

Small specimens of large predatory characins occasionally appear in aquarium stores, either imported to order or arriving as contaminants in

▶ *Its teeth alone should give a clue to the eating habits of the African Pike* (Hepsetus odoe)! *It is not suitable for keeping in a community aquarium.*

Tank Conditions and Care

HABITAT: Large aquarium which may or may not be planted depending on the eating habits of the fish being kept. A fine sand substrate should be used.

Tank size	Min 48x18x18in (122x46x46cm)
pH	6.0–7.5; check species requirements
dH	To 20°; check species requirements

Temperature 22–28°C (72–82°F); check individual species requirements.

Water changes For some species up to 50% every week, for others 20–25% weekly will suffice.

Filtration Type of filter is not critical provided the one chosen is working efficiently.

Lighting Spotlights provide shaded areas while allowing plants to grow.

FEEDING: Carnivores, a mixed diet consisting of pieces of meat and fish, prawns, mussels, earthworms, aquatic invertebrates, etc. Herbivores should be fed lettuce, spinach, peas, etc. For omnivores, same requirements as for carnivores and herbivores plus flake and tablet foods.

HEALTH: No particular problems if good water conditions are maintained and companion fish are selected wisely!

consignments of other fish. Probably the most common of these species is the Pink-tailed Chalceus (*Chalceus macrolepidotus*), which is very popular with aquarists because of its striking silvery body covered in large scales, and the contrasting bright pink caudal fin. Despite the fact that it is a piscivore, it adapts quite well to tank conditions and will take dead foods such as pieces of meat and fish, as well as flake (when young) and tablet foods. These fish are aggressive towards one another if kept in a group of less than ten, but tend not to attack other fish. A single specimen can be kept in a community tank with companions large enough not to be considered as food.

Clean, well-oxygenated water is a prerequisite for keeping most large characins. This is best achieved by coupling a very efficient biological filter, to break down their plentiful waste products, with an external canister filter to remove the debris. One exception is *Erythrinus erythrinus*, which is able to use its swim bladder as a respiratory organ and can therefore survive in the oxygen-deficient waters of pools and sluggish streams by going to the surface to take gulps of air – however, this does not mean that stagnant water conditions should be replicated in the aquarium!

Sometimes it can be difficult to get the carnivorous fish to feed (see Foods and Feeding, page 63) and you may need to offer them live foods; if you are squeamish about doing this, then the carnivores are not for you! It is also a good idea to vary their diet by using a selection of different commercial frozen foods, as they sometimes go off their food for no apparent reason. When feeding young fish, you should ensure that the pieces are large enough for them to eat without choking themselves, but not so small that they ignore them.

Breeding the larger characins is no easy matter. Many have not been spawned in captivity. Some are known to make migratory spawning runs in the wild. So, if you are looking for a challenge these fish could provide it.

Large Gouramis FAMILY: BELONTIIDAE

ALTHOUGH THESE FISH ARE CALLED LARGE Gouramis, this is a relative term – most of the Asian species only grow to around 4–6in (10–15cm). Like all anabantoids, they possess an auxiliary labyrinth organ at the rear of the head, which can extract oxygen from the air above the water surface as a supplement to the gills.

Gouramis are graceful, peaceful fish that tend to swim slowly or remain fairly still. They are well-suited to the community tank. Only during spawning can the males get a little aggressive – particularly with the females.

Some species have been hybridized to enhance or change the coloration. *Trichogaster trichopterus* is naturally silver with barely discernible pale blue vertical bands and two small blue spots. (It is known as the Three-spot Gourami – the third spot being the eye.) This species has been hybridized to produce a blue mottled strain (the Opaline or Cosby Gourami) and a golden

▲ *Though relatively small, the Lace Gourami (Trichogaster leeri) is one of the hardier types of gourami, and is tolerant of most water conditions. It enjoys great longevity, living for seven or eight years provided it is properly looked after.*

Representative Species

	maximum adult size
Trichogaster trichopterus Three-spot Gourami	4in (10cm)
Trichogaster trichopterus var. Blue, Cosby, Opaline and Golden Gouramis	4in (10cm)
Trichogaster leeri Lace Gourami	4.5in (11.5cm)
Trichogaster pectoralis Snakeskin Gourami	8in (20cm)
Trichogaster microlepis Moonlight Gourami	6in (15cm)

Tank Conditions and Care

HABITAT: Best suited to a well planted aquarium with slow water movement. Avoid mixing with excessively active fish or inveterate fin-nippers.

Tank size	Min 36x15x15in (91x38x38cm). If separated for breeding, 18x10x10in (46x25x25cm) will suffice for one pair. Use a tightly-fitting cover glass and keep out of draughts.
pH	6.5–7.8
dH	To 25°
Temperature	24–28°C (75–82°F)
Water changes	10% every 14 days. Replace with mature water of the same temperature.
Filtration	Use an internal mechanical/biological filter with gradual flow and keep the water surface undisturbed by strong current. For the breeding

aquarium use a small internal air-lift corner filter but ensure the air-lift is not supplied with cold air. Place it near a radiator or similar.

Lighting	Fluorescent tube over the aquarium

FEEDING: Omnivorous. Provide vegetable matter (lettuce leaf, for example) and aquatic invertebrates. Flake foods will be accepted.

HEALTH: Can suffer from tumours and lymphocystis, which appear as small lumps on the flanks of the body. There is no cure. Careful selection when buying is recommended. Specimens that develop this disease should be isolated. For damage through fin-nipping, apply disinfectant (methylene blue or malachite) directly onto the affected region.

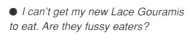

● *I can't get my new Lace Gouramis to eat. Are they fussy eaters?*

... Gouramis are omnivorous, and once acclimatized will accept all kinds of food including flake foods. However, some of the gouramis, such as your Lace Gouramis, take time to settle into a new environment. Try offering some live *Daphnia*. It could also be that other more aggressive species are dominating the feeding ritual; and, as a last resort, isolate the offending individuals.

● *What is the best method of getting my gouramis to breed?*

Assuming your fish are sexually mature, Nature will generally take her own course. The main obstacle is the presence of other fish, especially species that swim frantically around the tank in a seemingly aimless manner. They can disturb the more graceful gouramis in their sexual activity. The best course of action is to isolate the gouramis in a separate breeding tank – an 18in (46cm) tank is more than adequate. This should have gentle filtration so as not to disturb the water unduly, and floating plants. Apply a tight-fitting cover glass. Try raising the temperature slowly (0.6°C/1°F per day) to 27°C (81°F). It is also advisable to remove the female after spawning to prevent bullying by the male.

▶ *A* Three-spot Gourami *(Trichogaster trichopterus)* surfacing in order to gulp air. This is the usual mode of respiration for anabantoids.

variety (the Golden Gourami). A lilac strain, the Amethyst Gourami, has also been produced, though this is not available in the trade.

Easy Breeding

Most of the species listed here breed readily in the home aquarium. Sexes can be determined by the shape of the dorsal fin (and the anal fin of some species) which is longer and pointed in males. The male makes a large floating nest of sticky bubbles and reinforces it with scraps of vegetation. He then entices the female under this nest and wraps his body around hers in such a way that his reproductive organ is close to hers. The eggs are thus fertilized as they leave the female. The male guards the eggs, chasing off all who come near the nest, including the female. The fry stay in the nest for the first week.

Dwarf Gouramis
FAMILY: BELONTIIDAE

THE BEST KNOWN DWARF GOURAMIS ARE THOSE belonging to the genus *Colisa*, which are native to India, Assam, Bangladesh, Burma and Borneo. They are popular aquarium fish, with some species being selectively bred to achieve new colour forms (for example, the Royal Blue Dwarf Gourami, a colour form of *C. lalia*).

Colisa labiosa and *C. fasciata* are often confused; some think *C. labiosa* is a colour morph of *C. fasciata*. They interbreed readily, and there are probably many hybrids in the trade. Spawning *Colisa* species is straightforward, but problems can arise in feeding the young which, on hatching, are tiny and require infusoria. It is imperative to time your breeding program so that you have cultured sufficient food for the fry.

Another group that is sometimes available is the croaking gouramis (*Trichopsis* spp.). Their common name is derived from their ability to "croak", usually when they are excited or they are spawning. Although they will survive with other small, peaceful fish, it is better to keep them in a species tank planted with fine-leaved plants and a few *Cryptocorynes* plus some floating plants such as Indian Fern or Water Lettuce. Males have a longer, more pointed dorsal fin. In *T. pumilis*, you can see a yellowish area of spawn within the female's body. Breeding can be tricky; try warm, shallow water, about 4in (10cm) deep. Their bubble-nest is small and usually placed beneath floating leaves. The fry are tiny and require infusoria as a first food.

Chocolate Gouramis (*Sphaerichthys osphronemoides*) are considered very difficult fish and are only suited to the advanced aquarist. The key to keeping them alive is good water management. Soft, acidic conditions and a mature tank with premium quality water are more important factors than temperature. An appropriate feeding regime should also be observed. They are not fond of prepared foods such as flake, preferring live *Daphnia* or bloodworm. If live foods are unavailable, they will take frozen foods.

Tank Conditions and Care

HABITAT: Mature, planted, community aquarium with other peaceful fish. Floating plants are beneficial. For some species, such as *T. pumilis*, a species tank is preferable.

Tank size 24x12x12in (61x30x30cm) if kept in a community; 18x10x10in (46x25x25cm) for spawning a pair provided there is plenty of cover for the female.

pH 6.0–7.5 for *Colisa* spp. and *T. vittatus*; 6.0–7.0 for *Sphaerichthys* spp.; 5.8–7.0 for *T. pumilis*.

dH To 15° for *Colisa* spp. and *T. vittatus*; to 4° for *Sphaerichthys* spp.; to 10° for *T. pumilis*.

Temperature 22–28°C (72–83°F). Some species may require higher temperatures for breeding.

Water changes 10–15% every 10–15 days. Spawning often follows a water change.

Lighting Reasonably high lighting levels, but with some darker regions for retreat.

FEEDING: Mostly omnivorous. Will accept flake foods, but for the best colour and to bring into breeding condition, bloodworm and mosquito larvae, live or frozen, are recommended.

HEALTH: Good water conditions are essential. This is very important for Chocolate Gouramis, which are prone to bacterial infections and infestation by skin parasites.

In sexing Chocolate Gouramis, adult males may be distinguished by the yellow edge to their anal and caudal fins. When they are ready to spawn, the females are more rounded in their body. These fish are mouthbrooders (although some reports state that they build bubble-nests) and produce small broods of 20–40 fry. The female collects the eggs and incubates them for up to 14 days in her mouth. Throughout this period she does not eat, so it is essential to condition the fish well with plenty of live foods before attempting to spawn them. Chocolate Gourami fry will accept newly hatched brine shrimp once they have been released.

● *Is it easy to tell the difference between male and female Honey Gouramis?*

The sexes look alike until they come into spawning condition, when the male takes on a rich golden-brown (honey) hue on his flanks, his throat becomes almost navy blue and the front of the anal fin looks black. The female remains drab brown with a darker brown stripe along the centre of her flanks.

● *Would you recommend dwarf gouramis for a new aquarium set-up?*

No; your tank should have been running for six months or more before you introduce these fish. Chocolate Gouramis, and to a lesser extent Honey Gouramis, are delicate and require a mature, well-planted aquarium.

● *Why are these fish sometimes called "labyrinths"?*

This common name relates to the entire Anabantidae family, and derives from the name of the accessory breathing organ on either side of their heads that allows them to breathe atmospheric air.

▲ *Although pairs of the Thick-lipped Gourami (Colisa labiosa) are a welcome and attractive addition to a community aquarium, they are best moved to another tank to breed.*

Representative Species

	maximum adult size
Colisa sota Honey Gourami	2in (5cm)
Colisa fasciata Giant Gourami, Banded Gourami	4in (10cm)
Colisa labiosa Thick-lipped Gourami	4in (10cm)
Colisa lalia Dwarf Gourami	2in (5cm)
Sphaerichthys osphronemoides Chocolate Gourami	2in (5cm)
Trichopsis pumilis Dwarf Croaking Gourami	1in (2.5cm)
Trichopsis vittatus Croaking Gourami	2.5in (6cm)

Giant Gourami
FAMILY: OSPHRONEMIDAE

THE LARGEST OF THE GOURAMIS, THE GIANT Gourami, is prized as a food fish in its native lands – eastern India, Malaysia, Java, China – where it is farmed commercially.

Young specimens of some 1–2in (2.5–5cm) are always available in the hobby, and people buy them without realizing that their growth rate is phenomenal and their potential adult size of 18in (46cm) frightening. Young specimens are quarrelsome among themselves but as they mature they become loners. Giant Gouramis should be kept with fish of a similar size to themselves, otherwise smaller fish will be eaten. You should only buy these fish if you can commit to keeping them for many years and if you can provide suitable accommodation for them.

Because of their size, few people choose to breed these creatures in an aquarium but, if you like a challenge, they can be bred at six months old. They build a floating nest of plant debris just below the water surface. The large eggs take up to 30 days to hatch; the male continues to guard it for a further 15–20 days until the fry are ready to fend for themselves.

Q&A...

● *I have a large Giant Gourami that I can no longer cope with. What can I do with it?*

There is no easy answer. Large specimens are virtually unsaleable. Public aquaria and retail outlets are swamped with offers of fish that have outgrown their tanks. If you can find someone willing to take the fish, be prepared to give it away.

● *Is it possible to sex Giant Gouramis?*

Yes. In males, the dorsal and anal fins are pointed and, during the spawning season, his lips thicken; in females they are rounded.

● *How large can I expect them to grow?*

In a home aquarium, they may attain 16–18in (41–46cm) but they can be larger. In the wild they can grow in excess of 24in (61cm).

▲ *The colour and body shape of the Giant Gourami (Osphronemus gourami) varies from juvenile to adult. Young specimens have a delicately pointed snout and a relatively slim body. As they mature, they develop a heavier, more thick-set appearance.*

Tank Conditions and Care

HABITAT: An aquarium with some cover provided by large pieces of wood to which Java Fern can be attached. Floating plants can also be used to provide shelter.

Tank size Min 48x18x18in (122x46x46cm), but be prepared to provide a larger aquarium.

pH	6.5–8.0
dH	To 25°
Temperature	20–30°C (68–86°F)
Water changes	15–20% every 7–10 days

Filtration Very efficient filtration – trickle combined with external canister filters.

Lighting Sufficient to be able to observe the fish. If growing large, robust specimen plants, spotlights are essential.

FEEDING: Omnivorous; will take flake and pellet foods, peas and pieces of banana.

HEALTH: Not susceptible to disease provided water quality is maintained.

Combtails FAMILY: BELONTIIDAE

COMBTAILS ARE FOUND IN SOUTHEAST ASIA, with the true Combtail (*Belontia signata*) occurring in Sri Lanka and Hasselt's Combtail (*B. hasselti*) in Borneo, Java, Sumatra and Singapore, where they inhabit still or slow-moving bodies of water.

Although they are fairly easy to keep, these fish are not generally recommended for beginners because of their belligerent attitude, which becomes more pronounced as they grow. Young specimens may be kept in a community tank, but when they mature and pair off they harass not only each other but also other fish. Adult *B. signata* reach about 5in (12.5cm), while *B. hasselti* can grow somewhat larger, up to 7.5in (19cm).

Combtails are fairly easy to breed. *Belontia signata* builds a single air bubble-nest beneath a large plant leaf and places its eggs in it. *Belontia hasselti* uses the more familiar bubble-nest, made out of a single layer of bubbles, in which to raise its offspring. As males can become very pugnacious at this time you may need to remove the female for her own safety. Raising the fry is relatively straightforward, using newly hatched brine shrimp and even fine flake.

Tank Conditions and Care

HABITAT:	Planted aquarium with plenty of cover in the form of caves and thickets of plants.
Tank size	Min 36x15x15in (91x38x38cm)
pH	6.5–7.5
dH	To 25° (*B. signata*); to 35° (*B. hasselti*)
Temperature	24–28°C (75–83°F)
Water changes	15–20% every 10–14 days
Filtration	Efficient filtration with gentle water flow
Lighting	Brightly lit to grow sufficient plants to provide sheltered conditions for the fish

FEEDING: Omnivorous fish, they take flake but frozen meaty foods such as bloodworm and chopped mussel or live foods are preferred. They also benefit from some vegetable matter.

HEALTH: Reasonably robust fish, so long as water conditions are well maintained.

Q&A...

● *My fish are spawning but the bubble-nest quickly breaks up. How can I prevent this?*

The parents will keep adding to the bubble-nest until the fry are ready to leave. In an aquarium, however, water turbulence may cause the nest to disintegrate before the fish can repair it. To avoid this, you should reduce or redirect the water flow from filter returns and airstones to create a calm area.

● *Each time my fish breed I get a few good-quality fish and a lot that don't grow very much. Why is this?*

In a word, bullying. The larger fish prevent the smaller ones from getting to the food. Move the larger fish to another aquarium, thus allowing the others to grow on. Repeat this process if necessary. You will still get some runts in the brood, but their numbers will be greatly reduced.

● *How do I differentiate the sexes?*

Males have pointed dorsal and anal fins, which are used for display during courtship. The colours of the male also deepen at this time.

▲ *The Combtail* (Belontia signata) *has a reputation as a bully in the community tank. You will need to choose its tank companions carefully.*

Fighters FAMILY: BELONTIIDAE

THANKS TO THE FLAMBOYANT FINNAGE OF THE males, Siamese Fighters are among the most popular fish with new aquarists. The trouble is, this finnage can be their downfall when they are kept in the community aquarium. Male *Betta splendens* are renowned for their belligerence: two males will fight to the death, and this character has been exploited for centuries in sporting bouts in their native Thailand. They were first bred in around 1850 to accentuate their pugnacious characters; they then became popular as ornamental fish and were bred to enhance their finnage and colour. Females are drab in comparison. Their finnage is shorter and, although they are available in the same colours as the males, their colour is less intense. Females may also have darker stripes along their flanks. Several females may be kept together but males should be kept individually.

Some of the other species of *Betta* are not so much trouble to keep. *Betta bellica*, for example, is an appropriate choice for a quiet community aquarium and several pairs can be kept together, although they should be separated for breeding. A pair of *B. pugnax* may also be housed in a peaceful community tank.

Breeding Fighters

The majority of fighters are bubble-nest builders. They require a tank with warm, shallow water (6in/15cm). Clumps of plants should be placed in the aquarium to provide an anchor for the nest and also shelter for the female. The water should be still, so disconnect filters and aerators. The male wraps himself around the female beneath the nest and she simultaneously expels eggs and milt. After the pair break their embrace, the male catches any eggs that are falling to the bottom and spits them into the bubble-nest. The process is repeated until the female is spent. At this time it is wise to remove the female for her own safety and leave the male to his parental guard duties. The eggs hatch in about

Representative Species

	maximum adult size
Betta splendens Siamese Fighter	2.5in (6cm)
Betta picta Java Fighter	2.5in (6cm)
Betta pugnax Penang Mouthbrooding Fighter	4in (10cm)
Betta bellica Striped Fighter	4in (10cm)
Betta imbelis No common name	2in (5cm)

▼ *The male Siamese Fighters (Betta splendens var.) shown here squaring up to one another would soon rip each other's fins to pieces. Two male fighters should never, therefore, be kept in the same aquarium.*

24 hours and the fry should be given very fine foods such as infusoria followed by newly hatched brine shrimp.

Betta pugnax, on the other hand, is a mouthbrooder. The female produces 10–20 eggs which are caught by the male in his cupped anal fin. The female then takes the eggs in her mouth and "spits" them into the male's mouth for him to brood. This process is repeated until the pair have produced up to 100 eggs. As with the other species of *Betta*, infusoria followed by newly hatched brine shrimp are the first foods for the fry of *B. pugnax*.

Q & A...

● *Fighters are kept in small pots in my local shop. Why? I thought they needed to be kept warm!*

For years, the fish trade kept their male Siamese Fighters in individual pots rather than putting each one into a separate tank with other fish because the other fish would often shred the fighter's fins. Fighters need to be kept warm, and also require good water conditions, and any reputable fish supplier will keep them like this. Partitioned fighter display tanks have been designed, but with a large enough system to allow the water to be kept heated and filtered.

● *Can I keep a male fighter in my community tank?*

Male fighters should only be kept in a very peaceful community aquarium. Their trailing fins are too tempting to other fish such as some of the barbs, livebearers and larger tetras, who harass the fighter, nipping at its fins. The fighter will hide away and may die. You have a choice; remove the fin nippers, or keep the fighter in another tank.

Tank Conditions and Care

HABITAT: Planted tank, either a species tank or a quiet community aquarium. For breeding, a specially set-up aquarium.

Tank size 18x10x10in (46x25x25cm) for species tank or breeding; 24x12x12in (61x30x30cm) if keeping in a community.

pH   Varied. Check according to species, especially if you are intending to breed them. *Betta splendens* will tolerate 6.0–8.0, others are more specific.

dH   Varied. Check according to species, especially if you are intending to breed them. *Betta splendens* will tolerate up to 25°, others, e.g. *Betta pugnax*, need softer water to 12°.

Temperature   22–28°C (72–82°F). Some have a very specific range – check first!

Water changes   10–15% every 10–15 days

Lighting   Enough to maintain plant growth, but with some darker regions.

FEEDING: Mostly omnivorous. Will accept flake foods. Bloodworm and mosquito larvae, either live or frozen, are recommended.

HEALTH: Some can be delicate and difficult to acclimatize to the tank. Fungal and bacterial infections are usually caused by fin nipping, poor water conditions or low temperatures.

Other Anabantoids

FAMILIES: ANABANTIDAE
AND BELONTIIDAE

THREE OTHER GROUPS OF ANABANTOIDS ARE worthy of mention: paradise fish, a commonly available Asian group; the Climbing Perch, also from Asia but less readily available; and bush fish from Africa, which are becoming increasingly popular in the hobby.

PARADISE FISH

Macropodus opercularis. Like all anabantoids, the Paradise Fish frequently takes in atmospheric air from just above the water line. This is stored in the cavity at the back of the head that houses the labyrinth lung-like organ. Here the oxygen is separated from the air and dispersed into the bloodstream.

The colour of Paradise Fish varies greatly with differing water conditions. Peaceful for most of the time, they do become a little aggressive, especially among their own species during breeding.

Male Paradise Fish can be easily distinguished from females, being far more colourful and with fin extensions that are lacking in the females. Breeding is relatively easy – indeed, it is hard to stop once pairings have been made. Eggs are deposited in a bubble-nest built at the surface, reinforced with bits of loose vegetation and guarded by the male. This process leads temporarily to an untidy-looking tank, but the thrill of breeding these fish usually makes up for this.

▼ *One of the earliest fish imported into Europe (the Goldfish was the first), the Paradise Fish* (Macropodus opercularis) *arrived in France in 1869. Since then, it has remained a popular species.*

▶ *The Brown Spike-tailed Paradise Fish* (Parosphromenus dayi) *from Southeast Asia is a gentle fish that is best kept in a planted aquarium with others of a similar disposition.*

Tank Conditions and Care
Paradise Fish

HABITAT: Fairly densely planted tank, with floating plants. Water movement should be slight. Do not keep fin-nippers such as Tiger Barbs as tank companions.

Tank size 36x12x12in (91x30x30cm) as a community tank, though 18x10x10in (46x25x 25cm) is adequate for breeding purposes.

pH	6.5–7.2
dH	8–18°
Temperature	22–26.5°C (72–80°F)

Water changes 10% once a month unless breeding, in which case leave changing the water until breeding is completed.

Filtration Small internal power filter with gradual flow, air-lift filter, or undergravel filtration. The last type should not be used for breeding purposes, as fry may be sucked into the gravel.

Lighting Moderate lighting levels required. Much of the lighting will be masked by the presence of floating plants.

FEEDING: Omnivorous, with a preference for small, live foods or their frozen equivalents.

HEALTH: Relatively hardy, though susceptible to the more common aquarium ailments such as whitespot. Avoid draughts of cold air just above the water surface, as these kill fry and can also take a toll of adult specimens. Provide a tight-fitting cover glass.

● *What is the best way to keep a Paradise Fish?*

... Although it is tempting when buying Paradise Fish to select only the more colourful and finer-finned males, if you wish your males to continue displaying their finery, then provide them with females to show off to! Paradise Fish like well-planted tanks, with abundant floating plants. Water movement should not be too strong. Finally, ensure there are places in the tank where the females can take refuge; males can become aggressive during spawning, so these retreats are much needed.

● *How can I get my Paradise Fish to start breeding?*

Paradise Fish will readily spawn in the community aquarium. However, a separate breeding tank will allow you greater control over the environment and save the fry from being eaten by other fish. Feed copious amounts of live foods such as *Daphnia*, mosquito and gnat larvae (glassworm) to bring both sexes into condition. Then gradually increase the water temperature over one week from 22–24°C (72–75°F) to around 25–26°C (77–79°F).

Representative Species

Paradise Fish	maximum adult size
Macropodus opercularis Paradise Fish	4in (10cm)
Pseudosphromenus cupanus Spike-tailed Paradise Fish	3in (7.5cm)
Parosphromenus dayi Brown Spike-tailed Paradise Fish	3in (7.5cm)
Climbing Perch	
Anabas testudineus Climbing Perch, Climbing Bass	8in (20cm)

Bush Fish	
Ctenopoma acutirostre Leopard Bush Fish, Leopard Ctenopoma	6in (15cm)
Ctenopoma ansorgii No common name	3.5in (8.5cm)
Ctenopoma kingsleyae Kingsley's Bush Fish, Kingsley's Ctenopoma	6in (15cm)
Ctenopoma oxyrhynchus Mottled Bush Fish, Mottled Ctenopoma	4in (10cm)

CLIMBING PERCH

Anabas testudineus. The Climbing Perch originates from the tropical freshwaters of India, Indonesia and the Malay peninsula. The species tends to be a little pugnacious but, like the bush fish of Africa, can easily be kept in an aquarium with other similar-sized species. It is very resilient to the misdemeanours of the aquarist and tolerates quite wide but gradual fluctuations in water quality.

Climbing Perch are known to migrate overland through damp grass in search of other bodies of water. This they do by writhing on their sides, using their comb-like operculum (gill cover) as a claw.

The common name of the species derives from the fact that the first specimen was found in a lower branch of a tree next to a stream. It was thought that the fish had climbed the tree in the course of overland migration. This is now known not to be the case. More likely, the individual found had either been caught by a fish-eating bird and discarded on the branch, or had settled on the branch while the tree was submerged, and had become marooned as the waters receded.

▲ *The Climbing Perch* (Anabas testudineus) *has a comb-like operculum which is extremely sharp. You should exercise great care when handling these fish to avoid getting cut.*

Tank Conditions and Care
Climbing Perch

HABITAT: Fairly densely planted aquarium with retreats.

Tank size	48x12x12in (122x30x30cm)
pH	6.5–7.5
dH	10–20°
Temperature	22–25.5°C (72–78°F)

Water changes Infrequent. Around 10% every six weeks.

Filtration Subgravel or internal power filter with only moderate flow.

Lighting	Subdued

FEEDING: Omnivorous; will accept flake, pellets, lettuce, peas, spinach, and a variety of live foods.

HEALTH: This species is quite hardy. It was one of the first tropical fish to appear in public aquaria across Europe.

Tank Conditions and Care
Bush Fish

HABITAT: A planted aquarium with abundant wood (bog wood or vine roots) in which to lurk.

Tank size	48x15x15in (122x38x38cm)
pH	6.5–7.2
dH	6–20°
Temperature	22–25.5°C (72–78°F)
Water changes	10–15% every month. Replace with matured water rather than straight from the tap.
Filtration	Sub-gravel or internal power filter with only moderate flow.
Lighting	Subdued

FEEDING: Carnivorous; feed small, meaty foods either live or frozen.

HEALTH: A pretty hardy group of fish, though they can succumb to the usual aquatic diseases. Sickly looking specimens can often be revived with a little peat extract (available from your local aquatic shop).

● *Can Climbing Perch be sexed?*

Yes, sexing them is straightforward. The anal fin is larger on males than on females, and males also exhibit slightly more striking coloration.

● *What foods are suited to Climbing Perch?*

Climbing Perch are omnivorous, accepting flake or pelleted food, lettuce and peas, and aquatic invertebrates such as insect larvae.

● *Can I keep bush fish with Climbing Perch and Paradise Fish?*

I see no reason why not, though Combtails would be preferable to Paradise Fish, as the latter are generally smaller. All these fish are anabantoids, and as such have auxiliary air-breathing apparatus, and so would make for an ideal "theme" tank.

● *What is the best way for me to keep* Ctenopoma ansorgii?

This is one of the smaller species, and requires a hardness of 5–15°, a pH of 6.5–7.5 and slightly warmer water (26°C; 79°F) than other bush fish. Provide these fish with lots of plant cover as a place of refuge, but also leave open areas in the aquarium for them to swim in.

BUSH FISH

Ctenopoma species are occasionally also referred to as "climbing fish" for similar reasons to the Climbing Perch. The bush fish are from the tropical freshwaters of west and central Africa. They are more voracious than Paradise Fish, with a predilection for live aquatic invertebrates and small fish. Although not normally aggressive, careful selection is required of fellow inhabitants in a community aquarium to avoid costly mistakes.

Bush fish have a protrusile jaw, carefully designed to shoot forward a considerable distance, and with a large gape. These features help them to capture their prey. For most of the time, bush fish remain still, camouflaged both by their inconspicuous coloration and by hiding among vegetation, constantly on the look-out for possible morsels of food.

The majority of bush fish tend to be drab; however, certain species are more colourful, such as *C. ansorgii* and *C. acutirostre*. Also, some adult specimens (generally males) of *C. kingsleyae*, though drab grey over much of their bodies, exhibit a striking thin pearl edging to their fins.

Bush fish generally prefer to be kept in small communities of four or six specimens, depending on the size of tank.

▲ *The Leopard Bush Fish* (Ctenopoma acutirostre), *which comes from Africa, is not a community fish in the accepted sense, as it shows a propensity to consume its smaller tankmates.*

Rainbow Fish ORDER: ATHERINIFORMES

IT IS NOT DIFFICULT TO SEE HOW rainbow fish came by their name. Not only are their colours very striking, but the iridescent sheen of their bodies also takes on different hues depending on how it catches the light.

There are three main groups. First the atherinids, with the better-known species *Bedotia geayi* from Madagascar and *Telmatherina ladigesi* from Sulawesi. Secondly, there are the melanotaenids from Irian Jaya, New Guinea and tropical regions of northern and eastern Australia. Representative species include *Chilatherina axelrodi*, *C. bleheri*, *Melanotaenia lacustris* and *M. boesemani*. For many years very few species were available to hobbyists, with only a handful more known to science. Since the late 1970s, however, newer species have been discovered, bred, and made available to the aquarist.

Finally, there are the *Pseudomugil* species from Australia and New Guinea. They are difficult to acclimatize to the aquarium, which is probably why they are rarely offered for sale.

● *What species would you recommend as an introduction to keeping rainbow fish?*

Many of the melanotaenids are both easy to keep and relatively straightforward to breed. The beautiful blue sheen of the male *Melanotaenia lacustris* intensifies as it displays to the females. *Melanotaenia herbertaxelrodi* mixes red, blue and golden hues, and can be spawned with little difficulty. Or try *Glossolepis incisus*, the Red Rainbow. The females of this species look a little drab compared to the males.

● *How do I sex rainbow fish?*

Males are more colourful than females and the first dorsal fin, when laid flat, extends beyond the start of the second dorsal fin. This can be used to distinguish juvenile specimens in a dealer's tank, where colour has not fully developed, and there may be more than one species in the same tank. Juveniles are cheaper, and you have the joy of watching them mature.

▲ *The Splendid Rainbow Fish* (Melanotaenia splendida) *is a slim fish when young, but the body deepens, especially in males, as the fish mature.*

Representative Species

	maximum adult size
Bedotia geayi Madagascan Rainbow Fish	6in (15cm)
Telmatherina ladigesi Celebes Rainbow Fish	2.75in (7cm)
Chilatherina axelrodi Axelrod's Rainbow Fish	3.5in (8.5cm)
Chilatherina bleheri Bleher's Rainbow Fish	4in (10cm)
Glossolepis incisus Red Rainbow Fish	4in (10cm)
Iriatherina werneri Thread-fin Rainbow Fish	2in (5cm)
Melanotaenia boesemani Boeseman's Rainbow Fish	4in (10cm)
Melanotaenia herbertaxelrodi Lake Tebera Rainbow Fish	4in (10cm)
Melanotaenia lacustris Lake Kutubu Rainbow Fish	4in (10cm)
Melanotaenia splendida Splendid Rainbow Fish	4in (10cm)
Pseudomugil furcatus Forktailed Rainbow Fish	2.25in (5.5cm)
Pseudomugil signifer Australian Blue-eye Rainbow Fish	2in (5cm)

Tank Conditions and Care

HABITAT: Planted tank with large open swimming areas. Fine-leaved plant or a spawning mop is required for breeding these fish.

Tank size 48x15x15–18in (122x38x38–46cm). *Pseudomugil* species, if using a dedicated species tank, can be raised and spawned in a 24x12x12in (61x30x30cm) aquarium.

pH Varies according to species: 5.7–6.5 for *Iratherina werneri*, to 7.5–8.0 for *Melanotaenia herbertaxelrodi*. *Pseudomugil* spp. prefer about pH 7.0. If unsure, then aim for a neutral pH (7.0).

dH 7–15°

Temperature 22–26°C (72–79°F). Some species require more than 27°C (81°F).

Water changes 10–15% every 10–15 days. Spawning often follows a water change.

Filtration Very efficient to maintain water quality. Use a power/trickle filter combination.

Lighting Reasonably high lighting levels, but with some darker regions for retreat.

FEEDING: Mostly omnivorous. Will accept flake foods, but for best colour and breeding condition, bloodworm or mosquito larvae, live or frozen foods.

HEALTH: Fairly hardy, except for the *Pseudomugil* spp. which are rather delicate. Expect the usual diseases such as whitespot, which can easily be remedied with commercially available cures.

▲ *The Madagascan Rainbow Fish* (Bedotia geayi) *can be difficult to acclimatize. Neutral to slightly alkaline, medium-hard water conditions are preferred.*

▲ *The long, trailing fin filaments and the lyre-shaped caudal fin of the male Thread-fin Rainbow Fish* (Iriatherina werneri) *make it an eye-catching fish.*

Keeping Your Rainbows

In the wild, rainbow fish live in small creeks, streams, rivers, lakes, or even brackish waters. Most are omnivorous, but should be fed live aquatic invertebrates such as mosquito larvae, and bloodworm. This is particularly recommended to bring the rainbows into breeding condition, and for new introductions to the tank.

Atherinids and melanotaenids are fairly hardy community fish, though many mclanotacnids grow to around 3–4in (7.5–10cm), need lots of open swimming space and may bully smaller fish. Atherinids on the other hand, especially the Celebes Rainbow (*Telmatherina ladigesi*), have flowing fins that attract fin-nippers. *Pseudomugil* species are best kept in a species tank.

Most rainbow fish can be bred fairly easily in a community tank. They scatter adhesive eggs among fine-leaved plants or a spawning mop (see Breeding, pages 56–57). No parental care is offered. The eggs should be removed to an isolated hatching and rearing tank. Hatching time varies with species. Newly hatched fry should be fed infusoria for the first few weeks, followed by newly hatched *Artemia* and small *Daphnia*.

Do not mix too many species in one tank, as some species will cross-breed. Ideally, stock one male to two females; since males can become aggressive during breeding, this will reduce the strain on the females. Better still, keep a small number (perhaps six to eight) of the same species, as rainbows do like to·shoal.

Snakeheads FAMILY: CHANNIDAE

SNAKEHEADS ARE TO BE FOUND IN TROPICAL Africa and southern Asia though, because of their economic value as a food resource, they have been introduced into other areas including Hawaii, Japan and Korea. Snakeheads are predatory, feeding on other fish, frogs and snakes. Their common name derives from the native name "Cobra fish" for the larger Asian species, so-called because of their painful (though non-poisonous) bite if handled carelessly.

Many species can reach a length in excess of 30in (76cm) and are very powerful swimmers and jumpers. They also grow extremely quickly, especially the larger species.

Using Air to Live

In common with the anabantoids, snakeheads have an accessory breathing organ at the back of the head. The gills are insufficient on their own to perform oxygen exchange from the water, and

▲ *You should beware of buying attractive young specimens of the Red-striped Snakehead* (Channa micropeltes), *as they quickly develop into large, mundanely coloured adults.*

Representative Species

	maximum adult size
Parachanna obscura No common name	12in (30cm)
Parachanna africana African Snakehead	12in (30cm)
Channa orientalis Oriental Snakehead	8in (20cm)
Channa striata Striped Snakehead	15in (38cm)
Channa micropeltes Red-striped Snakehead	39in (1m)
Channa argus Spotted Snakehead	34in (86cm)

so this supplementary organ is essential, even when the waters in which they live are abundant with dissolved oxygen. Thus snakeheads must have access to the atmosphere in order to survive. Newly hatched snakeheads lack the ability to utilize air, but within one month are capable of doing so.

Particularly during seasonal periods of low, poorly oxygenated water, this ability to utilize air comes into its own. At such times, snakeheads can migrate overland through moist vegetation in search of other bodies of water. They can also survive by burrowing into the mud until the next rainy season replenishes the waters.

One of the main problems for the aquarist in purchasing snakeheads is that the colour of juvenile specimens may differ quite considerably from that of adults. For example, Red striped Snakeheads (*Channa micropeltes*) only have the striking coloration that gives them their name while they are young. Also bear in mind snakeheads' dietary requirements and potential size before deciding to buy. Yet despite their drawbacks, ownership of these inquisitive fish can be highly rewarding. Over time, many species become reasonably tame, and can recognize – and, more importantly, refrain from biting – the hand that feeds them.

Q & A

● *Are there any species suitable for a smaller, 4ft (1.2m) tank?*

... *Parachanna obscura*, from West Africa, grows to around 12in (30cm) and is rather attractively coloured. Another African species is *Parachanna africana*, which again grows to 12in (30cm). The Sri Lankan species *Channa orientalis* can attain a similar size in nature, though only around 8in (20cm) in the aquarium. Ensure that fellow tank inmates are large enough to remain uneaten.

● *Can these smaller species be bred in captivity?*

Although *Parachanna africana* has been bred, this is not a practical proposition for the hobbyist as it requires a very large tank. In their natural habitat, snakeheads build a floating raft-like nest at the water's edge out of vegetation harvested from the plants that grow there. This would be extremely difficult to emulate in the home.

● *Do I have to feed live fish to snakeheads?*

No, in most cases alternatives can be used. Try chunks of beef-heart and fresh fish, fed in moderation to avoid fouling the tank. Smaller specimens will readily accept frozen fish foods such as shrimp, prawn and mussel, though here it is even more imperative to ensure all food is eaten and not left to rot in the tank. They may also be fed earthworms, but grade the size of the worm to the size of the fish being fed – small fish cannot eat large worms!

Tank Conditions and Care

HABITAT: Gravel substrate; aquarium can be planted, though snakeheads are not particular about tank decor. Provide a heavy cover glass, weighted down to prevent escapes.

Tank size For smaller species 36–48x15x15in (91–122x38x38cm). For larger species from 60x18x 18in (152x46x46cm). A well-fitting cover over the tank is required.

pH	6.5–7.5 (not critical but avoid extremes)
dH	To 20°
Temperature	23–28°C (73–83°F)

Water changes Approximately 10% once a month. Snakeheads are fairly tolerant of varying water conditions, but the water should not become polluted with uneaten food.

Filtration Water should not be too turbid. For larger specimens an external power filter, with a gradual flow, is best. Smaller snakehead tanks can be filtered internally with a submersible power filter.

Lighting Not too bright. Snakeheads, particularly sub-adults and adults, lead a sedentary existence and prefer subdued light conditions. The juveniles of the larger species are more active and inquisitive.

FEEDING: Garden worms, and frozen foods such as mussels, prawn, whitebait, and beef-heart. Try using maggots to raise small juvenile specimens.

HEALTH: Fairly hardy. Ensure the temperature does not fall too low, as this is probably the greatest threat to their wellbeing. Jumping out of the tank is a common problem, particularly with the larger Asian species, though if your prized snakehead is found on the floor, seemingly dead, try to resuscitate it by returning it to the tank. Suspend it in a net near the water surface where, if still alive, it can exercise both its gills and its accessory breathing apparatus. Bacterial infections can be a problem if conditions are poor.

Gobies
FAMILIES: ELEOTRIDAE AND GOBIIDAE

THE GOBIES THAT WE SEE IN THE AQUARIUM trade belong to two families: the Eleotridae (sleeper gobies) and the Gobiidae (true gobies). They are distinguished by the ventral fins, which are separate in the Eleotridae and united to form a cup-shaped sucker in the Gobiidae. They have elongate bodies and two separate dorsal fins, the first of which has short, flexible spines while the second has soft rays and, in some species, a single spine. The caudal fin is rounded. Many are fairly sedentary, bottom-dwelling fish that dart rapidly about the tank in search of food. All can be territorial, especially when breeding, so be sure to provide suitable nooks and crannies.

Gobies inhabit fresh, brackish and marine waters around the world. Some species are totally freshwater, some live in brackish waters and others are totally marine. Species such as *Tateurndina ocellicauda* are suitable for softwater, community aquaria. Of those listed here, most prefer brackish conditions in a specially set-up aquarium, not necessarily a species tank, but one with other brackish-water fish and plants.

▲ *Given the right conditions, the Peacock Goby* (Tateurndina ocellicauda) *will breed readily in your tank. Raise the fry on brine shrimp.*

● *What are the ideal conditions for keeping Bumblebee Gobies?*

... Although sold as freshwater fish, Bumblebee Gobies actually prefer harder, slightly saline water. To accommodate them, set up a hardwater aquarium and add 1–2 tablespoons of aquarium salt per 2.1 gallons (10 litres) of water. Don't try to introduce them to a well-established community tank containing soft, slightly acidic water – under these circumstances, the Peacock Goby is your best option.

● *I have bought a* Gobioides broussonnetii. *Is this species suited to a community tank?*

These fish are predatory, and so are definitely not suitable community fish. They can grow to a considerable size and are territorial and belligerent, even among themselves. Therefore, set up a species tank for them, containing brackish water. A soft substrate is essential as they like to bury themselves and to create a number of hiding places in the tank. Provide them with plenty of meaty foods, which they will take from the substrate. Small worms, aquatic insect larvae (e.g. caddis grubs) and *Asellus* (water louse, or sow bug) are avidly eaten. They will also accept dead foods such as bits of shrimp and fish.

Representative Species

	maximum adult size
Brachygobius xanthozona Bumblebee Goby	1.75in (4.5cm)
Periophthalmus papillio Butterfly Mudskipper	6in (15cm)
Stigmatogobius sadanundio Spotted Goby	3.5in (8.5cm)
Gobioides broussonnetii Violet Goby, Dragon Fish	24in (61cm)
Oxyeleotris marmoratus Marbled Sleeper Goby	20in (51cm)
Tateurndina ocellicauda Peacock Goby	3in (7.5cm)
Hypseleotris compressa Empire Gudgeon	4in (10cm)
Butis butis Crazy Fish	6in (15cm)

Several smaller species have been regularly bred in captivity – *T. ocellicauda* and *Brachygobius xanthozona* are prime examples. Breeding strategies vary; some species spawn in caves and under stones, while others place their eggs on rocks, wood or plants and others scatter their spawn among plants. Most practice some form of parental care, defending their eggs and fry in the same way as many of the cichlids do. Feeding the young fry is easy, as they will take newly hatched brine shrimp. Growth rate is good.

Of all the gobies, the mudskippers are probably the most bizarre. To keep them successfully, set up a long aquarium, 12in (30cm) high, with shallow water, wood, perhaps a salt-tolerant plant or two, and a sand or fine gravel "beach" at one end. Mudskippers like to come out of the water and rest with just their tails in the water; because of this, ensure that your tank has a very tight-fitting cover glass to maintain humidity.

The Crazy Fish (*Butis butis*) has the disconcerting (and unexplained) habit of floating belly-up, apparently dead. But if you attempt to take out the "body", it rights itself and swims away!

▼ *Bumblebee Gobies* (Brachygobius xanthozona) *often squabble. Check their finnage for bites and subsequent secondary infections, and treat as necessary.*

Tank Conditions and Care

HABITAT: Sand or fine gravel substrate, with plenty of caves and other hiding places. A well-planted aquarium for preference. They are territorial, so allow space for them to create and defend territories, especially when breeding.

Tank size	36x12x12in (91x30x30cm) for the smaller species; 48x15x15in (122x38x38cm) for the larger ones.
pH	6.5–7.8; check species requirements
dH	7–18°; check species requirements

Temperature 10–30°C (50–86°F) depending on species. You must check the requirements of the particular species you are keeping.

Water changes	15% every week
Filtration	Very efficient filtration to give well-oxygenated water with a slight flow.
Lighting	Fluorescent lighting sufficient to maintain plant growth.

FEEDING: For the larger species, a meaty diet, for example insects, maggots, pieces of fish and meat, and so on; smaller species will accept frozen bloodworm or brine shrimp. Live foods (*Daphnia*, bloodworm, mosquito larvae) will help to bring them into spawning condition.

HEALTH: No particular problems provided water quality is maintained.

Arowanas FAMILY: OSTEOGLOSSIDAE

THIS ANCIENT FAMILY OF FISH CAN BE TRACED back some 35–55 million years, to the Eocene period. The osteoglossids are represented in South America by *Arapaima* (one species) and *Osteoglossum* (two species), in Africa by the genus *Heterotis* (one species) and in the Indo-Australian region by *Scleropages* (three species).

They are referred to as "bony tongues" on account of a toothed bone on the floor of the mouth (the "tongue") which bites against teeth on the roof of the mouth. The swimbladder and pharynx are linked by a duct and are used for respiration. The fourth gill arch is modified into a screw-shaped organ; at one time, this was also thought to be used for respiration but recent research on *Heterotis* has showed that it is used for filter feeding.

Keeping Large Fish

These large, imposing fish are built for swimming and spend most of their time cruising the aquarium. They therefore need equally large, imposing tanks and life-support systems, and should only be kept by the dedicated aquarist who is able to provide suitable conditions, or by public aquaria. The filtration system is particularly important. Not only do these fish require clean, well-oxygenated water, they also produce copious amounts of high-protein waste. External power filters coupled with trickle filters are suitable; alternatively use a separate undertank biological filter.

Arowanas are easily frightened. They react by sweeping the body into an S-shape and leaping from the water. In an aquarium this has obvious drawbacks, so avoid frightening them. If floating plants or plants that grow to the surface are provided, the fish will take refuge among or beneath them. But for extra security, provide a heavy cover glass.

Both *Osteoglossum* and *Scleropages* species are mouthbrooders. In the wild, *Osteoglossum* is often caught with its mouth full of fry. The fry

Representative Species

	maximum adult size
Scleropages formosus Dragon Fish, Asian Arowana	36in (91cm)
Osteoglossum bicirrhosum Arowana	39in (1m)
Osteoglossum ferreirai Black Arowana	39in (1m)
Heterotis niloticus No common name	36in (91cm)

▼ *Arowanas* (Osteoglossum bicirrhosum) *can snap at each other and cause split and bitten fins. To prevent this from happening, ensure that they are not kept in cramped conditions.*

● *What companion fish can I keep with my Arowana?*

... Bottom-dwelling species such as the doradid catfish, *Oxydoras niger*, any of the larger loricariids (*Panaque* spp. or *Hypostomus* spp.), or perhaps the African bagrid, *Aucheoglanis occidentalis*, are ideal.

● *I have a large heated pond in my conservatory, partially below ground and partially above. Could I keep an Arowana in this?*

There is no reason why not; these fish are active surface dwellers and would be easily seen. The solid sides to the pond would mean the fish would not be so easily frightened. However, large specimens kept in ponds in public aquaria and zoos have been known to leap from the water and take small birds from overhanging branches! Make sure cats with tempting tails don't sit on the edge of the pond!

● *What can I use to catch my Arowana?*

You should use a deep, fine-meshed net or a home-made linen net to catch these large, nervous fish.

are then released, collected and sold to the aquarium trade. It is not uncommon to see fry offered for sale still with their yolk sacs. Such young fish are often difficult to keep alive because the yolk sac is liable to damage, especially in transit, and the resultant infections can cause death.

The Asian Arowana (*Scleropages formosus*) is listed on CITES II, which restricts the export of wild-caught specimens (see Fish and the Law, page 203). As a result, it is now being bred commercially for the aquarium trade in East Asia. Young specimens are tagged, logged and sold with a certificate, so that ownership of a particular individual can be traced. Australia prohibits the export of its two Arowana species, the Silver Barramundi (*Scleropages jardini*) and the Spotted Barramundi (*Scleropages leichardti*)

Tank Conditions and Care

HABITAT: Large aquarium with a substantial cover glass. Roots for decor; these can have Java Fern attached and perhaps specimen Amazon Swordplants. An area where the plants reach the surface or a small mat of floating plants will give the fish a "safe" haven and deter jumping. Avoid anything that the fish can dash against and dislodge their scales.

Tank size	Min 48x18x18in (122x46x46cm) for small specimens. These fish can grow quite quickly, so be prepared to rehouse them.
pH	6.5–7.0
dH	To 10°
Temperature	Around 24°C (75°F)
Water changes	15% every week

Filtration Very efficient filtration – external canister filter combined with a trickle filter to give well-oxygenated water with a good flow.

Lighting Fluorescent lighting sufficient to maintain plant growth.

FEEDING: They require a meaty diet – insects, maggots, pieces of fish and meat – but they will also take some vegetable matter such as peas. Youngsters may only take live food at first, but they can be weaned away from it. Three meals a week is enough.

HEALTH: No particular problems, provided water quality is maintained. If the fish dislodge scales or damage themselves jumping, you may need to treat for fungus or a bacterial infection.

Passive Electrogenic Fish

▲ *Peter's Elephant-nose* (Gnathonemus petersi) *can be difficult to acclimatize to the aquarium. Providing it with a diet of small live foods will help.*

PASSIVE ELECTROGENIC FISH ARE THOSE SPECIES that are capable of emitting a weak electrical signal. This creates a force field around the fish similar to that generated by a bar magnet. The fish can pick up any disturbance in this field caused by an object or another fish. By measuring the electrical potential of this interference, the fish can tell what caused it. Not only does the fish recognize the signature of the disturbance, it also knows its location and distance. One of the organs of the Electric Eel (see page 178) operates in a similar manner.

Seeing in Murky Water

There are freshwater representatives of this type of fish in Africa and South America. Almost all live in dimly lit or sediment-laden water, where visibility is poor. These fish are not related, and their electric organs have developed independently through the process of parallel evolution.

A surprisingly large number of fish – more than 200 species living in both freshwater and marine habitats – are recognized as being able to generate electricity. Whereas some employ this capacity actively for defence or predation, others use it passively, as here, as a means of finding their way around in murky waters.

The passive electrogenic fish vary enormously in size and shape. There are the mormyrids from Africa, often referred to as elephant-nose fish, which range in size according to species from around 4in (10cm) to over 2ft (61cm). Their common name derives from the long, trunk-like snout found on many mormyrids. Another African species is the large *Gymnarchus niloticus*, a belligerent eel-like fish that is predatory but uses its weak electrical generation purely for electrolocation. From tropical South America come various species, again eel-like, including *Gymnotus carapo*, and the rather delicate South American knife-fish of the genera *Apteronotus*, *Eigenmannia* and *Sternopygus*.

Representative Species

	maximum adult size
Gnathonemus petersi Peter's Elephant-nose	14in (36cm)
Campylomormyrus tamandua Elephant-nose	16.5in (42cm)
Gymnotus carapo Banded Knife-fish	24in (61cm)
Apteronotus albifrons Ghost Knife-fish	15in (38cm)
Eigenmannia virescens Transparent Knife-fish	12in (30cm)
Gymnarchus niloticus Aba Aba	60in (1.5m)

▼ *Transparent knife-fish (Eigenmannia virescens) are distinctive, in that they lack both dorsal and caudal fins. They are timid fish that are best kept as a group in a species tank.*

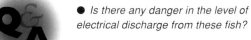

● *Is there any danger in the level of electrical discharge from these fish?*

... None whatsoever, either to the aquarist or to other tank inhabitants. The signal is very weak, only detectable by the use of sensitive measuring equipment and the fish themselves.

● *Should these fish be kept in isolation like the electric eel and electric catfish?*

Many of the passive electric fish prefer to live as a small community of like species. This is particularly true of the smaller elephant-nose fish from Africa, which appear to have quite a sophisticated social structure for fish. These fish have even been known to support and care for others that are sick.

● *If these fish are kept in small communities, don't they become confused by all the stray electric emissions? How do they know which is their signal?*

If a companion is "jamming" a fish's signal, then one or other will change the frequency to a different level. That way each individual can recognize its own signal.

● *Could I start a "theme tank" of passive electric fish?*

Yes, but mixing representatives from different continents may prove a problem, as their social structures may not be compatible. Most of the African elephant-nose mormyrid species can be kept together provided they are of similar size, as can the South American knife-fish. Both the smaller mormyrids and the knife-fish are shy, and will not take kindly to other skittish fish species. The large African *Gymnarchus* is aggressive and not suited to the conditions in a community aquarium.

Tank Conditions and Care

HABITAT: Both African and South-Central American species require reasonably dense vegetation, with secluded areas in which to hide. The elephant-noses require a soft sandy substrate.

Tank size	36–48x15x15in (91–122x38x38cm)
pH	6.0–7.5 (to 7.0 for knife-fish)
dH	To 18°
Temperature	22–27°C (72–81°F)

Water changes Approximately 15% once a month. Replace with mature water of similar temperature and chemical composition.

Filtration Slow-flowing, external mechanical filter.

Lighting Subdued, just enough to promote plant propagation.

FEEDING: Most of the species listed above are insectivorous, particularly in the juvenile stage of their development. Well-washed *Tubifex* is ideal for elephant-noses.

HEALTH: Both the elephant-noses and the knife-fish can be delicate, particularly in the early introductory period. They are susceptible to whitespot, in which case careful treatment is required. Dose with zinc-free malachite green at half the recommended strength.

Active Electrogenic Fish

FAMILIES: MALAPTERURIDAE
AND ELECTROPHORIDAE

ELECTROGENIC FISH ARE THOSE THAT POSSESS the means to generate an electric current, using either high-energy emissions for predation and defence – here defined as active – or very low electrical emissions as a form of radar (passive). Of the active emitters of electricity, there are only two freshwater varieties: the Electric Eel (*Electrophorus electricus*) and three species of electric catfish (*Malapterurus* spp.). The Electric Eel originates from the waters of the Amazon basin in South America, while electric catfish are found in the freshwaters of west and central Africa, and the Nile.

The electric organs of both the Electric Eel and electric catfish can be likened to the battery of an automobile. Each organ consists of a series of modified muscle cells, separated by a jelly-like substance that acts as the electrolytic medium. The muscles and medium are encased in tissue to form a tubular structure. The muscular action of every creature, including humans, generates a very weak electric current, but in these fish the circuitry of the electrogenic organs amplifies this into a far more potent charge.

The electrical organs of the Electric Eel are highly complex. There are three of them, each of which performs a specific task. One emits a very weak discharge, used as a form of radar to navigate the muddy waters that are the eel's habitat, while two others of varying intensity output are used for defence and predation. The more powerful organ can deliver 450 volts from an adult specimen. They are located in different areas of the fish; the main one covers much of the upper part of the body, the secondary (Hunter's) organ is located ventrally, and the weak signal used for radar purposes is situated near the tail.

In the case of the electric catfish, the electrogenic organ encapsulates almost the entire body, from just behind the head to the base of the tail. Adult electric catfish can emit some 300 volts, both for defence and for knocking out prey.

Little is known of their natural lifestyles. All active electrogenic fish are sedentary creatures, and probably only come together as a pair for short periods for spawning purposes, under which circumstances they would most likely not use the powerful electrical discharge.

Tank Conditions and Care

HABITAT: Aquarium with few if any other inhabitants, dimly lit, with plenty of hiding places. Note the comments in the Q&A regarding handling.

Tank size Electric Eels are not recommended for the domestic aquarium, but if you do decide to keep them at home, then using a large tank (6–8ft/ 183–244cm) right from the outset will obviate the need to transfer the fish as it grows. Ensure it has a strong, tight cover. A minimum 3ft (91cm) tank will suffice for an electric catfish; rarely do the fish realize their full natural size in the aquarium.

pH	6.5–7.5; not critical for any species
dH	To 15°
Temperature	22–25°C (72–77°F)

Water changes 10% every month. Be careful not to disturb or frighten the fish in the process.

Filtration High-efficiency mechanical external devices needed. These can be muck-generating fish.

Lighting Dim lights. Place the aquarium away from direct sunlight in order to avoid shadows that might frighten the fish.

FEEDING: Both the Electric Eel and electric catfish are predators. Live foods in the form of other fish is required, though electric catfish will often accept live earthworms.

HEALTH: These are hardy fish, more likely to suffer damage from contact with sharp objects or aquarium heaters than through disease. Having no scales, they can easily be burned by lying against the aquarium heater for warmth. Position the heater carefully so as to avoid this.

Representative Species

	maximum adult size
Electrophorus electricus Electric Eel	79in (2m)
Malapterurus electricus Electric Catfish	24in (61cm)
Malapterurus minjiriya Electric Catfish	39in (1m)
Malapterurus microstoma Electric Catfish	26in (66cm)

▲ *Electric Catfish* (Malapterurus electricus) *require nooks and crannies to lurk in, otherwise they may hide beneath heaters and suffer burns.*

▼ *The Electric Eel* (Electrophorus electricus) *should only be kept by experienced aquarists.*

● *How do I handle my Electric Eel or catfish?*

... With extreme caution! The level of electrical discharge is weak in young specimens, though in juveniles of both groups it will be noticeable. The main hunting and defence organs work like the condenser in a camera flashgun: once the discharge is released it takes time to regenerate – for an electric catfish around 10–15 minutes. However, you do not know whether the full discharge has been emitted! Remember the Electric Eel has two powerful electric organs, so while one may have been discharged, the other may still be on full charge. Use a plastic rather than a wire-framed net when handling very young specimens. Water is a good conductor of electricity, so wear rubber gloves.

● *What size of Electric Eel or catfish can I keep?*

An Electric Eel can grow to 6.5ft (2m) or more, and any specimen larger than 8–10in (20–25cm) will be too big for most domestic installations. The discharge of an adult Electric Eel is strong enough to be felt though electricians' gauntlets. Unless you can detect the state of charge, leave well alone. Electric catfish, on the other hand, can be kept in the home aquarium. The discharge is most unlikely to be fatal to a healthy human, thanks to the relatively low amperage. But make no mistake – you will know all about it should it happen! The precautions above hold good for sub-adult electric catfish. This species will probably not attain full size, in excess of 2ft (61cm) in the tank at home, so its full electrical power is unlikely to be achieved. Even after death, electric fish can still emit an electrical discharge. The charge will gradually decay over a period of about 48 hours.

● *What would you say to someone wishing to keep an electric catfish?*

Electric catfish, though not recommended to the novice fishkeeper, can provide an interesting challenge. These are solitary creatures. Most other tank inhabitants may be sought-after as food. Larger fish may suffer electrocution as the catfish seeks to defend itself from what it may perceive as a threat. This is a fish that prefers live food, mainly fish, though specimens will often take live earthworms. (Hand feeding, naturally, is not recommended.)

Bichirs and Reedfish
FAMILY: POLYPTERIDAE

THE POLYPTERIDAE OR LOBE-FINNED PIKES ARE natives of tropical Africa. Their lineage can be traced back 60 million years or more through the fossil record to the Tertiary or even late Cretaceous periods. Nowadays they are represented by two genera, *Polypterus* and *Erpetoichthys*. Elongate, sinuous fish, they have ganoid (diamond-shaped) scales covering the whole of their bodies. For continuous swimming the fish move with a snake-like body motion, but for short distances they just use their fan-shaped pectoral fins to execute gentle manoeuvres. The dorsal fin is composed of several small finlets.

The Polypteridae are unusual in having a lung linked to the intestine. This structure acts as an accessory breathing apparatus, allowing them to survive in oxygen-deficient waters. However well-oxygenated your aquarium, these fish must be allowed access to the water surface to take in air, otherwise they will die.

Preventing Escapes

Keeping these fish poses no real problems. They should have a planted tank for preference – they are fond of lying among and beneath plants – otherwise be sure to provide other hiding places. Given enough space, these creatures are generally placid but, if overcrowded either with their own kind or with other fish, they can become territorial and very belligerent. A tightly fitting cover glass is essential, as they will get out of even the tiniest of openings, Reedfish especially.

Tank Conditions and Care

HABITAT: Planted tank with sand or rounded gravel substrate. Use a tight-fitting cover glass.

Tank size	Min 36x12x12in (91x30x30cm)
pH	6.5–7.0
dH	To 10° depending on species
Temperature	22–28°C (72–82°F) depending on species.
Water changes	15% every 10–14 days
Filtration	Efficient filtration
Lighting	Fluorescent lighting sufficient to maintain plant growth.

FEEDING: As carnivores, they require a mainly meaty diet – morsels of fish and meat, worms, insect larvae, etc, all chopped to a size that the fish can take without choking. Established specimens will also eat tablet and pelleted foods.

HEALTH: No particular problems.

▶ *Marbled Bichirs* (Polypterus palmas) *are, for the most part, peaceful with other fish that are too large to be considered as food, and those that do not aggravate them. However, they have a tendency to be aggressive towards their own kind.*

Catching and moving fish can also be tricky. Use a deep net that you can close with your hand at the top, just beneath the frame, thus preventing the fish from slithering up the side of the net and out onto the floor.

It is also advisable to choose companion fish with care. If they are too small, they will become food for a hungry bichir or Reedfish; if too quarrelsome, the Reedfish or bichirs may be harassed by the other fish picking at their fins until they become ragged and torn. Ideal tank companions would be midwater fish, such as the larger barbs.

Some species have been bred in captivity but reports are sketchy. In *Polypterus ornatipinnis*, the male initiates the courtship proceedings. The fish become restless and chase around the tank. Then, when spawning occurs, he positions his cupped anal fin beneath the female's anal orifice to collect and fertilize the eggs which are then placed among vegetation. At 26°C (79°F) the eggs hatch in about four days.

Representative Species

	maximum adult size
Erpetoichthys calabaricus Reedfish, Ropefish, Snakefish	15in (38cm)
Polypterus ornatipinnis Ornate Bichir	17in (43cm)
Polypterus delhezi Armoured Bichir	14in (35cm)
Polypterus palmas Marbled Bichir	12in (30cm)
Polypterus senegalensis Senegal Bichir, Cuvier's Bichir	12in (30cm)

● *What is the difference between a Reedfish and a Bichir?*

... *Polypterus* species (bichirs) have pelvic fins, whereas *Erpetoichthys* species (Reedfish) do not.

● *However hard I try, I cannot keep my Reedfish in the aquarium. I have a close-fitting cover glass with just a narrow gap for the filter pipes but it still manages to get out. What would you advise?*

You should cover all entry points for wires and pipework with a piece of net curtain and tape this all round the edges with sturdy tape (such as that used for insulating electrical wiring); large specimens of Reedfish are powerful enough to dislodge ordinary Scotch tape! If you do find your Reedfish shrivelled on the floor, put it back in the aquarium – it may surprise you and survive.

● *Is it possible to sex and breed my Reedfish?*

It certainly is possible to sex them. The caudal fin of the male has 12–14 bars and is olive in colour, whereas the female has 9 bars and the fin colour is ochre. However, no reports of captive breeding could be found.

● *I saw some very small bichirs for sale, but noticed that they had what appeared to be growths on either side of their heads. Should these make me wary of buying them?*

The young of some species (for example, the Marbled Bichir) have external gills, and it is probably these that you saw. They are perfectly normal and nothing to worry about, so you can confidently buy the fish. However, you should take great care when handling the young fish to avoid damaging them. As the fish grow, these external gills disappear.

Spiny Eels   FAMILY: MASTACEMBELIDAE

THESE FISH ARE NOT TRUE EELS BUT DO HAVE an elongate, eel-like profile. Whereas true eels are roughly cylindrical in shape, most spiny eels are compressed. They originate mainly from the Malay archipelago, but there are examples from the Middle East, India and Africa. Many of the larger species are fished as a food resource, particularly in East Asia.

Close examination of the back, just anterior to the long dorsal fin, reveals a series of short sharp spines – hence the common name of the fish.

Coming and Going

Spiny eels mostly prefer to live among reeds, their natural habitat being the muddy lower levels of the water column. They have the unusual ability to swim both forward and backward with equal dexterity. Their food mainly comprises aquatic invertebrates, though large specimens will eat other small fish.

Some of the larger species, for instance *Mastacembelus erythrotaenia*, can become extremely belligerent, even attacking their owners during tank maintenance. On the other hand, the smaller representatives of this group can be quite rewarding to keep, although their shy nature means that they are not always readily visible.

▲ *Take care when handling large specimens of the Fire Eel* (Mastacembelus erythrotaenia), *as their spines can easily cut your hands.*

Representative Species

	maximum adult size
Mastacembelus armatus Tyre-track Eel	20in (51cm)
Mastacembelus erythrotaenia Fire Eel	39in (1m)
Macrognathus aculeatus No common name	12in (30cm)
Afromastacembelus plagiostomus Lake Tanganyikan Spiny Eel	14in (36cm)

Tank Conditions and Care

HABITAT: Among secluded thickets of reeded plants (*Vallisneria*, etc). Juveniles require a sandy substrate. The Lake Tanganyikan Spiny Eel needs the same water conditions and rockwork as used for Lake Tanganyikan cichlids (pages 72–74).

Tank size	Min 36x15x15in (91x38x38cm). A tight-fitting cover is essential.
pH	Around 7.0–7.5 for the Asian species, and 7.5–8.0 for the Lake Tanganyikan Spiny Eel.
dH	15–20°
Temperature	24–28°C (75–82°F)
Water changes	10–15% every 10–14 days
Filtration	Avoid subgravel filters. Use external or internal mechanical filters. Ensure the young eels cannot enter the inlet pipe if fitted.
Lighting	Not too strong

FEEDING: Adults eat small fish. Juveniles prefer live foods such as *Tubifex* and bloodworm (gnat larvae). Dried foods are taken by most specimens.

HEALTH: Body lesions are common; juveniles may burrow through the gravel and adults graze themselves on sharp rocks. Provided the wound does not become infected with fungus, it should heal quickly, leaving no scar. Temperature drop is the main concern – avoid cool water for long periods.

Freshwater Stingrays

FAMILY: DASYATIDAE

TWO SPECIES OF FRESHWATER STINGRAY FROM South America are occasionally available: the Ocellated Freshwater Stingray (*Potamotrygon motoro*) growing to 15in (38cm); and the Freshwater Stingray (*Potamotrygon laticeps*) growing to 24in (61cm). The natural habitat of the Freshwater Stingray is in fairly shallow, moderately clear water, with a sandy or alluvial bed.

The "sting" of a stingray is a serrated spine on the top of the long elongate tail. As the stingray's body is compressed, its eyes are located dorsally on the head. This fish lives in shallow, clear water, so to avoid "sun blindness" most species, including marine representatives, have a flap over the eye to protect the retina.

Freshwater Stingrays are reasonably active for most of the day, in search of morsels of food on the bottom of the tank. Despite their size, they are quite peaceful fish, though they should not be trusted with small fish.

Q&A

● *How do I transport a Freshwater Stingray home?*

... With a sharp spine on the dorsal surface of the slender tail section of its body, a stingray should obviously not be carried in a plastic bag. Use a plastic box with a sealable lid. If the journey is long, then ensure you have something to retain the heat such as an old blanket or newspaper in which to wrap the box. Place only one fish in each box, as it is not unknown for one stingray to spike another by mistake in such confines and, if one stingray dies, the water quality will quickly decay, leading to the death of the other specimens.

● *Is the spine poisonous?*

Yes, though not life-threatening to humans. The pain inflicted can still be quite intense, though whether this is due to a true venom or a result of blood poisoning caused by the mucus covering entering the bloodstream is not known. The spine is serrated, like a bread knife, further exacerbating any wound. Normally the Freshwater Stingray is peaceful, and the spine is mainly used for defence.

Tank Conditions and Care

HABITAT: Planted aquarium with a sandy substrate in which the fish can burrow.

Tank size Min 48x24x15in (122x61x38cm). The floor area of the tank needs to be as large as practically possible for this bottom-dwelling and bottom-feeding fish.

pH	6.5–6.8
dH	Max 12°
Temperature	23–26°C (73–79°F)

Water changes *Potamotrygon* are sensitive to changing water conditions. Water changes should be slow, using matured water of similar chemistry to that in the tank.

Filtration High-efficiency filtration is essential. Try external or internal power filters.

Lighting Not too high a level

FEEDING: Live foods such as *Tubifex* and earthworms are preferred, although frozen shrimp, cockle, etc., will suffice.

HEALTH: This depends largely on water quality rather than on disease. Freshwater Stingrays will quickly succumb if the water conditions are not optimal.

▲ *The Ocellated Freshwater Stingray* (Potamotrygon motoro) *is one of around a dozen species native to South American rivers. As it requires very precise water conditions, it is definitely a fish for the specialist.*

Lungfish

LUNGFISH HAVE BEEN INHABITANTS OF THIS planet for some 400 million years. The earliest fossilized examples have been discovered in rock strata of the Lower Devonian geological period. At this time Australia, South America and Africa all formed parts of a supercontinent known as Gondwanaland, which later broke up and drifted apart. Lungfish therefore came to be distributed across all these three continents.

All lungfish are elongate and have their dorsal, caudal and anal fins united. Both *Lepidosiren* and *Protopterus* species are covered with very small scales, the unrayed ventral and pectoral fins are filamentous and the swimbladder is paired.

South American Lungfish (*L. paradoxa*) are by far the easiest to maintain in captivity, and youngsters adapt quickly to the confines of a tank. Small specimens are particularly attractive, being mottled yellow and brown, but by the time they reach about 4in (10cm) in length they become a dull grey. Although potentially large, they are quite tolerant of other fish big enough not to be considered as food.

By contrast, African lungfish (*Protopterus* spp.) are highly belligerent and need a tank to themselves. Small specimens may tolerate companion fish, but not for long. Extreme care is needed when handling these fish or when carrying out routine tank maintenance. They have very powerful jaws, which they use against filtration pipes, nets and even fingers. They are also great escape artists – should you find your fish on the floor, take care when picking it up, even if it is dried out, as it will try to bite you. Coaxing it into a thick, deep, wet, linen net makes handling easier.

When spawning, both the South American and African lungfish build nests, which are guarded by the male.

As a protected species, the Australian Lungfish (*Neoceratodus forsteri*) is not available commercially. It differs from its South American and African counterparts in that it has large scales, its body is compressed, its paired fins are paddle-like, its swimbladder is unpaired and it does not aestivate. Its breeding strategy is also different – it lays its eggs among plants.

Tank Conditions and Care

HABITAT: Sand or fine gravel substrate, planted for South American Lungfish. Wood and smooth rocks for decor. Avoid sharp-edged rocks that may damage their bodies. Provide a heavy cover glass, weighted down if necessary to make sure the fish cannot escape; this particularly applies to any of the African species.

Tank size Min 48x8x18in (122x46x46cm) but be prepared to provide a larger aquarium.

pH	6.5–7.5
dH	To 15°

Temperature South American Lungfish 23–28°C (73–83°F). African species 25–30°C (77–86°F).

Water changes 15–20% every 10–14 days

Filtration Very efficient filtration – external canister filter. For African species a separate biological filter can be used.

Lighting Fluorescent lighting strong enough to maintain plant growth for the South American Lungfish, or to observe the African species.

FEEDING: South American Lungfish are basically carnivorous and will eat shrimps, worms, fish, water snails or pieces of fish and meat. African species are even less fussy, more predatory, and will consume anything, dead or alive, from aquatic bugs (when small) to fish.

HEALTH: Not susceptible to disease, provided water quality is maintained and sharp objects are avoided. If the water quality deteriorates, then some degeneration of the filamentous fins occurs. This can be rectified by changing the water and checking on the efficiency of the filtration unit. Under prime conditions, scratches on the body will heal of their own accord.

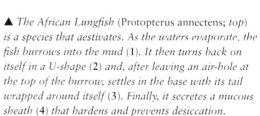

● *My lungfish keeps coming to the surface and taking gulps of air. Is this normal?*

Yes it is. These fish survive in very oxygen-deficient waters by taking in air and using the paired airbladder as a lung – hence the common name. If you prevent a lungfish from reaching the water surface it can drown.

● *What is aestivation?*

It is a state of dormancy brought about by periods of adverse conditions in the wild, when the water courses dry up in summer (see diagram above).

● *What is the best way to transport my lungfish?*

In a large plastic bucket with sufficient water to cover the fish. This will help to discourage it from trying to leap from the container either as you put the fish in or just as you open it. Ensure that your bucket is equipped with a tightly fitting lid.

▲ *The African Lungfish* (Protopterus annectens; *top*) *is a species that aestivates. As the waters evaporate, the fish burrows into the mud* (1). *It then turns back on itself in a U-shape* (2) *and, after leaving an air-hole at the top of the burrow, settles in the base with its tail wrapped around itself* (3). *Finally, it secretes a mucous sheath* (4) *that hardens and prevents desiccation.*

Representative Species

	maximum adult size
Lepidosiren paradoxa South American Lungfish	49in (1.25m)
Protopterus aethiopicus Ethiopian Lungfish	79in (2m)
Protopterus annectens African Lungfish	32in (81cm)
Protopterus dolloi Lungfish	52in (132cm)

Aquatic Plants

Part of the joy of the aquarist's hobby is
creating an environment that is not only sympathetic to
the types of fish you are keeping, but that also appears natural
and aesthetically pleasing. Plants will form an integral part of most
of the set-ups you may wish to make. The range of aquatic plants
offered for sale is great, and a good selection, imaginatively
combined with rocks and wood, can produce
a beautiful aquarium display.

There are many criteria for choosing your plants.
First, check whether those that appeal to you will prosper
in a tank; the majority of aquatic plants are "marginals" rather
than "true" aquatics (i.e. plants that grow permanently submerged),
but not all such plants will adapt successfully to life in the aquarium.
You should also consider the compatibility of your plants and livestock. Will they thrive in the same water conditions? And will
some of your fish tend to eat certain types of plant? Finally,
plan the overall layout of the aquarium, so as to achieve
an attractive and practical mixture of plant heights,
leaf shapes and textures, and colours.

This section covers the various types of aquatic
plant and offers advice on how to tend and propagate them.
As well as describing the plants that you will want to thrive,
it also includes treatment of the ones that you will definitely
want to eliminate: the nuisance algae that are
the bane of the aquarist's life!

▶ *Plants make a stunning visual display*
and create an interesting home for your fish.

What is an Aquatic Plant?

AQUATIC PLANTS, FOR THE PURPOSES OF THE aquarist, are those that will grow underwater. This broad term in fact encompasses both those plants that spend all of their time underwater (often referred to as "true aquatic plants") and those that spend only part of their time submerged ("marginals"). The latter term will be familiar to pondkeepers, as it is these plants that provide a floral display around the edge, or margin, of the pond.

Aquatic plants behave in the same way as terrestrial plants. They vary widely in form, from single-celled algae to more complex organisms, in which each part (leaf, stem, flower, etc.) has evolved to perform a particular function that ensures its survival. The two things that link all green plants are photosynthesis and respiration. Photosynthesis is the process by which plants harness the energy of light. During photosynthesis, the plants absorb carbon dioxide through stomata (tiny pores) on their leaves and release oxygen. During the day, carbon dioxide and water are combined chemically to produce sugars, which are quickly converted to starch, releasing oxygen as a by-product. This process occurs in the chloroplasts, which contain chlorophyll, a pigment that gives plants their green coloration.

● *Can I use marginal plants in my aquarium?*

... Yes – the majority of plants sold for the aquarium are marginals, including rooted plants, such as *Echinodorus* and *Cryptocoryne* and cuttings, such as *Hygrophilia*. However, certain marginals are best confined to pond use. If in doubt, check with your aquarium or garden store.

● *When I bought my plants they were standing in trays of cold water, and I transported them home in a plastic bag. It was a cold day, and I lost a lot of them. Is it possible for aquarium plants to become chilled?*

Yes. Tropical plants, like tropical fish, should not be exposed to low temperatures. They should be displayed for sale in water at the correct temperature (touch the glass of the tank or dip a finger in the water to check) and transported in water at a similar temperature. Use an insulated polystyrene box to transport them if the weather is cold or the trip is long.

● *How do I tend the plants in the aquarium without disrupting my fish?*

Most plant care can be carried out quickly and with the minimum of disturbance whenever you do a water change and conduct your general tank maintenance. The lower water level will also make it easier for you to reach the plants.

▶ *Aquarium plants affect the balance of oxygen and carbon dioxide dissolved in the water. With the tank lighting on, the net result is the release of oxygen into the water and the absorption of carbon dioxide from it (photosynthesis exceeds respiration). With the tank lighting off, oxygen is removed from the water and carbon dioxide is released, since respiration is occurring.*

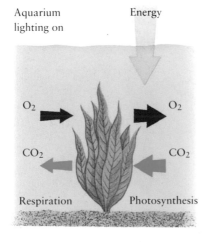

Aquarium lighting on

Energy

O_2 → → O_2

CO_2 ← ← CO_2

Respiration   Photosynthesis

Aquarium lighting off

O_2 →

CO_2 ←

Respiration

▶ *Like fish, plants are affected by the water quality and temperature and by light levels. Overhead light is best, and some light must fall directly on or into the water.*

Chlorophyll is the agent that allows the conversion of the energy from light into the energy combined in the sugars during photosynthesis.

Respiration uses the sugars and starch to provide energy for growth and other life processes. It occurs continually, in the light and the dark. During respiration, carbon dioxide is produced and energy is released for use by the plant. At night, when photosynthesis is suspended, plants absorb oxygen and release carbon dioxide; during the day more oxygen is released by photosynthesis than is used by respiration, so in the course of a day, oxygen is produced and carbon dioxide absorbed. If grown in the dark, green plants lose their colour and become very pale and yellowish.

Iron deficiency can also cause plants to grow pallid, and it may be necessary to add iron to the substrate to ensure healthy growth. Other trace elements are also essential for good growth but, in the main, these will be introduced naturally into the aquarium by regular water changes. As their name implies, trace elements are only present in minute quantities, so be sure not to overfeed your plants. In the confines of an aquarium, this is as easy to do as overfeeding your fish.

Reproducing the Natural Environment

Plants, like tropical fish, come from areas with water conditions ranging from soft acidic to hard alkaline. Fortunately for the hobbyist, most plants can tolerate and adapt to a wider variety of water conditions than fish. Likewise, the flow of water through the tank can play a large part in growing plants successfully. A gentle current gives the best results. Fine-leaved plants should be kept away from turbulence, as their leaves quickly bruise and tear. Temperature requirements vary, but the majority of plants respond well to a range of 21–27°C (70–81°F).

To provide the correct degree and duration of light for aquarium plants, consider their native tropical environment. Here, throughout the year, each 24-hour period comprises 12 hours of light and 12 hours of darkness. Discounting the first

Guide to Minimum Lighting Levels

tank size	number of tubes
24x12x12in (61x30x30cm)	3 x 15 watts
36x15x15in (91x38x38cm)	3 x 25 watts
40x18x18in (102x46x46cm)	3 x 30 watts
48x18x18in (122x46x46cm)	3 x 40 watts
62x18x18in (157x46x46cm)	3 x 65 watts

and last hours of daylight, there are 10 hours of intense light in each day that need to be reproduced in the aquarium. To ensure that the lights are on and off at the right times, use time switches. The plant's location in the wild is also an important factor where lighting is concerned. For example, a plant in a shaded forest pool requires less light than one in a shallow, open stream. The accompanying table gives the level of lighting that is needed for different sizes of planted tank. Although this might seem too bright for the fish, recall their natural habitat. If the light becomes too intense for them, they will retire to the shade, where, if the set-up is correct, they will still be visible. (See also Lighting, pages 16–17.)

Cuttings

CUTTINGS, WHICH ARE OFTEN CALLED "BUNCH plants", form the mainstay of aquarium plantings. They are relatively cheap to buy and the appearance of a wall of plants in your tank can be achieved in next to no time.

Many of these plants are marginals (see What is an Aquatic Plant?, pages 188–189); parts of their lives are spent submerged, while at other times they protrude from marshy ground or shallow water. During these latter periods, they are most easily harvested for the aquarium trade. In planting these cuttings in our tanks, we are reproducing the conditions they would encounter during the rainy season when the marshes become inundated. In order to survive, the plants must rapidly adapt to aquatic conditions. Many of them shed their leaves, and become bare stems. At this point, you should resist the temptation to throw them away. Leave them undisturbed and, in time, some (but not all) will sprout side shoots, which will have leaves that are usually of a lighter colour and different shape to the ones that have died. Such shoots represent the plants' underwater growth phase, and it is these that we are interested in propagating for our domestic aquaria.

Although some aquarists use lead weights and plant cuttings in bunches, this practice is not recommended, as it may damage the plants. Any damage allows infections to take hold, and the plants will rot from the base.

▶ Ammannia *species thrive in a bright aquarium. These are plants that can easily be propagated from cuttings.*

Planting

Plant a single species at a time, keeping any other plants warm in their plastic bags until you are ready to use them. Lay them out on a tray and grade them according to height. Check each one for damage, removing bruised leaves or stems. Cut off the damaged stem just below a leaf joint and then remove the bottom pair of leaves.

Make the effort to plant each cutting separately. In this way, you will avoid bruising or breaking the stems, which would occur if you simply thrust a bunch of plants into the substrate. You will also get far fewer yellow and dying leaves at the base of the plant because all the leaves are receiving sufficient light to photosynthesize.

Think of your tank as an underwater garden, and give the individual cuttings ample space.

To create the appearance of a wall of plants, stagger your rows. Looking from above, you should be able to see substrate between each plant, while from the front you will be faced with a wall of vegetation that hides the back of the tank. If you are careful, you can grade the height of the plants so as to have shorter species at the front and taller ones at the back.

Propagation

The table (right) lists some of the easiest plants to propagate. Most will root from cuttings – that is, after all, how you bought them! Alternatively, they can be layered. Bend down a healthy stem and anchor it, but take care not to cut or bruise it (hair pins are useful for this). From each node roots will appear, followed by a shoot. Once the shoot is long enough, it can be nipped off and used as a cutting.

● *How can I tell if a cutting has been grown underwater or not?*

... If grown underwater, the plant is supported by the water and therefore does not need a very strong stem. If you hold the base of the stem in your hand, the plant will flop over. Those grown out of water usually have strong, sometimes woody stems which may, or may not, have little hairs on them. When you hold these at the base, they remain upright.

● *Is there a general guide that I can use for the planting distance?*

As a general rule, the distance between your plants should be the span of their leaves so that, when viewed from above, each plant doesn't touch, or only barely touches, its neighbour in any direction.

● *My Bacopa is growing too tall. What advice can you offer for cutting it back?*

The following technique applies to all cuttings. Take out the complete section of Bacopa (or whatever). Replant the shorter front plants at the rear and cut back the taller ones, replanting the top cuttings in the front of your grouping. Do not throw away the bottom parts of the stem; these can be planted in another tank and will throw off side shoots which you can use to increase your stock.

Popular Species

	lighting requirements
Alternanthera rosaefolia Red Hygrophila	Very bright
Ammannia senegalensis Red Ammannia	Very bright
Bacopa caroliniana Giant Bacopa	Not critical
Cabomba aquatica Green Cabomba	Bright
Cabomba caroliniana Green Cabomba	Bright
Cabomba piauhyensis Red Cabomba	Very bright
Didiplis diandra Water Hedge	Subdued
Egeria densa Giant Elodea	Bright
Heteranthera zosterifolia Water Stargrass	Bright
Hygrophilia polysperma Dwarf Hygrophilia	Bright
Hygrophilia salicifolia Willow-leaf Hygrophilia	Bright
Limnophilia aquatica Giant Ambulia	Bright
Ludwigia repens Ludwigia	Bright
Ludwigia mullertii Red Ludwigia	Bright
Myriophyllum hippuroides Miriophyllum	Bright
Nomaphila stricta Giant Hygrophila	Bright
Rotala macandra Red Rotala	Very bright
Synnema triflorum Water Wisteria	Bright

● *I used some Bladderwort for my fish to spawn on. The fry hatched but, despite feeding them (and watching them feed), I am suffering numerous losses. Why is this happening?*

Your plant is to blame. Bladderworts (*Utricularia* sp.) are carnivorous plants that sometimes appear in the aquarium trade. Their small bladders, which resemble air bubbles, catch tiny aquatic organisms – including newly hatched fry – which are then dissolved as food.

Rooted Plants

ROOTED AQUARIUM PLANTS, SUCH AS AMAZON Swordplants (*Echinodorus* spp.) and *Cryptocorynes*, are sold either ready-potted or with bare roots. The former are grown in fertilizer and contained in a small basket, from which they can root into the substrate, and are usually healthy and pest-free. Bare-rooted plants are cheaper, but take months to establish themselves, and so are unsuitable if you are after "instant" results.

An average-sized aquarium can only hold one or two large Amazon Swordplants. The dwarf variety (*E. tenellus*) is more practical, and will carpet the front of the tank. They are avid feeders and, like the *Cryptocorynes*, benefit from the addition of some clay pellets to the substrate.

Planting

Many hobbyists prefer to remove basket-grown plants from their containers, gently shake off the potting medium and plant them "bare-rooted". This method is particularly recommended for *Cryptocorynes*, as it yields several small plants, each of which, given enough space, will grow into a larger one. When planting them (especially the broad-leaved varieties), make sure that you do not overshadow other plants that need bright light. Use the shade for lower-growing species such as Dwarf Anubias, which will grow well in such conditions. The full leaf span of each mature plant is a good guide to spacing them: tall, narrow plants such as *Vallisneria* can be grown closer together than, say, *Samolus parviflorus*. As with cuttings, always plant individually.

Certain plants, notably the African Water Fern (*Bolbitis heudelotii*) and Java Fern (*Microsorium pteropus*), should not be planted in the substrate, but are best attached to wood or rocks. These grow from rhizomes that send out slender roots to anchor the plant. Initially, the rhizome can be held in place with elastic bands, fishing line or plastic-coated garden wire. To attach the plant to wood, drill small holes through the wood,

▲ *Hair Grass* (Eleocharis acicularis) *is an attractive fine-leaved rooted plant for the aquarium.*

Popular Species

	lighting requirements
Anubias nana Dwarf Anubias	Subdued
Bolbitis heudelotii African Water Fern	Subdued
Cryptocoryne balansae No common name	Bright
Cryptocoryne ciliata No common name	Bright
Cryptocoryne nevillii Dwarf Crypt	Bright
Cryptocoryne wendtii No common name	Moderate
Echinodorus cordifolius Radicans Sword	Bright
Echinodorus major Ruffled Sword	Bright
Echinodorus paniculatus Broad-leaved Sword	Bright

▼ *The Pennywort* (Hydrocotyle vulgaris) *makes a good foreground plant if kept under strict control.*

thread wire through the hole and gently twist the ends together. Be careful – if you damage the rhizome it may rot. This technique is very useful for growing plants at different levels in the tank.

Propagation

Many rooted plants produce runners that either travel along the substrate (e.g. Vallis and the Dwarf Amazon Sword) or that run below it and then emerge at the surface, where a small plant develops (e.g. *Cryptocorynes*). Allow the young plant to grow to around 1–1.5in (3–4cm) before detaching it from its parent. Alternatively, leave the new plants to colonize an area of substrate, and the attachment will break down naturally.

Some plants are clump-forming (e.g. *S. parviflorus*). The clump can be lifted and the individual plants gently eased apart.

Yet others produce adventitious shoots. These grow at various points on the mother plant; for example, on Amazon Swordplants they are on the flowering stem above the water, while Java Ferns have them on the leaf margins. To propagate Swordplants, peg down the flower stem and let the shoots take root in the substrate before cutting the stem. With Java Fern, attach the plantlets to wood or rock and they will grow on.

Echinodorus tenellus Pygmy Chain Sword	Moderate to bright
Eleocharis acicularis Hair Grass	Bright
Hydrocotyle vulgaris Pennywort	Bright
Microsorium pteropus Java Fern	Subdued
Sagittaria platyphylla Giant Sag	Very bright
Sagittaria subulata Dwarf Sag	Moderate to bright
Samolus parviflorus Water Lettuce	Bright
Vallisneria spiralis Straight Vallis	Bright
Vallisneria tortifolia Twisted Vallis	Bright

● *My Amazon Swordplant is rapidly outgrowing the tank. Is there anything I can do to curb its growth?*

The one way you can check it temporarily is to grasp the plant firmly at its base and gently pull upwards until you feel, and sometimes hear, some of the roots break. This is usually sufficient to halt its growth in the short term, but be prepared to repeat this as necessary.

● *My* Cryptocorynes *have become overcrowded. Do I need to remove all of them from the tank or can I just thin them out?*

You can simply thin them out. Be careful, though, as a number of the plants will still be joined together by their runners, which you will have to cut if you find you are removing too many.

▶ OVERLEAF *A huge variety of plants can be observed in this imaginatively planted tank, including* Cryptocoryne, Echinodorus *and* Hydrocotyle *species.*

Bulbs and Corms

THIS GROUP CONTAINS SOME OF THE MOST highly prized aquarium plants, which are also some of the most difficult to succeed with. Bulbs and corms are often imported "dry" and introduced into dealers' tanks, where they begin to sprout. The majority are then offered for sale with just a small growing point in evidence. If you are fortunate, they will have a few leaves attached. This can make transportation home difficult, as the shoots or small plantlets are easily damaged or knocked off the bulb, corm or rhizome in transport and, if there is no other growing point, nothing else will be forthcoming.

The Aponogetons are some of the most well-known plants of this type, and make wonderful specimen plants. But be warned – they will thrive for 6–9 months and then shed most of their large leaves, leaving only a basal rosette. At this time, they should be removed from the aquarium and placed in cooler waters for about 8 weeks, before being returned to the main tank to resume their growing. One major problem with these plants is that their soft leaves are easily damaged by turbulent water conditions, rough handling or snails. Keeping your tank free of snails is difficult, but is an essential prerequisite for growing such plants as the *Nymphaea* species (the tropical water lilies) and *Barclaya longifolia*.

● *I have been trying to grow a Tiger Lotus but I just get green leaves. It was red when I bought it. What am I doing wrong?*

You are using too little light in your aquarium. If you want to retain the red coloration of these plants, you must provide them with a very intense light. To achieve this, increase the number of tubes over the aquarium, not the length of time that you are lighting the tank (which should always stay at 12 hours).

● *My* Barclaya *looks as though it is flowering underwater. Is this normal?*

Yes it is. The flowers may open fully, but it is more normal for the flower buds not to open, and yet still produce viable seed. To grow them on, you should sow them as soon as they are ripe, and on no account allow them to dry out.

● *What sort of fertilizer should I use for my plants?*

You can purchase liquid fertilizers, but these have one major drawback: they tend to feed everything, including nuisance algae. It is far better to use pellets, which can be inserted directly into the substrate at intervals around the plant. There are a number of commercial products available. However, an excellent alternative fertilizer is rabbit droppings! These are a convenient size, and are available free from rabbit-keeping friends or neighbours. In addition, they dry well, and can be stored hygienically in an airtight tin.

Popular Species

	lighting requirements		lighting requirements
Aponogeton crispus Wavy-edged Aponogeton	Moderate to bright	Crinium thaianum Onion Plant	Moderate to bright
Aponogeton madagascariensis Lace Plant	Moderate	Nuphar japonicum Spatterdock	Bright
Aponogeton ulvaceus No common name	Moderate to bright	Nymphaea maculata Tiger Lotus	Very bright
Aponogeton undulatus No common name	Moderate to bright	Nymphaea stellata Red and Blue Water Lilies	Bright
Barclaya longifolia Orchid Lily	Moderate to bright	Nymphoides aquatica Banana Plant	Bright

▲ *Dwarf water lilies* (Nymphaea *sp.) need a large air gap at the top of the tank to flower. They are not seen at their best if you are using a hood on your aquarium.*

Planting

Plant so that the growing point is just at the surface. Especially for water lilies, feed well with fertilizer pellets inserted into the substrate within the plant's root run. Allow plenty of space between these plants, as some of them can grow quite large. Also, bear in mind that the natural tendency of water lilies is to grow a profusion of pads and flowers, which would quickly cover the water surface and exclude the light from all your other plants. The part of the lily that is of particular interest to the aquarist is the basal rosette of soft, pink-to-reddish underwater leaves that it has during its resting phase. To maintain this, you must nip off any leaf or shoot that looks as though it is heading for the water surface.

Propagation

Many of the Aponogetons and others produce seeds freely. The flower spikes are sent up above the water surface (*Barclaya* is an exception), and you can aid the fertilization process by using a very soft brush to stroke the flowers. The seeds will form and can be gathered for growing on elsewhere. Even if they are left in the tank, a few will survive and grow on. The sole exception is the Lace Plant (*Aponogeton madagascariensis*), which is best propagated by dividing the newly imported rhizomes.

Some of these plants (such as the Onion Plant, *Crinium thaianum*) form small offsets on their bulbs, and these may be removed and grown on. Growing any aquarium plant from seed is a long process. Because the tiny plants are extremely susceptible to damage by snails and fish, it is a good idea to set aside a separate, fish- and snail-free tank for the purpose of growing them.

Floating Plants

As a general rule, floating plants are only offered for sale on a seasonal basis. The two main exceptions to this are Crystalwort (*Riccia fluitans*) and Java Moss (*Vesicularia dubyana*). Both of these grow readily in aquaria and, once you have them established, form large masses, sometimes to the point of becoming a nuisance as they deprive other plants of light.

Although it is not strictly a floating plant, Java Moss is included here because it can grow well without being attached to anything. Most commonly, it is found growing from wood, rocks and bark. If growing on wood, it will even flourish above the waterline, provided the humidity is high enough. Clumps of this plant should be split if they become too large.

Crystalwort forms large floating mats at, and just below, the water surface. It is highly prized by aquarists because it forms a natural spawning site, fry nursery and hiding place for small fish. Indeed, any of the plants with long, flowing root systems perform a similar function, for example Water Lettuce (*Pistia stratiotes*) and Indian Fern (*Ceratopteris thalictroides*). Fish make good use of the roots and broad leaves to lay eggs, while bubble-nest builders such as the gouramis find them a useful foundation for their constructions. Crystalwort will also anchor itself to wood and stones, and can grow out of the water in the right circumstances. Only one floating plant is able to root itself in the substrate – the Indian Fern.

The Water Hyacinth (*Eichhornia crassipes*) is usually available in summer, when it is a popular purchase for garden ponds. This tropical species has large, fleshy leaves and a thickened, spongy, fibrous stem that retains air. It propagates by sending out shoots. Though it is too large for the normal tank with a hood, it is ideal for a heated indoor pond or open-topped aquarium, where, if conditions are favourable, it will also flower.

Whatever floating plants you are using, you should ensure that enough light can still reach the lower levels of the aquarium, otherwise the

Q & A ...

● *I had a good growth of Crystalwort in my tank, but over the summer it all died. What could have caused this?*

Too high a temperature. If the waters get too hot, above 25°C (77°F) for more than a few days, then the plant tends to disintegrate.

● *Why are parts of my Butterfly Fern rotting?*

The leaves are protected by fine hairs. Unfortunately, these hairs also retain any drops of condensation that fall from your cover glass. These cause the plant to rot.

● *Should I add fertilizer for my floating plants?*

It may be necessary if you have a mass of them. They feed from the water, so use a liquid fertilizer. Take care not to overdose and upset the balance of the tank. If you are doing regular water changes, though, it is not normally necessary to fertilize floating plants.

▼ *The attractive and unusual leaf shape of the Water Lettuce (Pistia stratiotes) makes it a popular choice of floating plant. In common with other floating plants, it is best suited to open-topped tanks.*

plants in the substrate may die. In tanks with a hood, it is also important to maintain a high level of humidity above the water surface; this prevents the leaves of plants such as the Water Lettuce from drying up and turning brown. All floating plants are delicate, so water movement should be extremely slow or even non-existent. A powerful flow of water will batter and bruise the plants and break them up.

Propagation

The floating plants reproduce by various strategies. The Water Lettuce produces runners, which may be divided up once the daughter plants are large enough. The Butterfly Fern (*Salvinia auriculata*) produces branches that can be broken off to form new plants. Crystalwort is an aquatic form of liverwort, whose thallus (plant body) forks frequently to form thick clumps. If these are broken up, each piece has the ability to form a new plant. When grown terrestrially, it produces spore capsules. Duckweed also reproduces vegetatively. Indeed, it seems to multiply before your very eyes, with a new plant being produced every 30–40 hours.

The Indian Fern produces adventitious buds, which develop into daughter plants on the older leaves. You should let them to develop to about 1.5in (4cm), and then either plant them in the substrate or allow them to float free.

● *Duckweed is overrunning my tank and clogging the filter. How can I get rid of this nuisance?*

This is difficult. Scoop out as much as you can with a net. Then clean the tank and implements thoroughly, removing all traces of the plant from the pipes, cover glass, buckets, and even your hands. Rinse the nets you used in very hot water. If even small pieces remain, they will multiply again. Duckweed does have one saving grace – some larger cyprinids like to eat it!

● *I have some Water Lettuce on my indoor pond in the conservatory. It is getting infested with greenfly. Is there anything I can use to dispose of them?*

Yes, but take great care. Insecticides are out, because they will kill the fish in your pond, but you could try cleaning the plants with a proprietary treatment. Alternatively, wash the greenfly off into the pond and let the fish eat them.

Popular Species

	lighting requirements
Ceratopteris thalictroides Indian Fern	Bright
Eichhornia crassipes Water Hyacinth	Bright
Lemna spp. Duckweed	Not critical
Pistia stratiotes Water Lettuce	Bright
Riccia fluitans Crystalwort	Bright
Salvinia auriculata Butterfly Fern	Very bright
Vesicularia dubyana Java Moss	Subdued

Algae

ALGAE CAN BECOME A SERIOUS NUISANCE IN the tropical aquarium. In the worst cases, they will pollute the tank and kill all your livestock and plants. Moreover, as many people (wrongly) attribute the growth of algae to excessive lighting, they are probably the single most common reason why many aquarists give up on growing aquatic plants. In truth, algae will proliferate if the lighting is too low, too bright or left on too long. Sunlight will also cause an algal bloom. Regular water changes are essential in reducing the levels of nitrates, phosphates, sulphates and carbonates, all of which provide food for algae.

Algae are extremely resilient. Their spores are carried over long periods by air currents in the upper atmosphere. Despite being exposed to the most intense cold, heat and radiation, the spores germinate once they encounter more favourable conditions. Some algae can survive long periods of desiccation, so leaving an old piece of rock or wood to dry out is no guarantee of killing them. They may simply remain dormant and become active when placed in a warm aquarium.

Types of Algae

This book is primarily concerned with four types: Green Algae, Diatoms, Whip Algae, and Blue-green Algae.

Green Algae comprise several different kinds of organism. Two of the most common nuisance varieties are *Chlorella*, which appears as a green film on the tank glass, and *Chlamydomonas* (filamentous or thread algae), which festoons rocks and plants. Some of the other, "colonial" forms of green algae are beneficial, as they may be cultivated to provide green water to feed some fry.

Diatoms are usually associated with plankton in the ocean. However, they occur in freshwater as well, and will multiply rapidly where there are high concentrations of nitrates and phosphates. In severe cases of infestation, they will even discolour the water, but it is more usual for them to coat rocks, gravel etc. in a brown slime.

Whip Algae use flagellae (whips) to propel themselves through the water. They require very high nitrogen levels to survive, so it is rare to find them in an aquarium – if you do, then it is likely that all your livestock will already have been killed by the pollution.

Blue-green Algae, or cyanobacteria, are by far the most troublesome variety. They can swiftly coat everything in the tank in a thick slime that suffocates plants and kills fish if left unchecked. Blue-green algae are not true algae; they possess characteristics of both algae and bacteria, hence the alternative name. They will proliferate where there is a combination of bright light and water that is rich in phosphates and nitrates.

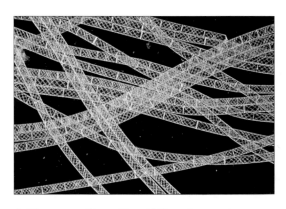

▲ *Filamentous Green Algae* (Chlamydomonas).

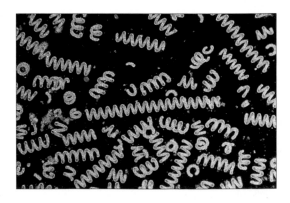

▲ *Blue-green Algae, or cyanobacteria.*

Q&A

● *How can I prevent algae from getting into my aquarium?*

... In short, you can't! Algal spores are carried in the air and float freely in water. They can be introduced with fish, on plants or rocks, or may be blown into the tank. The best you can do is to check all plants, rocks, etc. for traces of algae before introducing them into the tank and, if necessary, sterilize them.

● *Are there any natural methods of controlling algae?*

The most obvious is to use fish that graze on algae. Depending on the other inmates of your tank and its maturity, you might try the Siamese Algae Eater (*Crossocheilus siamensis*), or some of the sucker-mouth catfish – *Hypostomus*, *Otocinclus* and *Farlowella* species. For newly set-up tanks, Kissing Gouramis (*Helostoma temminckii*) are particularly useful, as are a couple of pairs of Swordtails or Platies (*Xiphophorus* spp.). Despite its name, the Algae Eater (*Gyrinocheilus aymonieri*) is not the most efficient fish at clearing algae, and has the additional drawback of harassing your other fish. In summary, you should not expect any of these fish to keep the whole tank spotless; you may still have to scrape the aquarium glass. What most of them are particularly good at is cleaning the plant leaves without damaging them.

▲ *Whatever type of aquarium you have, the control of algae is a matter of striking the correct balance of light, fish stocking levels, water quality and plant growth. As long as algae can be kept under control, as in the tank pictured here, they may even help you achieve an informal, natural look in your aquarium.*

● *Is there any easy way of removing thread algae?*

There is no way to eradicate them completely. However, one of the more effective methods of keeping them down is to use one of the rough canes that support house plants. Poke this into the centre of the algal mass and twirl it between your fingers, thereby wrapping the filaments around the cane. When you pull the cane out you will remove the algae with it. Repeat as often as necessary. Doing this doesn't get rid of the problem, but it does help to keep it under control.

● *Can I use an algicide to control algae?*

Yes, you can, but you should only do so as a last resort. Be careful not to overdose, and always follow the manufacturer's instructions to the letter. It is just as important to siphon out all the dead algae that tend to gather on the substrate, otherwise they will overload the filtration system as they decompose. This, in turn, may give rise to further problems.

Glossary

Activated carbon Material used in mechanical and chemical and chemical filtration systems to remove dissolved products.

Adsorption The means by which organic molecules are chemically bonded onto the surface of the filter medium. Not to be confused with "absorption".

Algae Primitive plants, often microscopic, which are almost exclusively aquatic and do not bear flowers. A food source for many tropical fish.

Anterior Front end; that which is in front of something.

Barbel Filamentous extensions, usually surrounding the mouth, by which the fish detect (taste) food.

Bifid spines Small, sharp, erectile spines often (but not always) positioned beneath the eyes of loaches.

Biological filtration A method of filtration using bacteria – *Nitrosomonas* and *Nitrobacter* – to convert toxic ammonia and nitrites into safer substances, such as nitrates.

Biotope The smallest geographical unit of the biosphere or of a habitat that can be delimited by boundaries and characterized by its own biota (plants and animals).

Black water Water with a high level of humic acids and low levels of nutrients.

Bottom sifter A creature that sifts the substrate for food.

Brackish water Water that is intermediate between fresh and marine in its level of salinity.

Brood Offspring of a single birth or clutch of eggs.

Broodstock A lineage or known source used in controlled breeding.

Bubble nest A "nest" of bubbles which harbours the eggs of some fish.

Buffering action The means by which a liquid maintains its pH value.

Caudal peduncle The narrow part of the fish's body, just in front of the caudal fin.

Congeneric Belonging to the same genus.

Conspecific Belonging to the same species.

Crepuscular Active at dawn and dusk.

Cyanobacteria A primitive life form that has some characteristics of both bacteria and algae but is regarded as being different from both. Commonly referred to as blue-green or slime algae.

Demersal Usually applied to eggs that sink or are laid on the substrate.

Dermal denticles Tiny bristle-like spines that cover the body (usually only applied to Sharks).

Dimorphism The incidence of two distinct types of individual in an animal species.

Electrogenic Applied to an organ that produces electricity.

Filter medium Materials used to remove solid or dissolved organic substances from the water.

Fry Young fish.

Genus A group of closely related species; the sixth division (in descending order) in taxonomy.

Gestation period The period of development between conception and birth.

Gills Organ through which the fish absorbs dissolved oxygen from the water and gets rid of carbon dioxide.

Glancing Usually of cichlids, feeding on the body mucus of the parents.

Gonopodium Copulatory organ of livebearing male fish.

Gravid patch Dark triangular patch close to the vent of female livebearers; especially prominent when they are almost ready to give birth.

Herbivore Plant eater.

Ichthyologist A scientist who specializes in the study of fish.

Impeller Fan within a power filter that drives the water through the filter.

Inferior mouth Located below the snout.

Infusoria Tiny organisms used to feed fish fry.

Introspecular spines Erectile spines behind the gills of some catfish; non-erectile in many others.

Labyrinth organ An accessory breathing organ.

Lacustrine Of lakes.

Larvae The first stage of some fish; newly hatched invertebrates.

Lateral line The series of pores along the flanks of the fish that allow it to sense vibrations on the water. It may appear as a single line or a broken line, but cichlids may have two – even three.

Line breeding A method of breeding father to daughter and mother to son. Used to develop new colour forms, etc.

Mandibular Of the lower jaw.

Maxillary Of the posterior part of the upper jaw.

Milt Fluid containing the male's sperm.

Mucus layer The protective slime coat on the body of the fish.

Mulm Organic debris, plant matter, fish waste, uneaten food, etc.

Mycobacteria Saprophytic or parasitic bacteria.

Mysis Small marine shrimp used live or frozen as food.

Nauplii The first larval stage of many crustaceans, especially brine shrimp.

Nuchal hump A pronounced hump which develops at the nape of the "neck" on some mature male cichlids.

Operculum Gill cover.

Osmosis The passage of molecules from a less concentrated to a more concentrated solution through a semi-permeable membrane.

Ovipositor Breeding tube extended by a female to place her eggs precisely on a surface.

Piscivore Fish eater.

Rays Small spines that support the fin membrane.

Rheophilic Living in running waters.

Riverine Of rivers.

Rotifers Small organisms cultured as first foods for some species.

Scutes Row or rows of overlapping bony plate. Sometimes each has one or several sharp hooks or spines.

Spawn Eggs of the fish; the act of producing the eggs.

Spawning mop Artificial spawning site made of yarn or similar material.

Species The basic unit of biological classification – any taxonomic group that a genus is broken down into. The members can interbreed.

Spermatopodium Modified anal fin of male goodeids which facilitates sperm transference to the male.

Substrate Bottom covering of sand, gravel, etc. in the aquarium.

Subterminal mouth Mouth below the snout.

Superior mouth Mouth above the snout.

Swimbladder Gas-filled bladder which allows the fish to maintain its position in the water column.

Terminal mouth Mouth at the end of the snout.

Trophotaenia Feeding structures developed by young goodeids while inside their mother.

White water Silt-laden waters.

Yolk sac A food source for the embryonic fish.

Fish and the Law

SINCE THE MID-1980S, MANY COUNTRIES HAVE come to recognize that fish should be given the same legal protection against exploitation that is afforded both to domestic pets and to more exotic species in the wild. Because fish kept by hobbyists live a secluded existence – most people's fish tanks are not on view to the public, and it would be difficult to prove a charge of cruelty to fish – most laws are written with the aim of conservation. They are of two main types: those governing the collection of species under threat, and those designed to prevent the introduction of species into habitats where they may pose a threat to the native fauna and/or flora.

Laws on keeping animals range from local to global applicability, and can sometimes be highly complex. Moreover, they often change quickly, particularly at local level, where they may be redrafted within weeks. The enactment of a new local law is typically a response to some unfortunate event caused by a careless hobbyist who has not taken adequate precautions with the species in his or her charge. It is part of your responsibility not only to provide proper care, but also to be aware of any regulations that apply to your location or the species that you keep. Importers and dealers are responsible for the legality of the stock sold, so a reputable shop is unlikely to offer prohibited species – but if you are in any doubt, ask.

INTERNATIONAL LAWS

The most universal of these is known as CITES (the Convention on International Trade in Endangered Species), which came into force in 1975 under the auspices of the United Nations. There are currently 143 signatory countries. The species under protection are reviewed at regular meetings and listed on appendices that specify different levels of control. The highest level of restriction is on Appendix I; these species are effectively excluded from trade except under special licence for captive-bred specimens. Under Appendix II, regulated (licensed) trade is permissible. Most species are found on Appendix III, the least stringent.

NATIONAL LAWS

While the primary aim of CITES is to protect wild species from over-exploitation, national authorities can protect indigenous fauna and flora by restricting or prohibiting the import and collection of species or varieties regarded as a threat to native species. National governments (in this case, Europe functions as a single nation) can restrict or prohibit the import of species not listed under CITES Appendix I or II.

LOCAL/STATE/REGIONAL LAWS

Local state or regional regulations range from restriction or prohibition on ownership of certain species or varieties which are seen as potential threats to local species, to the movement of specimens across state boundaries, or the export of specimens below a certain size, or the requirement that specimens must be certified free of certain diseases (such as *Salmonella* bacteria).

Acknowledgments

ABBREVIATIONS

AOL	Andromeda Oxford Ltd
AQ	Aquapress
BCL	Bruce Coleman Limited
JB	Jane Burton
MS	Mike Sandford
PM	Photomax, Max Gibbs

1, 2 PM; 3 AOL; 7 JB; 8–9, 11c, 11bl MP. and C. Piednoir/AQ; 11br AOL; 12–13, 14 MP. and C. Piednoir/AQ; 15 AOL; 17 Dennerle, Germany; 19, 20 JB; 22 MP. and C. Piednoir/AQ; 23tl Tetra; 23tr Trevor McDonald; 24 JB; 27 AOL; 32t JB/BCL; 32b, 34 MP. and C. Piednoir/AQ; 35 AOL; 36–7 MS; 37 AOL; 39 JB/BCL; 41 PM; 42 JB; 45, 46–7 PM; 49t MP. and C. Piednoir/AQ; 49b, 50t, 50b PM; 51t MP. and C. Piednoir/AQ; 51c, 51b, 52 PM; 53 JB; 55 MP. and C. Piednoir/AQ; 56 JB; 57 MS; 59 JB/BCL; 60, 62, 63, 65, 67 MP. and C. Piednoir/AQ; 68 Christer Fredriksson/BCL; 69cr, 69b PM; 70–1 MP. and C. Piednoir/AQ; 71 PM; 73, 74 JB; 75, 76 PM; 76–7 JB; 78 PM; 80–1 JB; 82, 83 PM; 84 MP. and C. Piednoir/AQ; 86 MS;

87, 88 PM; 89 D. Allison; 90 JB; 93t PM; 93c, 94 MS; 95, 96–7 PM; 98 JB; 100, 101 PM; 102–3 JB; 104 PM; 105 Dave Bevan; 107 JB; 108 PM; 109 JB; 110 PM; 111 MS; 112, 113t, 113b PM; 114 MS; 115, 116, 117 PM; 119 JB; 121 MP. and C. Piednoir/AQ; 122 PM; 123, 124 MS; 125 W. Tomey; 126t, 126b, 128, 129, 130, 131 PM; 132 JB; 133 PM; 134–5 MP. and C. Piednoir/AQ; 136t, 136b PM; 137 MP. and C. Piednoir/AQ; 138 Hans Reinhard/BCL; 138–9, 140 PM; 141 JB; 143 W. Tomey; 144l, 144r PM; 145, 146 JB; 149 Hans Reinhard/BCL; 150, 150–1 PM; 152 Hans Reinhard/BCL; 153, 154–5, 156 PM; 157 JB; 159, 160, 161, 162–3, 164, 165, 166, 167, 168, 169t, 169b, 170 PM; 172 MP. and C. Piednoir/AQ; 173 PM; 174–5 JB; 176, 177 PM; 179t MS; 179b, 180–1, 182, 183, 185, 187 PM; 189 MP. and C. Piednoir/AQ; 190 PM; 192 W. Tomey; 193 PM; 194–5 MP. and C. Piednoir/AQ; 197 Trevor Barrett/BCL; 198–9 PM; 200t, 200b Kim Taylor; 201 MS

Artwork by Julian Baker, Richard Lewington, Michael Loates & Graham Rosewarne

Further Reading

Allen, G.R. *Rainbowfishes* (Tetra Press, Melle, Germany, 1995)

Allen, G.R. and N.J. Cross. *Rainbowfishes of Australia and Papua New Guinea* (TFH Publications, Neptune City, New Jersey, USA, 1982)

Amlacher, E. *A Textbook of Fish Diseases* (TFH Publications, Neptune City, New Jersey, USA, 1970)

Andrews, C., Excell, A. and Carrington, N. *The Manual of Fish Health* (Salamander Books Limited, London, UK, 1988)

Boyd, K.W. *The Complete Aquarium Problem Solver* (Tetra Press, Melle, Germany, 1990)

Breder, C.M. and D.E. Rosen *Modes of Reproduction in Fishes* (TFH Publications, Neptune City, New Jersey, USA, 1966)

Burgess, W.E. *An Atlas of Freshwater and Marine Catfishes* (T.F.H. Publications, Neptune City, New Jersey, USA, 1989)

Dawes, J. *Livebearing Fishes* (Cassell plc, London, UK, 1995)

Ferraris, C. *Catfish in the Aquarium* (Tetra Press, Melle, Germany, 1991)

Gery, J. *Characoids of the World* (TFH Publications, Neptune City, New Jersey, USA, 1977)

Konings, A. *Cichlids and all Other Fishes of Lake Malawi* (Cichlid Press. http://www.cichlidpress.com)

Konings, A. *Malawi Cichlids in Their Natural Habitat* (Cichlid Press. http://www.cichlidpress.com)

Konings, A. *Tanganyika Cichlids* Verduijn Cichlids and Lake Fish Movies, Holland and Germany, 1988)

Lake, J.S. *Freshwater Rivers and Fishes of Australia* (Thomas Nelson (Australia) Limited, Melbourne, Australia, 1976)

Linke, H. and W. Staeck. *African Cichlids 1: Cichlids from West Africa* (Tetra Press, Melle, Germany, 1995.)

Linke, H. and W. Staeck. *American Cichlids 1: Dwarf Cichlids* (Tetra Press, Melle, Germany, 1995)

Loiselle, P.V. *The Cichlid Aquarium* (Tetra Press, Melle, Germany, 1995)

Merrick, J.R. and G.E. Schmida *Australian Freshwater Fishes* (J.R. Merrick, Macquarie University, Australia, 1987)

Muhlberg, H. *The Complete Guide to Water Plants* (EP Publishing Limited, 1980)

Rataj, K. and T.J. Horeman. *Aquarium Plants* (TFH Publications, Neptune City, New Jersey, USA, 1977)

Riehl, R. and H.A. Baensch, *Aquarium Atlas Vols. I–III* (Mergus Verlag GmbH, Melle, Germany, 1987, 1993, 1994)

Sandford G. and R. Crow. *The Manual of Tankbusters* (Salamander Books Limited, London, UK, 1990)

Sandford, G. *An Illustrated Encyclopaedia of Aquarium Fish* (Quintet Publishing Limited, London, UK, 1995)

Scheel, J.J. *Atlas of Killifishes of the Old World* (TFH Publications, Neptune City, New Jersey, USA, 1990)

Seuss, W. *Corydoras* (Dahne Verlag GmbH, Ettlingen, Germany, 1993)

Spotte, S. *Fish and Invertebrate Culture* (John Wiley and Sons, New York, USA, 1979)

Sterba, G. *Freshwater Fishes of the World* (Studio Vista, London, UK, 1967)

van Duijn Jnr., C. *Diseases of Fishes* (Iliffe Books Ltd., London, UK, 1967)

Vierke, J. *Bettas, Gouramis and Other Anabantoids, Labyrinth Fishes of the World* (TFH Publications, Neptune City, New Jersey, USA, 1988)

Wischnath, L. *Atlas of Livebearers of the World* (TFH Publications, Neptune City, New Jersey, USA, 1993)

Zupanc, G.K.H. *Fish and Their Behaviour* (Tetra Press, Melle, Germany, 1985)

Useful Addresses

American Cichlid Association, Howard Schmidt, P.O. Box 5351, Naperville, IL 60567-5351, USA.

American Killifish Association, Darrell R. Ullisch, 3084 East Empire Avenue, Benton Harbor, MI 49022-9718. e-mail: rivulus@compuserve.com. http://www.aka.org/

American Livebearer Association, Timothy Brady, 5 Zerbe Street, Cressona, PA 17929-1513, USA. http://petsforum.com/ala/

Aqua-Terra International, Henk Koenzen, Hillsestraat 37, 4269 VH Babylonienbroek, The Netherlands

Australia and New Guinea Fishes Association, P.O. Box 673, Ringwood, Victoria 3134, Australia

Belgische Bond Voor Aquarium– en Terrariumhouders, c/o W. Dossler, Stalkerweg 60, B-3601 Zutendaal, Belgium

British Aquatic Resource Centre http://www.cfkc.demon.co.uk

British Cichlid Association, Karen Horrocks, 70 Morton Street, Middleton, Manchester M24 6AY, England

British Killifish Association, A. Burge, 14 Hubbard Close, Wymondham, Norfolk NR18 0DU, England

Canadian Association of Aquarium Clubs, 95 East 31st Street, Hamilton, Ontario L8V 3N9, Canada

Dansk Akvarie Union, Humlemarksvej 13, 2605 Brondby, Denmark

Federación Ibérica de Sociedades Acuariofilas, Apartado de Correos 259, 48990 Algorta (Vizcaya), Spain

Federation of American Aquatic Societies, Hedy Padgett, 4816 E. 64th Street, Indianapolis, IN 46220-4828, USA.

Federation Associazioni Aquarilogiche ed Erpetologie, Corso Regina Marghrita 194, I-10152 Torino, Italy

Federation of British Aquarists Societies, 9 Upton Road, Hounslow, Middlesex TW3 3HP, England

Fédération Française des Associations d'Aquariophilie et de Terrariophilie, 34 Rue Sainte Catherine, F-54000 Nancy, France

Federation of New Zealand Aquatic Societies, 8a Faulkland Dr., Witherlea, Blenheim, New Zealand. e-mail: simtron@xtra.co.nz

Fédération Luxembourgeoise des Aquario- et Terrariophiles, 3 Chemin du Kohn, L-9191 Welscheid, Luxembourg

Federation of Northern Aquarium Societies, Brian Walsh, 9 Marsh Terrace, Darwen, Lancs. BB3 0HF, England

International Aquarium Societies. e-mail: silvah@spectra.net Homepage: www.spectra.net/~silvah/ aquarium.htm

International Killifish Association. http://www.killi.net/

North American Fishbreeders Guild, D.L. Sponeberg, R.R.#2, Box 67-L, Orangeville, PA 17859, USA. e-mail: onsiteina@juno.com

Northern Area Catfish Group, Steve Pye, 12 Ashwood Avenue, Abram, Wigan EN2 5YE, England

Verband Deutscher Vereine für Aquarien- und Terrarienkunde, I. und H. Stiller, Luxemburg Str. 16, D-44789 Bochum, Germany

Index

Major treatment of a subject is indicated by **bold** page numbers. References to illustration captions and annotations are *italic* page numbers.